1/3

JOHN F. KENNEDY

JOHN F. KENNEDY

THE LONDON STORY

April '24

Bernard A Marshall

Matador
Unit E2 Airfield Business Park,
Harrison Road, Market Harborough,
Leicestershire. LE16 7UL
Tel: 0116 2792299
Email: books@troubador.co.uk
Web: www.troubador.co.uk/matador
Twitter: @matadorbooks

ISBN 978 1803136 172

British Library Cataloguing in Publication Data.
A catalogue record for this book is available from the British Library.

Printed and bound by CPI Group (UK) Ltd, Croydon, CR0 4YY
Typeset in 11pt Adobe Caslon Pro by Troubador Publishing Ltd, Leicester, UK

Matador is an imprint of Troubador Publishing Ltd

For my dear parents and to those who inspire us, and for my adventurous brother Peter, and his two talented daughters Laura and Julia.

President Kennedy had the gift of imagination
(Sir Alec Douglas-Home)

*To understand the man, you have to see what was happening in the
world when he was twenty*
(Napoleon Bonaparte)

Ask not what my country can do for me, but ask what I can do for my country
(John F Kennedy, 20 January 1961)

Contents

1

JACK ARRIVES SOUTHAMPTON
(4 JULY 1938)

*Parties and politics, joyous sister Kathleen, introduction to the
aristocratic cousinhood, intensive days to shape a future.*

*Jack arrives at Southampton on American Independence Day, 4 July 1938, alongside
his father the Ambassador and elder brother Joe Jnr.
(Courtesy JFK Library)*

An English morning breeze swept around the sleek liner *Normandie* as it
slowly moved into its berth in Southampton docks. About to step onto solid
ground on American Independence Day was a 21-year-old student known to
his family as Jack. He smiled, as he felt the breeze on his face on that summer

morning of 1938 and hurried forward, smartly dressed in a grey striped suit, white shirt and dark tie with white stripes. Now six foot tall and slim, he was as tall as his elder brother and his famously brash and proud father. British officials recognising the American Ambassador gave him a friendly smile before all three Kennedys, greeted by embassy staff, were guided to the waiting boat train. As the train picked up speed, Jack looked intently out of his carriage window at England's rolling green fields and wondered in a relaxed yet excited way what lay ahead in this country he had read so much about. What would this land of kings and queens and noble warriors show him?

The Stars and Stripes fluttered on the side of the bonnet of the gleaming embassy car as it left Waterloo Station to cross the river. Jack peered up as they came alongside Big Ben; much taller than he had imagined from listening to the chimes on the radio, back in Boston. Turning onto a leafy tree-lined Mall, they soon came under the gaze of Queen Victoria, atop a white stone circle in front of the Palace and turned right for the greens of Hyde Park. Minutes later, the car drew to a halt at Prince's Gate. Jack spotted his seven younger brothers and sisters rushing towards them and as he jumped out, first to touch him was Kathleen holding a small bunch of flowers. Now eighteen and called 'Kick' by everyone, she hugged him tightly. She had always adored him. The red-headed and proud ambassador, beaming a Kennedy smile from behind his spectacles, gathered up the younger children with his wife Rose and led them up the steps of their new embassy home. The cream-coloured Georgian residence at 14 Prince's Gate facing the trees of Hyde Park, would become Jack's home that summer and the next.

Kick raced up the staircase alongside her brothers, talking excitedly with clipped Boston accent. She paused for a second and saw Jack with his open playful smile. In that glimpse she caught her breath quite involuntarily, wondering what lay ahead for Jack.

Four months earlier on 4 March, Joe had been transported by horse and carriage to present his credentials to the King. Eight days later, Nazi troops had streamed into Austria and Joe had quickly returned to America to confer with the President. Now on American Independence Day, two embassy vehicles waited outside Prince's Gate as Kick and Rose quickly changed into their evening gowns and jewellery. Five glittering dynamic Kennedys now jumped into the cars. As they sped along Hyde Park, the Stars and Stripes flag whipped into permanent salute as they headed to the Dorchester hotel. The setting sun had not yet given way to night as the Kennedys entered the lobby on that 'Fourth of July', 1938.

The guests in the elegant ballroom of the Dorchester fell silent as Ambassador Joe rose to explain America's stance to Hitler's latest demands. Reflecting America's isolationist view at this point, and his own rigid stance, he told the assembled audience, "If the British government really chooses to go to war, they must not expect us to pull British chestnuts out of the fire!"

Antony Eden, the young political star who had just resigned as Foreign Secretary in protest against the government's policy of appeasement, had been invited to reply. He told his American audience that he saw the need for an Anglo-American alliance in order, 'to protect the freedom of the individual, now almost rare in this troubled Europe'. He turned to the American Ambassador and suggested, "While we do not expect America to pull all the chestnuts out of the fire, there are beginning to be quite a few chestnuts that concern us both."

From his very first evening in London, Jack was hearing the call for an 'Anglo-American alliance'. He was about to see how the democracies of America and Britain were to deal with a bully and dictator. This theme would become the exact challenge that student Jack would face and be measured by two decades later.

London was at the heart of an empire that ruled almost a quarter of the world's population. It was the world's largest and wealthiest city. This was the stage on which the American Ambassador would try to influence Britain and world events. And it would be on this very stage that his son was to receive an education that would turn him into a legendary statesman.

Four days after Jack arrived, Kick, who had not stopped talking to her friends about him and had become a star amongst her new circle of British friends, arranged a dinner party. His young sister, and kindred spirit, had acquired full membership of a little circle known as the 'aristocratic cousinhood'. That Friday night, she tugged at Jack's sleeve, moving him excitedly from one group to another, young faces shining bright and all delighting in each other's company. Chandeliers and candles added sparkle to eyes eagerly exploring each moment. Under bright lights at Prince's Gate that night, this confident circle of youth took Jack into their close-knit circle as rapidly as they had taken in Kick.

At that moment, none could have possibly foreseen how close they would become. Or, the surprising part they were to play in each other's lives. At the very core of this noble circle, all around twenty years old, were the two brothers, Billy and Andrew Cavendish; their cousin David Ormsby-Gore and his girlfriend, Sissy Lloyd-Thomas, and Deborah Mitford. They came from families that had helped shape the history of Britain.

On that first Friday evening, a guest saw Jack, 'moving about with a sort of careless grace, not arrogant but simply confident. Boyish and rather lanky, but very, very handsome'. The Duchess of Devonshire remembered Kick and Jack that night. "Everybody who met her just loved her – her extreme good nature and high spirits, so like her brother Jack. They both had the same thick gold brown hair and bluey grey eyes. Both shared the same magnetic quality."

Expectation of war had infused the daily lives of the aristocratic cousinhood with great intensity. Jack would see pages of history turn with new fascination. He would watch his literary hero, Winston Churchill thundering warnings in Parliament, and share new ideas with his aristocratic friends on the lawns of Buckingham Palace as the King and Queen stood 'while different foreign princes came and bowed'.[1]

Inspired by boyhood books of noble adventure and stories of King Arthur and his court at Camelot, he was discovering the image of the man he wanted to be. These intensely lived pre-war days in London were key to his destiny. They would forever influence Jack's ideas and character. They would shape him before he came to shape our world.

2

THE FUN-LOVING BOY
AND FAMILY BONDS

*Jack survives scarlet fever, Grandpa Honey Fitz, 'proper'
Bostonians, perfectionist Rose, fisticuffs with Joe Jnr, Hyannis Port
– the crucible of competitive life.*

Jack arrived in the world just a month after America joined Britain in the Great War. The comfortable, spacious home in which he was born on 29 May 1917 stood in a leafy tree-lined suburb of Boston, a historic city that had been at the forefront of the American Revolution – from the Boston Tea Party to the evacuation of British troops in March 1775. Located a short tram ride from the centre, the New England-style timbered home had seven rooms, a sloping roof and large porch. His father, Joseph Kennedy, was a banker who would take the tram from 83 Beale Street to his bank in East Boston, each morning. When his children were born, the newly rich banker would tell his wife, Rose, "This is the only happiness that lasts." Two years earlier, when Joe Jnr was born, grandfather Honey Fitz told reporters, "He is going to be President of the United States." No such predictions were made for the second son.

Jack was already three when his sister Kathleen, with whom he was to form a special bond, was born. On 20 February 1920, the moment she was taking her first breath, Jack was breathing heavily and fighting for his life. He had a fever and probably a version of the deadly Spanish flu which had just swept across the world. In desperation, his father offered the priest at his son's bedside half his worldly wealth for his church if Jack pulled through. (He later wrote a cheque to the church for a bus to transport disadvantaged children to hospital.)[2] It took little Jack two months to recover and he returned home with his hospital nurse. Her heart had been so taken by him that she begged to be allowed to stay with her 'fun-loving humorous boy who never complained'![3]

In 1921, Joe moved to a larger home five minutes away. They were now the wealthiest family in a solidly middle-class neighbourhood. A shiny black Rolls-Royce and English chauffeur replaced Joe's Model T Ford. The new home at 51 Abbotsford Road was an imposing colonial-style residence on an acre of ground that had fourteen rooms and a wrap-around porch with curved bay windows. Life for the children was often played out on that wrap-around. It had been divided up into territorial play areas by Rose, using folded gates 'so that way they could be with each other and entertain each other for hours at a time'. From the veranda, Rose and the children in the 1920s had 'the full panorama of neighborhood life to entertain them: cars passing by, people walking along, many of them who waved, the letter carrier, the milkman with his wire basket loaded full as he came to our house and empty as he left, the policeman passing by on his patrol, the grocery boy, tradesman, visitors and friends… everybody with a smile and cheerful greeting for the children'.[4]

Rose was a rigid perfectionist with a fetish for 'proper behavior'. But her emotional and physical absences – her 'management' rather than maternal approach to child rearing – would have an effect on her sons who fought for her attention. She was unhappy with her long drawn-out love match that had gone wrong. When expecting Kathleen, she moved to her parents' home in despair at her husband's infidelities. Honey Fitz insisted she return to Joe, saying, "The old days are gone… you've made your commitment. You must now honor it."[5]

When not engaged in competitive fisticuffs with his brother, Jack turned more and more to books. He probably found solace in his books from the domestic tension between his parents when home, and solace when they were not. Books would fuel a growing curiosity in sensitive Jack, about the world beyond his Boston veranda.[6]

Formal education began a few blocks away from home at the Edward Devotion Kindergarten. At age seven, Jack joined his brother at Noble and Greenbough School. They were the only Catholic children in this elite and private school peopled by families with Anglo-Saxon names: Barbour, Brewer, Huntingdon and Wright. Moving into this new social world was an important change for Jack and his brother. The school was friendly and strict, run by female teachers. Since many of the parents would have nothing to do with the Kennedy family, the two brothers suffered taunts at school. The local view was that Joe 'had made money in ways that were known in banking circles as unsavoury'.[7] A contemporary recalled that grandfather Honey Fitz was considered 'a scallywag if there ever was one and the boys must have had a hard time'.[8] Despite the prejudices they suffered, Jack and Joe Jnr enjoyed their school, headed by the brilliant Myra Fiske, a preacher's daughter. Jack, with his wit and passion for history, became her pet. Interviewed at ninety-four, the extraordinary Miss Fiske explained her love for the boys: "Discipline was never a problem to me – it never worried me. How did I keep discipline? I simply feel the thing. I felt it so keenly that they, the children, felt it.

"Love," she went on, "doesn't that take care of a lot? And you know, they are twice as smart as you are!"[9]

Even if 'proper Bostonians' did not appreciate him, Honey Fitz was popular amongst ordinary Bostonians. He had been elected the youngest-ever mayor in 1905. At five feet two and known as the little Napoleon, he was a bundle of blarney, energy and song. Rose Kennedy was initially ignorant of the hostile world her sons encountered at school in this new world of Yankees. Her response, as with her husband's infidelity, was to avoid any unpleasant reality as much as possible. Rose never took her children to school, this being left to the chauffeur in the black shiny Rolls, nor did 'she attend any school social activities'.[10] However, she often took Jack and his brothers and sisters all over Massachusetts, educating them in local history: "This is Plymouth rock where in 1620… this is where the tea was dumped in Boston harbor…'[11] etc.

Jack was fond of Honey Fitz and loved his stories, imploring him to "Tell that one again, Grampa."[12] Jack's first ten years were filled with memories of his beloved grandpa who took him and Joe Jnr to Red Sox games and boating in the public gardens. Jack got his first glimpse of campaign politics when the Mayor took him around town when he ran to become governor in 1922. At his sixtieth birthday party in 1923, Honey Fitz clasped his two grandsons and told newspaper reporters his secret. "Mingle with the young people. Go through life good-natured and friendly. You will derive the greatest pleasure from making others happy."

Honey Fitzgerald's father had been an Irish emigrant who worked as a farm labourer and then as an itinerant peddler in the streets of northeast Boston. He married Rosana Cox, herself a daughter of Irish emigrants, and six years later he went into business with his brother in a small grocery store. Honey Fitzgerald was born on 11 February 1863 and attended Boston Latin

School. It was one of the finest schools in America and in 1884 Honey Fitz was accepted by Harvard Medical School – a big achievement for a second-generation Irish immigrant. Nine months later, his father died of pneumonia and, since his mother had already died six years earlier, he gave up medical school to look after and bring up his six brothers whilst working as head of a customs house. Unusually for a man recognised as a calculating politician, he married a shy farmer's daughter, Josie Hannon, whom he had idealistically and romantically pursued for a number of years. They married on 7 September 1889 and their first daughter, Rose Elizabeth Fitzgerald, was born on 22 July 1890. Being brought up in youth without women in the family, Fitzgerald regarded his daughter Rose as a miracle and she duly became, outside his life of politics, the centre of his attention. He became mayor in December 1905, an ambition he had harboured after becoming a local state senator and then congressman, all with the help of his six younger brothers. As a hugely popular and dynamic mayor, he 'roared from dinner to dinner and dance to dance'. As one reporter put it: "1,500 dances, 200 picnics, 1,000 meetings, 3,000 speeches and shared 5,000 dances with girls – all proud to have had a dance apiece with Fitzy."[13]

Jack's great-grandfather on his father's side, Patrick J Kennedy, came to America in the spring of 1849 on the *Washington Irving* at the age of twenty-four. Leaving Ireland as a young farmer from County Wexford, he met Bridget Murphy, two years older, also travelling alone from Wexford. They married six months later and he found work as a 'cooper', making beer barrels, with Bridget's cousin. The family had two girls and a boy but, aged just thirty-five, Patrick died of consumption. (Irish immigrants lived on average only for fourteen years, possibly dying at an even higher rate, it was said, than the kinsmen they had left behind after the potato famine.) Their son, Patrick, was then looked after by his younger sisters and his mother, Bridget, went out to work as a domestic, in 'Yankee houses'. After getting work as an assistant in a grocery and clothes store near the ferry terminal at 25 Border Street, Bridget somehow managed to buy the shop and then a second. Despite being unable to write, she had become a woman of property and chose to send Patrick to Lyman Public School. On leaving school, Patrick took a job as a stevedore before Bridget helped him buy a tavern near the docks, and then a second. He now read books whilst he poured drafts of beer and 'listened'. Despite lacking the usual 'gift of blarney', after expanding his wholesale liquor business, he decided to go into politics. In January 1886, Patrick was elected at twenty-eight to the State Legislature. He married Mary Augusta, who came from a socially established family from east Boston. Their first child, Jack's father Joseph Patrick Kennedy, was born on 6 September 1888. Two sisters then followed and in 1901 Joe entered Boston Latin, one of America's finest public schools. Despite needing to repeat a year at school, he became president of his class and a popular baseball player. If there was a disconcerting note, it was the prediction in the 1908 school yearbook that he would earn his fortune 'in a very roundabout way'.[14] Joe entered Harvard as a hardy athletic and outgoing youth and married Rose, the former mayor's daughter, in October 1914.

Both sides of the family, united by Joe and Rose, had reaped the rewards from a history of hard work, grocers' shops, public houses and politics. It was banking and business that would now propel Joe forward. After becoming the youngest president of a bank in America at twenty-five with the help of a loan from his father, he would eventually set himself up independently. Commuting by train each morning from his leafy suburb into Wall Street, he made his first big killing in the winter of 1923. Using insider information to manipulate prices in the stock market, he earned half a million dollars with just an outlay of $14,000 on credit. He followed this in the spring of 1924, sitting with a fund of five million dollars in a Waldorf Astoria hotel room for nine weeks, with specially installed ticker tape. He saved the John Hertz Yellow Cab company into the bargain, and Mr Hertz gave Kennedy a secret cash sum, as well as a generous share of stock in his company. (Hertz soon regretted his action when Kennedy promptly dumped the stock, leading to a fall in the share price.) Joe's growing reputation as a shrewd and ruthless market operator did not make him any new friends.

In 1925, Joe rented a two-and-a-half-acre estate and white clapboard house overlooking Hyannis Port that would be their summer home and become the crucible of Kennedy competitive family life. Two years later, he moved the family from Boston nearer to New York 'where the money was to be made'. After renting a place in Riverdale for a year, he bought a 'statement house' with a wide view overlooking the Hudson River on six acres of ground on the exclusive Westchester estate at 294 Pondfield Road, Bronxville. In 1927, he moved into the film business and for a brief period owned four studios, including Pathé DeMille. When he met film star Gloria Swanson, he persuaded her to let him manage her film career. His affair with this married star became an open secret in Hollywood.

Hyannis Port summer home purchased in 1928. It became the crucible of competitive Kennedy family life. (Courtesy JFK Library)

In 1928, Joe bought the big white summer home with green shutters they had rented. Situated at the end of Scudder Avenue, it cost $25,000. It was part of a cluster of houses that resembled a self-contained outpost rather than a town. Famed for its long Cape Cod summers and fronting the ocean with tennis courts, a pool and a green lawn big enough for playing football, it now became the Kennedys' spiritual home.

Charles Spalding, one of Jack's closest childhood friends, described his weekends with the family. "There was endless action... endless talk... endless competition... people drawing each other out and pushing each other to greater lengths. It was as simple as this: the Kennedys had a feeling of being heightened and it rubbed off on the people who came in contact with them. They were a unit. I remember thinking to myself that there couldn't be another group quite like this one." Another visiting friend recorded, "Bedlam would be pouring through the windows... we could hear their raucous competing voices and laughter, high-spirited insults and then tramping on the stairs, as telephones rang, dogs barked, radios blared and someone banged out a few notes on the living-room piano, en route to somewhere else."[15]

People saw that Jack had inherited his father's sandy hair, blueish eyes and squarish face; but his jaw and wide mouth with prominent teeth belonged to his mother, as did his cooler temperament. Joe Jnr, by contrast, took after his father: aggressive, mercurial and quick to fly into a temper, characteristics which became the bane of Jack's life. Rose would recall, "During some of the earlier years there were real battles… Joe Jnr was older, bigger, stronger, but Jack, frail though he was, could fight like fury when he wanted to,"[16] which also revealed her loss of control of the boys when Joe was absent, as was often the case.[17]

Joe Jnr adapted to his mother's strict rules by performing the role she expected of him – he was neat, orderly, responsible and even fatherly towards his younger siblings, though not towards Jack, his nonconformist rival. Rose said that she often gave Jack an extra portion of food at table, much to Joe Jnr's indignation. Jack got the extra portion "…because he needed it. He had a rather narrow face and his ears stuck out a little bit and his hair wouldn't stay put, and all that added, I suppose, to an elfin quality in his appearance. But he was a very active, very lively elf, full of energy when he was not ill and full of charm and imagination. And surprises – for he thought his own thoughts, did things his own way, and somehow just didn't fit any pattern".[18] Unlike her other children, Rose saw that Jack "was unconcerned about dress. His shirt never seemed to stay in his trousers, nor would his collar stay down".[19] Rose sometimes felt Jack's mind "was only half preoccupied with the subject at hand, doing his arithmetic homework, or picking up his clothes off the floor, and the rest of his thoughts were far away weaving daydreams."[20]

Jack's home life revolved around his father, his fiercely competitive elder brother and a vivacious younger sister. His emotionally distant mother, Rose, played a lesser role. Joe was the dominant force. He made his high parental expectations very clear. He wanted only winners. "Don't come in second or third," he admonished his children. "That does not count."[21] The children accepted all this because they knew their overpowering dad was motivated by an intense desire to ensure their well-being.[22]

Joe, imbuing every aspect of his children's lives with fever-pitched competitive intensity, turned the dinner table into another playing field. He was constantly quizzing his two sons and Kathleen about events in the world. He would push them to give a point of view, and to make up their own minds. Joe was not entirely blind to the fact that he was an overbearing, demanding and insistent character who dominated almost everyone and everything he touched. He sensed how destructive this could be, so he made a point of encouraging a measure of independence and even irreverence. Lem Billings recalled that whilst mealtime conversations never consisted of small talk, Joe "never lectured – he would encourage them completely to disagree with him and of course they did disagree with him".

Joe, the master of competitiveness, was a strong golfer and would beat his sons readily. He played tennis, shrewdly hitting and placing the ball as a strategist might in the boardroom. The sports field and dining room was where their competitive instincts were honed, rivalries worked out and the ties that bound them together made. When Joe was not there, Rose would take over the questioning, reading from a prepared list. Rose kept a very strict eye on the children's daily neatness, deportment, correct social and religious training, as well as ensuring perfect teeth. Rose's lack of emotional warmth and frequent absence of both parents, led to a degree of emotional neglect. Shipped off to convent and boarding schools increased the children's sense of independence, emotional and otherwise. Kick and Jack would later feel close affinity to their English counterparts from noble families who had experienced similar schooling and sense of independence.

To Joe, life itself was an epic competition that went to the daring and determined. There was exceptional pressure to live up to 'Kennedy standards', to stand out and not just from the crowd but to be the best of the best! After Joe had offered his sons the best education and introductions to the highest levels of society, they all had to pass through the crucible of experience on their own to become the kind of men he wanted them to be. Joe always 'trusted experience as the greatest creator of character'.[23]

Like many wealthy parents, Joe was concerned that love of mindless ease might spoil his children, and he sent them to private schools to instill a sense of purpose, destiny and responsibility. When Jack was displaying signs of terrible carelessness about his clothes, appointments and money, his father wrote anxiously to Jack's schoolteacher admitting he had 'possibly contributed as much as anyone in spoiling him, by having secretaries and maids following him to see that he does what he should do'.[24] As a rich young man, Jack would see wealth not as something to be earned or maintained, or something others might try to wrest away, but as something that was simply his, as much a part of him as his feet and his fingers.[25]

Joe imbibed the family with a remarkable sense of loyalty. He taught his children, particularly Jack and Joe Jnr, to rely on family unity as a shield against competitors and opponents. He once introduced Jack to one of the Fisher brothers, and car designers for General Motors saying, "I wanted you to meet him just to show you what success brothers have who stick together." It was a lesson that Jack and none of the Kennedy children ever forgot.[26]

In this authoritarian family however, neither of the two elder boys willingly conceded superiority to the other – neither would back off. Jack was not to be intimidated, as a cycle race once around the house showed. A frontal collision between the two which left Joe unhurt, had Jack needing twenty-eight stitches! Another time, Jack was caught putting on Joe's new bathing suit by mistake. "Joe was furious," Rose recalled, "and when four days later Jack made the same mistake again, Joe, with a mercurial aggressive temper like his father, exploded and took after his younger brother. Jack sensibly took flight, over the lawn, through the marsh and down the beach. He then ran along the old breakwater. Joe was gaining on him when, thank goodness, Eddie Moore [her father's secretary] arrived on the scene and, sensing the situation was serious, shouted, 'Stop that! You two get yourselves back here. Right now!'"[27] Jack seemed to develop his hit-and-run style of attack, provoking Joe into unsuccessful chases, that turned his flight in front of all his brothers and sisters into a kind of triumph.

"Jack," as one young woman dating him as a teenager remembered, "would always talk about his brother all the time – e.g. Joe plays football better, Joe dances better, Joe is getting better grades. Joe just kind of overshadowing him in everything as a teenager." When asked later if anything really bothered him as a child, Jack could only think of this competition with Joe and the games and roughhousing on the porch and in the garden which could descend into hostilities. Jack would recall, "Joe had a pugnacious personality. Later on, it smoothed out, but it was a problem in my boyhood."

If Jack felt that he lived under the shadow of his elder brother, his sister Kick was the one member of the family who always put him in first place. Three years younger, she had always adored Jack. They shared the same sense of humour, quicksilver wit and talent for making and attracting friends. Jack soon developed a special bond with his sister. All the children, except for Joe Jnr, were beset with health problems. Jack was by far the sickliest child, and Kick often worried deeply about Jack's health. She herself suffered from asthma and allergies.

Jack, though not in charge, was always mindful of his younger brothers and sisters, who looked up to him. He made sure Rosemary was not left out at parties. Eunice recalled, "Jack would take her to a dance at the club and would dance with her and kid with her and would make sure a few of his pals would cut in, so she felt popular. He'd bring her home at midnight. Then he'd go back to the dance."

Fun-loving Kick, who needed no special attention, was extremely popular at school. She was rarely moody or temperamental, always sunny and full of jokes and quick to laugh. One of her friends from Noroton would say, "Wherever Kathleen went, sunshine followed."[28] Jack, taking along his schoolmates to visit Kick at the Noroton Convent, would see his friends invariably falling in love with his kid sister. Kick, as one of her nuns described it, had a personality and "a fund of energy with the power of charm and persuasion, with trustfulness in good and with an optimistic outlook on the world that wins its way and succeeds in its undertakings, making its appeal to the will rather than to the mind."[29] Despite her sunny manner, Kick was sometimes unhappy at the convent, and Jack knew this. He visited often and wrote her amusing letters. When Kick told her father how much she adored and admired him, he wrote to Jack, 'She really thinks you are a great fellow. She has a love and devotion to you that you should be very proud to have deserved. It probably does not become apparent to you, but it does to Mother and me. She thinks you are quite the grandest fellow that ever lived, and your letters furnish her most of her laughs in the convent."[30] Joe would later say of Kick, "All my ducks are swans… but Kick was especially special."[31]

For the winter, Jack's father acquired a large Mediterranean-style villa at 1095 Ocean Boulevard in Palm Beach. With a red-tile roof and white stucco walls, it spread over seven bedrooms. It had a pool, and occupied two acres of prime oceanfront. Joe had got it for a bargain $115,000 after the Florida market collapse. It became the Kennedy winter home for several weeks at a time. It was here after a spell at Canterbury Preparatory School where he became ill, that he spent the spring of 1930 in their sunny Palm Beach home with a private tutor. Jack then entered Choate, the boarding school where he was about to play out his adolescent years.

3

CHOATE – THE AMERICAN ETON

Rebellious nature, love of history, King Arthur and Churchill,
clever individualistic mind, bouts of unexplained illness, talent for
making friends, the Muckers' Club, boy 'most likely to succeed'.

Jack, turning fourteen, entered Choate in Connecticut on Friday, 2 October 1931. He would spend four years at this boarding school run on the lines of an English public school. Though recently built, wealthy parents regarded it as a kind of American Eton. It employed a few Englishmen on the faculty staff[32] and was ruled over by a formidable headmaster, the Reverend George St John. It was whilst developing his playful love-hate relationship with Choate that Jack's light-hearted nature and a certain rebellious quality came to the fore. It was here he would show his first signs of leadership.

Within weeks of his arrival, housemaster Earl Leinbach noted in a report, 'Jack has a pleasing personality and is warmly received by all the boys in the house, but rules rather bother him a bit.'[33] Leinbach was a war hero who had escaped capture by the Germans and had a beautiful blonde wife who all the boys fancied. Jack respected him and Leinbach soon recognised Jack's determination and 'wholehearted tenacity when faced with a problem.'[34]

After Joe Jnr had done well and won the school prize for best combining studies and sport, Rose wrote to the headmaster about Jack. 'He has a very attractive personality, we think, but he is quite different to Joe. He hates routine work but loves History and English – subjects that fire his imagination.'[35] 'We are reading *Ivanhoe* in English', Jack wrote in one of his earliest letters about one of his favourite subjects, 'and though I might not be able to remember material things such as tickets, gloves, and so on, I can remember things like *Ivanhoe,* and the last time we had an exam on it, I got ninety-eight.'[36] A friend recalled, "He seemed to absorb what he read much better than the rest of us."[37] Jack's history teacher too was impressed, telling his father, "Jack has one of the few great minds I have ever had in history."[38]

Jack showed a determination from an early age to be himself rather than conform to his mother's mould. He wanted to find an identity of his own at Choate and not that of his dutiful elder brother. Though loyal to each other, the competitive spirit promoted by their father ensured an intense rivalry. With Joe excelling at sport, Jack felt he had to prove himself at sport as well. Swimming and golf were his main choices and he did his best at football. But whilst Joe was also a model pupil, Jack seemed intentionally sloppy. He did not do his work on time, was deliberately unpunctual and had an 'inability to concentrate'. As the director of studies put it, 'Jack has a high IQ and is one of the most undependable boys in the third form... I cannot see how we can guarantee that he won't have to tutor this summer.'

In his first summer term, Jack promptly failed his French and Latin exams. So, whilst elder brother spent August sailing and swimming in Hyannis Port with the family, Jack stayed behind to take extra classes. From then on, he made sure he never failed his exams again. In his second year, Jack complained that his new housemaster proved no challenge at all. "Down where I am now, I can get away with anything and it's no fun." Fun – as it would be for the rest of his days – was fast becoming the leitmotif of Jack's existence. That was when he was not ill – and even then he would make the best of it. That winter he fell ill, exhibiting flu-like symptoms. "Jack's winter report sounded more like a hospital report," recalled the headmaster's son.[39] The wife of the headmaster, Clara St John, visited Jack in hospital and reported to Rose, "Jack's humor hasn't left him for a minute even when he felt most miserable." In an early display of elegant appreciation, Jack wrote to Clara. 'Thank you for your numerous kindnesses to me when I was in hospital. I will never be able to repay them, so I'll have to be satisfied just letting you know my appreciation'.

The following summer, Jack's elder brother sailed with his parents to England. Jack's father and Choate decided it would be better to keep Jack's nose to the grindstone because he 'has a tendency to be careless in details and really is not determined to be a success'. To add to Jack's misery of missing out on holidays, he was now put under the direction of a highly disciplined master, J J Maher. 'He had the reputation that his floor was where the kids were on time, were neat and they knew and obeyed the rules'. Mr Maher's only answer to people wanting to fight him "was more discipline and more toughness. Jack got tossed into that and wanted no part of it", recalled the headmaster's son. What Jack needed was great teachers, like the headmaster George St John and Mr Leinbach, able to provide that underlying love (as displayed once before by Myra Fiske) without which Jack could not perform.[40]

Rose did not visit Jack at school; not once. She spent much time away from home and when planning another long trip to California, was confronted by Jack who at the age of five bravely remarked, "Gee, you're a great mother to go away and leave your children alone."[41] It was a mark of his daring quality against a mother who seemed emotionally aloof yet ruled her children with strict precision. Rose took refuge in religion and adopted a rigid code to shield her from disappointment. It was unsurprising the children called her 'Mother', whilst Joe was called 'Dad' or 'Daddy'.

In 1933, Joe went to see his eldest son receive Choate's trophy Harvard award. He was appalled to see sixteen-year-old Jack sloppily dressed and cavorting with a gang of buddies – all lacking that earnest posture of self-discipline and determination that so marked Joe Jnr for success. Looking for an explanation, he turned to housemaster Mr Leinbach, who reported, "Jack's papers are chaotic and he invariably forgets books, pencils or paper. Impulsive actions characterize his every move. Whenever he wants a clean shirt, he has to pull every shirt out of his cupboard and then 'does not have time' to put them back. His room is inspected night and morning every day, and I always find the floor cluttered up with articles of every description. When he sees me, he remarks, 'I never get away with anything in this place.' To fasten his mind upon an assignment task is his most difficult job, for he is bubbling over with a host of half-formed ideas of a different type." But then Mr Leinbach added, "What makes the whole problem difficult is Jack's winning smile and charming personality... it is an inescapable fact that his actions are really amusing and evoke real hilarity."[42]

Joe advised the school on 21 November 1933 that he wanted Jack to eventually continue his education in England. He had already placed his eldest son at the London School of Economics and Political Science (LSE). 'Joe you would be proud of', he wrote, adding, 'I would very much like Jack to follow in his footsteps and he can only do that if he senses his own responsibilities. I'm worried about his happy-go-lucky and clownish manner combined with a degree of indifference which does not portend well for his future development'.

The headmaster, George St John, responded in a surprising and insightful manner. He believed, he said, that behind that sloppy façade Jack had, 'a clever individualistic mind. It is harder to put it into harness than Joe's, and harder himself to put it into harness. Jack is so pleasantly optimistic that we all want to help him. He challenges the best that's in us. When he learns the right place for humor and uses his individual way of looking at things as an asset instead of a handicap, his natural gift of an individual outlook and witty expression are going to help him'. The headmaster concluded, '…the fact of the matter is that I cannot feel seriously uneasy or worried about Jack. The longer I live and work with him, the more I talk with him, the more confidence I have in him. I would be willing to bet that within two years you will be as proud of Jack as you are of Joe.'

A photo of Jack taken in that summer of 1935 shows a good-looking and healthy youth on the verge of manhood. Biographer Geoffrey Perret tells us, 'His gaze is fresh and blank – still to be written on. The knot of his tie is crammed up against the large soft collar, so tiny it disappears. No other Choate graduate of 1935 sports a knotted tie like this, as the yearbook shows. The tie is of no interest at all; the way he wears it says *he* is.'[43]

Jack's great success in the five years he spent at Choate, until he left at eighteen, was to find ways to have fun. Before his final year, he had formed the 'Muckers' Club', named after people who had the task of collecting horse manure from the streets. The club consisted of a gang of twelve friends – Lem Billings, Rip Horton and others, who behaved like Robin Hood's band of Merry Men, all staying fiercely loyal to him. A Muckers' plan to pile a heap of manure onto the school dance floor one night in front of the boys and their dates was exposed before they had a chance to come to the rescue with their shovels 'to save the day'! Joe was called in by the headmaster, and he had to plea to save Jack and the boys from being expelled. Joe, a ruthless rule breaker himself, now took positive notice of the spirit shown by his younger son. After placating the headmaster, he told Jack with a glint in his eye that if he had formed the club, its name would not have begun with an 'M'! This was a big moment in Jack's life – when he first won – in his own right – the attention and love of his father.

Jack had shown his ability to attract a loyal following. He made people laugh and had the gift of not taking himself or his health too seriously. Given the many solitary hospital stays he experienced, lying in bed waiting for visitors, he developed a yearning to share fun and attract friends. Left to himself for long periods in his younger life, he never relished being alone. Whilst not a 'bookish boy', Jack developed a serious interest in reading. A friend, Kay

Halle, visiting Jack recuperating from illness, found him "lying in bed, very pale, which highlighted the freckles across his nose. He was so surrounded by books I could hardly see him. I was very impressed, because at that point the very young child was reading *The World Crisis 1914–1918*, by Winston Churchill".[44] It wasn't knowledge for its own sake but the grander world he glimpsed through it, that was important to Jack. He had a method of finishing a piece of reading and then closing his eyes to recall each of its main points. By such discipline, and seeing history through the eyes of the Anglo-American aristocrat Churchill, the 'first glimmerings of the man he was shaping to become' were now evident, according to biographer Nigel Hamilton.

Jack probably held the record for the number of days spent in the school's hospital section. The staff of Choate School were sincerely frightened by Jack's frequent and sudden periods of illness and after one such time the headmaster confided to Joe, "Jack is one of the best people that ever lived – one of the most able and interesting. To see how sorry everyone is, when Jack is ill, proves the kind of fellow he is."[45]

It must have been troubling for a young boy that no doctors were able to really explain why he became ill. And, rather challenging to be living under the burden of a father who would not tolerate 'losers'. But it was in those conditions, whilst the other boys were playing baseball or football, that Jack started his passionate reading of history and heroes. Here, he could dream intensely about the adventures of King Arthur and Ivanhoe, where fealty was sworn to an outstanding leader. Here, he could sense the courage and excitement displayed by chivalrous knights and princes.

From early childhood, Jack was clearly his own master. This independent and open-minded boy was keen to come to his own views on life. Within certain bounds, Jack had rebelled against school and, indirectly, against parental authority at Choate. His schoolwork continued to be uneven, strong in English and History, which interested him, but mediocre at best in languages, which required the sort of routine discipline he found difficult to maintain. But, in certain ways, Jack was able to show he might outgun his elder brother. The far-sighted Choate headmaster St John again: 'Jack has a clever, individualist mind... and the gift of "individual outlook". The final product is often more interesting and more effective than the boy with a more conventional mind who has been to us parents and teachers much less trouble.'[46]

Jack displayed a confident but delightfully unassertive manner that often comes to those who harbour few doubts about their own talents or social standing. The Kennedys' social standing in the spring of 1934 improved after Joe and Rose spent a weekend at the White House with President Roosevelt. Rose made sure to write to the children on White House paper, allowing Jack at seventeen to reply, 'Got your White House letter. It must have been swell.'[47]

Like many young rebels, Jack fought against calls to duty in his youth. The headmaster, George St John, would recite to the boys at evening chapel, "The boy who loves his *alma mater* will always ask not what can she do for me but what can I do for her?" The Choate headmaster must have felt both surprised and deeply satisfied, when he listened to his once rebellious pupil recite this idea twenty-six years later on taking the presidential oath.

When Jack graduated from Choate in the summer of 1935 he was nominated by his classmates as the one 'most likely to succeed'. Coming sixty-fourth in a class of 112 and no outstanding varsity athlete, somehow they were already aware of qualities in him that neither his grades nor his athletic prowess showed. His loyal classmates knew he had a capacity for leadership, not yet fully formed or always apparent to others. The assistant headmaster, Wardell St John, in his final letter to Jack's parents: 'Jack has it in him to be a great leader of men, and somehow I have the feeling he is going to be just that.'[48]

Now six feet tall and looking the picture of health, Jack spent the summer of 1935 sailing and celebrating with his brother Joe. The parties could be pretty boisterous. After an Edgartown regatta, the two boys threw a party which turned into a mini riot. The police were called and the brothers shared a cell that night.[49] Despite their fierce rivalry, Jack, overshadowed then, by his bigger brother, admitted later that he would rather have 'spent an evening or played golf, or in fact done anything with him.'[50]

Jack had an outstanding talent: 'The thing about Jack in school was his ability to win the friendship and admiration of everyone,' recalled a friend.[51] In this, he seemed to follow his grandfather's advice that one of the most important missions in life is to make friends and keep them: show kindness at all times.[52] This 'outstanding talent for making friends and enjoying friendships', as Rose put it,[53] would prove priceless, as he and Kick were about to make new friends for life in England.

4

LSE, PRINCETON AND HARVARD

False starts at LSE and Princeton, Kick's year in Europe, Jack enters Harvard, Shy boy to 'playboy', King Francis and medieval history.

Jack heard he had been accepted by Harvard on 23 July 1935. He had achieved marks of eighty-five per cent for his favourite subjects, English and History, and had come sixty-fifth in a class of 110. Seeing a chance to assert his independence from his father and elder brother, he suddenly transferred his choice to Princeton as soon as he saw his friend Billings had been accepted there.

Then came another change. After Joe had organised funding for Roosevelt's 1932 campaign, he had expected to be rewarded with a position in government. This did not happen until 1934 when Roosevelt appointed him – as he said privately, a thief to catch a thief – to be in charge of the new Securities Exchange Commission (SEC) to tidy up America's stock market. After a year in the job, in which he did well, he resigned from the SEC declaring grandly he was 'through with public life'. After failing to get a 'better job' from Roosevelt, he packed his bags and headed for a vacation in Europe. He insisted on taking Jack, to sign him up for a year at the London School of Economics where he had sent Joe Jnr to study under the renowned left-wing socialist professor Dr Lasky. It was a move to help his sons understand a socialist view of things 'in order to better protect their money'. "These boys," the arch capitalist would say, "when they get a little older and have a little money, I want them to know the whatnot of keeping that!"[54] Meanwhile Kick was about to go to a Catholic convent near Paris and to be educated there in the same way as her mother. They all left New York aboard the new French liner *Normandie*, on 25 September 1935.

It was Jack's first-ever trip to England and was destined to be short. When he reached London, Jack stayed at Claridge's and attended LSE's freshers' first week. He found a house with a maid and wrote gleefully to Billings, 'They say it is only a stroll through from Buckingham Palace so I shall shortly be hurling stones at the King. I have met a number of royals + lords here and I'm getting rather royal myself'. No sooner had he posted this letter than he fell badly ill with suspected hepatitis and his father decided to return him to America for specialist treatment.

When Jack re-entered Princeton on 24 October, they managed to squeeze an extra bed into Billings' bedroom, that he shared with Rip Horton. The view from Jack's living room on the fifth floor of South Reunion Hall overlooked the main college entrance which was topped with ivy and a white lantern, put up in 1780. Although delighted to be with his old school friends, Jack seemed disappointed by the country club atmosphere and what he saw as the provincialism of Princeton. Some weeks later, doctors, who had not yet found a cure for his illness, recommended he be withdrawn from college for proper monitoring and treatment until the next fall. That winter, Jack took many tests and examinations in hospitals in Palm Beach and Boston. In between these tests he lived for the weekends, where he indulged in dances, girls and action. His Princeton roommate Rip Horton recalls Jack "liked to be sloppy, liked to play golf, he liked girls. But he would never give himself over entirely to anything. He would love to come to New York and stay with me and we would go to those nightclubs. He was a guy who lived very hard for twenty-four hours a day". With his sense of adventure and mischief, the occasional misdemeanour would occur. That October, Jack was interviewed by officials after a woman complained he had deliberately bumped his car into hers four or five times, "which story has some truth although I didn't know I was leering", Jack told Billings, and asked him to take the blame, suggesting he write to the police telling them, "you're sorry and realize you shouldn't have done it, etc…"[55]

Kick had made an unhappy start at the Sacred Heart Convent in St Maux. She wrote, 'It's so strict in its rules and stuck out in the country', and pleaded to go to the Holy Child Convent in Neuilly, Paris. Kick soon settled there, sharing a room with an English girl who 'seems very nice'. She enchanted everyone with her good humour and curiosity, earning the nickname 'Mademoiselle Pourquoi' for her habit of questioning the rules. On her sixteenth birthday, she was given

Family line up with baby Jean, Bobby, Pat, Eunice, Kathleen, Rosemary, Jack and Joe Jnr. at Hyannis Port, August 1928. (Courtesy JFK Foundation)

Swimming in Nantucket Sound, Cape Cod circa 1925/26.
Rosemary, Jack, Eunice, Joe Jnr, and Kathleen. (Courtesy JFK Foundation)

*Kathleen (Kick) prepares
to dive at The Breakers at
their Palm Beach home,
March 1934. (Courtesy
JFK Library)*

Jack together with his 'kindred spirit' and sister Kick with whom he developed a special bond, Palm Beach, Christmas 1939. (Courtesy JFK Library)

'The fun loving boy who never complained' was often precariously ill. Looking cheerful but with a suspected bout of jaundice in London in 1937, Jack was unable to start his studies at the London School of Economics. (Courtesy JFK Library)

Seated on the bumper of his soft top Ford, Jack with his dachshund 'Offie', picked up in Germany during his European car tour with his friend Lem Billings, The Hague, August 1937. (Courtesy JFK Library)

Jack juggling in a street in Germany, perhaps in Cologne, August 1937. (Courtesy JFK Library)

Kick to the left of her mother, Rose, and Rosemary about to leave Prince's Gate to be presented at Court before the King and Queen, 11 May 1938. (Alamy)

Photographers besiege Ambassador Kennedy and his family in the gardens behind Prince's Gate on 16 March 1938, shortly after their arrival. From the left, Kick (soon to break into London society to become a star in her own right), Joe, Teddy, Rose, Rosemary, Jean and Bobby. (Courtesy JFK Library)

Ambassador Kennedy and Jack greet guests on 22 June 1939 for Eunice's 'coming out' party at 14 Prince's Gate , Kensington. (Magnum)

Sharing an intimate moment with Kick's friend, Jane Kenyon Slaney at Prince's Gate. (Magnum)

Jack dances with Jane, the granddaughter of the Earl of Abercorn, 22 June 1939. (Magnum)

Joe Jnr, Kick and Jack race to the House of Commons to hear Prime Minister Chamberlain declare war on 3 September 1939. (Courtesy JFK Library)

Kennedy family gathered at Eden Roc, Cap Antibes, on the French Riviera, early August 1939. (Courtesy JFK Library)

a picture frame by her English friends and received a huge box of crackers from her Irish friends. Every fortnight, the girls from the convent went to the Louvre to gaze at the *Mona Lisa*. 'I'm really getting too cultured for words', Kick wrote home.

In the following Spring, the convent girls took an Easter holiday with the sisters by train, over the Alps into Italy. Kick was enchanted by Venice. 'Last night we all went out in a gondola for an hour. Never have I seen such a night. We have all decided to come back to Venice for our honeymoons. We sleep and are awoken by the sound of singing gondoliers', she wrote from Hotel Gabrielli Sandwirth on 29 March.[56] At a Mass in San Marco, they laughed when one of the girls taking communion was told by the priest that her lips 'were too red.' 'So that's that',[57] quipped Kick. They swam at the beach on the Lido and, getting back, she wrote to her parents, 'not very funny here as all the men talk to the girls on the street. We had about six in a cavalcade following us all over Venice today!'

In Florence they stayed at a *pensione* overlooking the River Arno where Dante once stayed. Kick, seeing a street parade, wrote, '…will be very Fascist by the time I get home'. Arriving in Rome, on her father's suggestion, she made contact with Count Galeazzi, who gave her three tickets for the Good Friday Mass in the Sistine Chapel as guests of Cardinal Pacelli. Next day, on the way to the Capitoline Hill, they were caught up in another big crowd. 'A policeman told us that Mussolini would probably appear in his office in response to the cheering and yelling… Lo and behold we had only been there an hour when Il Duce came out with a big stride and bigger grin – I was wedged in trying to take his picture.' She also had an audience with the Pope: 'The Holy Father spoke a few words to us in French and gave holy cards',[58] she wrote after seeing both Mussolini and the Pope on the same day. Before they left Rome, Kick wrote about meeting 'another convent from Switzerland – nine girls all English and are they English! Am still getting very fat and spaghetti is helping plenty – Love to all.'[59] They then headed for the Amalfi Coast. 'Never have I seen such blue water and as the road twisted and turned above the sparkling sea we were saying our prayers continuously.'

After this four-week Italian escapade, Kick got back to Paris to read a telegram from her mother. 'Sailing today on *Ile de France*. See you Ritz twenty-ninth'.[60] Missing her family, Kick wrote to Bobby, 'Mother shall be here in three days and just can't wait to see her. I haven't seen any beautiful Kennedy faces for seven months. Long long time that'.[61] Rose would recall the moment they met at the Ritz. "She looked so pretty and sophisticated in the moment she saw me and dissolved in tears of happiness as if she was still a little girl. I realized then so clearly how lucky I was to have this wonderfully effervescent and adorably loving and extremely pretty child as my daughter and friend."[62]

Kick was pretty but not in a sense that could be readily captured on camera. She was a 'soft Kennedy' without the angular lines. She was not tall, had tiny feet, wavy hair and deep-set eyes. She had a sensuous appeal that made nearly all the boys and men she met adore and fall in love with her. She had a personality of such vivacity that one biographer described it as, 'like quicksilver, skewing her older brothers with her wit, filling a languid afternoon with laughter and humour so the hours overflowed with life. She was a girl and then a woman, whom no one ever forgot.'[63]

Rose liked to travel – she made seventeen visits to Europe in the 1930s. In May 1936, she took Kick with her to Moscow. Her interest in Russia had been roused by Joe Jnr's visit the previous year with Professor Laski of the LSE. They stayed with 'the perfect host', Ambassador Bullitt, who was to form a bitter dislike of Stalin and Communism. He advised them to exercise caution when speaking on the phone 'as the operator was a spy' and warned them each time they left the Embassy they would be 'followed by a little car'! They saw the Bolshoi Ballet and the new Moscow subway, 'where every station is a work of art and mosaic', and took the train to Leningrad to visit the Hermitage. Rose found 'travelling with Kick was such a joy.'[64] It had been an education for Kick to see both the Soviet Union and Italy, and Rose took a balanced view of the Soviet system where, 'many of its aims, if not many of the methods, were worthy of respect and discussion.'

After Rose sailed home on the *Queen Mary*, Kick made her first independent trip to England. She had been invited by Derek Richardson, an American student at Cambridge who she had met skiing. Taking along her friend Ellie Hoguet from their Paris convent, they stayed at a vicarage in Cambridge, sleeping on air mattresses 'rolling all night!' At night, she and Ellie went to 'a great tent lit by lanterns overlooking the river' for a college dance, where young man after young man asked her to dance. This American Cinderella so long hidden away in a convent now spun quite carefree round the dance floor. Fresh from adventures in Moscow, her conversation was filled with laughter and wit. They partied until dawn, Kick telling her diary, 'seemed rather funny – walking around in evening clothes in broad daylight.' It had been a splendid four days of freedom for Kick. She had been a hit in England. Her year in Europe had been a thrilling experience. Still only sixteen, she now had a certain polish and sophistication. As her father said, experience was proving the most important thing in life for building character! Happy in her own skin, she had that streak of Kennedy independence and spirit that was extremely appealing. The more aloofness she exhibited, the more people were drawn to her extraordinary warmth and charisma. Jack had this same trait. She now returned to America as he was preparing to enter Harvard.

The Harvard School of Government was new and Jack was part of its first class in that autumn of 1936. Eager to prove the value of their new discipline, the teachers were the sort of enthusiastic and open-minded professors that Jack needed. He possessed that gift of an objective mind – curious and able to think independently. Donald Thurber, a fellow student, noted Jack's intellectual curiosity. "He was a person who would always ask questions of you, who would challenge your assumptions, not unpleasantly but he'd say, 'Why do you feel that way? What makes you think so?'."[65] In many ways, Jack was a spectator to his own life. But he was never content just being an observer. "Just as he refused to feel sorry for himself, when sick, he demanded action, not delay, fun not frustration, companionship and not lonely contemplation."[66]

Jack was determined to find his own niche. Joe Jnr had already established himself as an exemplary Harvard man; a football player and hugely popular. Jack shared a room in Weld Hall with Torby MacDonald and, like all of Jack's friends he came to adore Kick and kept a framed picture of her on his desk. As Jack had to nestle into his brother's world again, he tried for the football team. At 160 pounds and six foot tall, his comparatively slight frame was being swatted away like a fly on the football field and he was quickly demoted to freshman 'B' team.[67] Swimming was a different matter, and with Jack excelling at backstroke, his college squad were rated best in a generation. Then in his first year striving for fun over academic excellence, he became campus chairman of the 'Freshman Smoker' – responsible for arranging the annual student ball. He hired, not the usual one but two jazz bands for the party and roped in a stunning singing star called Gertrude Nielsen. It proved a great success. A classmate recalls: "It was a leadership activity at Harvard and a big deal." Jack had made his mark. And by inviting five of his football team home to meet four attractive girls over a weekend and attend a riotous party in Hyannis Port, he became ever more popular, playfully boasting to Billings, "I am now known as 'Playboy' amongst my team mates!"[68]

Jack had at first been a hesitant boy where girls were concerned. Kick had become interested in boys when she was no more than twelve years old. She seemed to know already how to deal with them – to flirt genteelly but always to keep her emotional distance. She had watched Joe Jnr and Jack in the beginning approach girls with great shyness and sensitivity. Jack had been so shy that he could have been the definition of the word. Kathleen enjoyed dance classes but Jack had to be dragged to them, and once, at the Gramatan Hotel in Bronxville he hid in the toilets until the dance teacher dragged him out. When girls chose boys to dance, Jack was always popular. One young girl that he liked was Betty Young, but he could not at first bring himself even to talk to her on the telephone. Jack eventually overcame his shyness. One day, watched by Kick and her sisters, he finally gave pretty Betty, 'a kiss under the mistletoe down in the front hall'. As younger sister, Eunice, reported to her mother, "Jack was a very naughty boy!"[69]

Having started late at Harvard and now nineteen, still suffering occasional stomach and back problems and not wanting to be left behind in his studies, Jack asked if he could undertake his four-year course in three. In his first year, he chose European History – medieval to the modern age. One of his first efforts was a ten-page essay, he wrote half in French and half in English. It was about King Francis I, the younger son of the Duke of Orléans, who had 'a bold and masterful bearing: the Prince in him'. Francis at twenty was a man of action with unbounded vitality who had studied the Italian Renaissance and wanted to introduce elements of it back into France. Jack much admired this Renaissance prince, describing him as, '*un homme de talente extraordinaire*', with a temperament 'rising above the commonplace of existence and declaiming a conception of royalty, lordly magnificence and pride'.[70]

Jack wrote, 'hardly on the throne, he had in a short time reached the zenith of his fortune, but his grip on it was somewhat superficial, trying to pick the fruits without nourishing the roots'. After a disastrous defeat at Pavia, 'the flaws in his character and lusty vitality once passed off as "youth", were now becoming apparent as moral weakness. It seemed almost a pity he could not have died at Pavia'.

In his first year, Jack got through a host of books on Mussolini and Hitler: *Dictatorship in the Modern World; Germany enters the Third Reich; Mussolini's*

Italy; Folklore and Capitalism; Essentials of Democracy. His academic tutor seemed only mildly impressed: 'Kennedy was ill part of the year and did no very large quota of tutorial work. Though his mind is still undisciplined, and will probably never be very original, he has ability, I think, and gives promise of development'.[71]

5

THE GRAND TOUR – JACK SEEN AS 'INTRINSICALLY ENGLISH'

France, Italy, and Germany, Observation and study deepening, Acceptance by Spee Club, Jack and Joe Jnr sail Harvard to victory in June 1938.

At the end of his freshman year on the first day of July 1937, Jack started out on the equivalent of a 'Grand Tour' as undertaken by generations of English scholars to see first hand those Medieval and Renaissance castles, chateaux and cathedrals. He boarded the SS *Washington* taking along Lem Billings and a fold-down Ford convertible.

After docking at Le Havre on 7 July, they headed in their open-top Ford for the cathedral at Rouen and the battlefields of the Great War around Soissons. Arriving too late to enter the war memorial, site to 7,000 American soldiers at Château-Thierry, Jack and Billings decided to climb over the closed gates. One of the first entries he made in the leather-bound travel book, which Kick had given him records them both being chased out of the huge grounds by a large guard dog!

They spent a costly first night in Paris and then moved to the cheaper Hotel Montana that faced the Gare du Nord, which charged 'only 80 cents for both of us'. They soon acquired the habit 'of leaving the car around the block to keep the price from going up'. Visiting the Moulin Rouge and Café of Artists, they met 'some of the well-known artists and Billings wanted to come home early, but didn't'. On Bastille Day, they went to Harry's Bar where they got lightly drunk on champagne, with Jack scrawling in his diary, 'Pretty interesting evening'. Attending Sunday Mass at Notre-Dame, Jack sat five seats from the French President. As Billings recalls, 'Jack went up to the VIP entrance and I was right behind him but I got stopped. How he did it, I don't know. Jack was always able to get into any place he wanted – I guess it was gall'.[72]

On 18 July, they visited the hunting lodge at Chambord belonging to Jack's Renaissance hero Francis, and picked up 'a couple of English fellows, one of whom went to Trinity College, Cambridge, and who considered Roosevelt the best dictator!' Jack's journal continues: 'French improving a bit + Billings' breath getting French', and recording the local view 'that there will not be another war, as France is much too well prepared for Germany'. Driving down the Loire, both were impressed by all the little farms they had seen in 'this neat and tidy but poor area. Americans do not realize how fortunate they are. These people are satisfied with very little'.[73] They visited Lourdes, fabled for its cures. 'Very interesting, but things seemed to become reversed as Billings became quite ill after leaving. Temp 103!'

They made a short trip to watch a bull fight in Biarritz. 'Very interesting, but very cruel, specially when the bull gored a horse.'[74] They could not get into Spain because of the civil war that had been raging for three years, but Jack got his first glimpse of fascism. After speaking to Falangist refugees close to the border at St Jean de Luz, he wrote, 'Not quite as positive now about Franco victory. Shows that you can be easily influenced by people around you if you know nothing and how easy it is for you to believe what you want to believe as people at St Jean do. The important thing in the question of victory is how far Germany, Italy and Russia will go in trying to secure victory for their side.' The fun-loving and girl-obsessed youth was beginning to engage a well-concealed intellect. "Jack was terribly inquisitive about what was happening in Europe," Billings recalled, "and made a point of picking up hitchhikers whenever he could. He would ask the French how they felt about Germany and whether there was going to be a war, and ask young German soldiers if they were pro-Hitler."[75]

After covering 350 miles in a single day, Jack, who liked to drive fast, entered Italy on 1 August. At Pisa, they picked up a German called Martin, 'rather interesting as he was anti-National socialist and anti-Hitler'. He told them how the Germans hated the Russians. 'Looks as if the next war would come from that direction', recorded Jack, with some foreboding. Arriving in Rome to explore the city at night on 5 August, they 'snuck into the Coliseum and found it filled with people. Very impressive by moonlight'.[76]

Jack thought Italian streets looked, 'more lively and full than in France', and got the impression that fascism seemed to treat Italians well, seeing 'pictures

Two German soldiers in shorts and hiking boots with Jack by his V8 Ford in Italy. 'Jack was terribly inquisitive in what was happening in Europe and made a point of picking up hitchhikers whenever he could. George and Heinz were with us for about a week; their general attitude was pro-Hitler'. (Courtesy JFK Library)

of Mussolini everywhere'. Billings remarked there was a lot less poverty than anticipated: 'The general public seemed not too unhappy'. Jack was prompted to question the nature of fascism: was it 'out-and-out socialism' as they had been told or 'a sort of secular version of authoritarian Catholicism or even the last agonies of Capitalism and a mere prelude to Communism?' He asked himself, 'What were the downsides of Fascism compared to Communism? Could there be any permanence in an alliance of Germany and Italy – or are their interests too much in conflict?'[77]

The pair drove down to Naples and visited Capri. 'Went to the Blue Grotto which is a cave under the water, the water having a beautiful blue color – although not blue and beautiful enough for 50 lira we scraped together!' complained Jack. In Pompeii, they learnt 'the only way… was to sneak in – which we did'. Driving up to Mount Vesuvius in their open-top V8 Ford, they picked up more Germans, two soldiers in shorts and hiking boots, called Georg and Heinz. 'They were with us for about a week and we gathered that their general attitude was pro-Hitler'. When they got back to Rome, the two frugal Germans slept in the car whilst Jack and Billings slept in a hotel, and after finding hotels in Florence, Jack complained, 'Once again we got our 25 lire rooms while the Germans got theirs for 8'.

In Venice they stayed at the Excelsior Hotel, swam at the Lido and wandered the canals and squares and called at the American bar. The leather-bound diary records, 'Listened to the concert in St Mark's Square where Billings finally had his picture taken with the pigeons… went out in a gondola which would've been quite romantic except as usual Billings managed to make a gay threesome'.[78] After five weeks of travelling, they were now tiring. 'Getting a bit fed up with spaghetti… put in our usual bad night with the mosquitoes as our net just seemed to lock them in'.

On 16 August, they headed for Germany with their two soldiers, and stopped en-route at a youth hostel in Innsbruck. 'The Austrian people impressed us very much as they were certainly very different to the Italians'. After halting at Garmisch where the Winter Olympics had been held, they reached the Pension Bristol in Munich. Before the night was out, they headed for the Hofbrau Haus, the scene of Hitler's first failed Putsch and now heavily festooned with pictures of him and Nazi insignia. Inside the Hofbrau they met a black-shirted Nazi trooper who gleefully encouraged them into believing they could depart with beer mugs as souvenirs. When they were promptly stopped at the door, 'we looked back and the German was laughing'. Jack was furious at being taken for a ride by a black-shirted Nazi on his first night in Munich. It 'gave us a very bad impression',[79] said Billings. 'The mood of the Germans we met was just insufferable. We just had awful experiences there. They were so haughty and so sure of themselves. The German people were going through a very strange period then'. Jack was absolutely overwhelmed with interest in the Hitler movement, recalled Billings, but at this point he simply noted, 'Hitler seems popular here, as Mussolini was in Italy, although propaganda seems to be his strongest point'. On leaving Munich, they started out as usual, 'except this time we had the added attraction of being spitten upon'.[80] They then bravely returned all the Nazi salutes and greetings they encountered with an enthusiastic and spirited, "Hiya Hitler!"

Hitler was due to speak three days later, at a massive Nürnberg Rally to 400,000 Party members brought from all over Germany by 400 special trains. The ancient and walled town was bedecked with blood-red Nazi banners emblazoned with black swastikas. Curiously, Jack and Lem missed the rally and instead headed north up the Rhine. 'Many castles all along the way. Towns are very attractive showing that the Nordic races certainly seem superior to the Latin. The Germans are too good – it makes people gang against them for protection'. On reaching Cologne, Jack marvelled at the tall spired cathedral. 'Really the height of Gothic architecture, the most beautiful of all we have seen'.[81] The beach at Ostend, when they got there was too cold for a swim or sunbathing so they headed for Calais, missing a boat, 'by ten seconds after a misunderstanding over Billings' passport… though Billings managed to get the good work-out he badly needed'. On this note, Jack and Lem ended their Grand Tour. They had been largely on their own and had lived as cheaply as possible, staying at twenty-six hotels, *pensions* and youth hostels and had often signed the visitors book, 'Not Gentleman'.

When they reached the private rooms of 17 Talbot Square in London, it felt more like home. They met up with Kick and Joe Jnr that first night and after shopping with his sister next morning, Jack went down to see her off at Southampton with her mother Rose, on the ship bound for America on 27 August. The Grand Tour travellers remained behind, to take up an invitation from Sir James Calder, who had once given Joe Kennedy the exclusive rights to import Haig Whisky, staying at 'a terrific big castle with beautiful furnished rooms. One room 40 yards long – a bedroom', noted Jack. They had grouse for dinner and stayed up till about three,[82] before leaving Herstmonceux Castle in Sussex for the Calder Estate in Scotland to shoot grouse. When they finally got back to America two weeks later, Kick was there to meet them and their grouse. On being presented the high-smelling bird, she chucked it straight over the side into New York's harbour, to the boys' great amusement.

Jack's 'Grand Tour' of 1937 had been invigorating. At twenty, he was sharpening his powers of observation and judgement – the freshman playboy was becoming a serious student. Having collected new ideas and questions for his professors, he now set out on his intensive course of twentieth-century isms: capitalism, fascism, communism, imperialism, militarism and nationalism.

Jack would trace British Liberal and Conservative attitudes from 1919 to 1938 in which he explored differences between idealism and realism. Curious about relations between nation states and the role of international law, Jack produced a paper on 'neutrality'. He tackled the issue of breaches of neutrality in war, and whether neutral pilots could guide ships of belligerent nations through their waters. He questioned whether 'a war zone is legal' and focused on the rights of submarines to attack neutral ships carrying munitions to an enemy power in so-called 'war zones'. Little could he foresee that one day he would be ordering a naval blockade and quarantine!

The student of government increasingly viewed England as the political anchor of Europe: 'the guarantor of peace between arrogant Germans, complacent French, noisy Italians and communist Russians'. In his own heart, Jack was not attracted to the Continental form of politics and patriotism. 'Fascism is the thing for Germany and Italy, communism for Russia and democracy in America and England'.[83]

The New York columnist Joe Alsop, who knew Jack better perhaps than any other journalist, wrote, 'There was something intrinsically English in the character of Jack Kennedy – for all his enthusiasm over girls and determination to have fun there was a level of reading and a commitment to balanced dispassionate judgement. He was an extraordinary man'.[84]

Jack, like his sister Kick, appreciated wit and irony, and instinctively understood the understated sense of British humour. They exhibited a very British sensibility: don't show your emotions, make light of your troubles and always keep a sense of humour.[85] Expanding on Jack's 'Englishness', Alsop would say, 'I still don't know what made him tick, quite. He was terrifically snobbish, you know. But not what people normally call snobbish. He was terribly old-fashioned, almost like, sort of English Grandee kind of snobbishness. It was a kind of snobbery of style – he liked people to be good-looking and hated people who let themselves go. He was snobbish about courage, and he was snobbish about experience. He didn't want us to be ordinary and routine, and kind of suburban vegetable living. He wanted experience to be intense'. The columnist concluded, 'Actually, I don't know how to put it quite. To my way of thinking he really wasn't like an American. He wasn't a foreigner either; but the normal successful American view of life was not really his view at all… What I am really talking about is a matter of style, of intellectual style, of viewpoint, of what you care most about, and what you like and dislike. It's very hard to pin down, but it's the best I can do after a long life of observing people, and I think it's not inaccurate'.[86]

When Jack resumed his studies in 1937, he was one of just eight students to be accepted by the elitist Spee Club of Harvard, deemed to be the heart of Boston's old establishment world. He would often enjoy breakfast and lunch in the ivy-clad Spee building over the next three years. His father had failed to be accepted by this quasi-English club with its leather chairs and Hogarth prints.

Now Jack could feel protected from any criticism his father had suffered for his Boston Irish background. Jack and club members took an oath that, 'for the rest of their lives they would do everything to aid one another'. When not at the club Jack would on occassion be seen mixing with celebrities and actresses at the Stork Club in New York.

To round off his summer term Jack, who enjoyed being on water, joined his brother, who was Harvard team leader in a sailing race. In separate boats they raced nine other college teams. Jack put them ahead in the sixth race and then took second place in the eighth race, ensuring a Harvard victory in this presiguous event.[87] With his father Joe watching, it was a thrilling way to end his second student year in 1938.

6

AMBASSADOR JOE – 'LONDON IS WHERE I WANT TO GO'

Ambassador Joe arrives March 1938, nine-child diplomatic sensation, Hitler marches into Austria, Easter with King and Queen at Windsor, Kick most exciting 'Deb', Jack and Joe Jnr arrive on Independence Day.

Life magazine in December 1937 greeted the news of Joe's posting to London with a full-page family photo of 'Nine children and nine million dollars'.

Joe had lobbied Roosevelt for the ambassadorship, telling the President's son Jimmy, "London is where I want to go. It is the only place I intend to go."[88] This sought-after diplomatic post was assuming great importance as Hitler's shadow sharpened over Europe.

By the 1930s, Joe had become America's fourth richest man. He had funded the President's election campaign as one of the few truly rich men in the Democratic party. He had known Franklin Roosevelt since 1917, when he was Assistant Secretary of the Navy and Joe was running the Fore River Shipyard. They were both strong-willed and highly opinionated men. They inevitably irritated each other whilst developing a wary mutual respect.

Rose now began to see her family as a kind of American nobility. London would give them the desired breakthrough she had always sought for her Irish Catholic family. Feeling vulnerable and insecure after devoting so much time to rearing nine children, she took conversation practice with a talented nun, Mother Patterson, from the convent at Noroton, before leaving Boston.

The moment the American Ambassador and his family stepped off the boat in Plymouth, they were treated as celebrities. Such a big and good-looking family had rarely been seen before amongst London diplomats. Conventional

Rose was eager to fit into her new role. Joe, an unconventional choice for ambassador, relished being the most undiplomatic of diplomats. He had no intention of changing his brusque style, and London took to this unpretentious forty-nine-year-old ambassador and his family with rare delight.

The Embassy was located just a fifteen-minute walk from their Prince's Gate home, in Grosvenor Square. When he first arrived at the Embassy, Joe was besieged by photographers and reporters before being greeted by his 195 staff. Occupying a post that had first been held by John Adams in 1785, Joseph Kennedy placed his business shoes in the footsteps where had formerly walked philosophers, poets, historians and members of the social elite. In all, five future presidents and four vice-presidents had been ambassadors in London. One of those whose portraits now gazed in stately manner down on him in the Ambassador's study, was the aristocratically urbane Joseph Choate, who held the post from 1899 to 1905.[89]

At his first embassy news conference, Joe made a show of his informality by putting his feet up on his desk whilst answering reporters' questions and declared, "You can't expect me to develop into a statesman overnight."[90] As an early indication of his isolationist and political stance, he quickly informed reporters that, "The average American, right now, is more interested in what he is going to eat and whether his insurance is good, rather than foreign politics."

Within a week of his arrival, Joe was being drawn in a royal carriage with white horses to present his credentials to King George VI at the Palace. During the half-hour ceremony, the King, dressed as an admiral of the fleet, standing with Foreign Secretary Lord Halifax by his side, chatted informally to Joe. The King, long fascinated with America, recognised the key role the United States could play in defending democracy and he now set out to win over the new ambassador. He did not forget to congratulate Joe on his recent 'hole-in-one' on the golf course, which the press had highlighted, and made a point of wishing to see the Ambassador's children as soon as they arrived.[91] Joe recorded privately, 'The King was almost boyish looking', and that Halifax, 'looks and acts like a Cardinal or Abraham Lincoln without the beard'. Joe later repeated some of his conversation with the King to the *Daily Telegraph* – the first of many diplomatic gaffes and breaks with protocol! Upset by the Ambassador's break with protocol by not wearing breeches at the ceremony, London's *Evening Standard* reported, 'Kennedy and the less important waiters were the only civilians at the presentation in trousers.'[92]

The day after Joe saw the King on 9 March, Austrian Chancellor Schuschnigg dared to flout Hitler's bullying and called for an immediate plebiscite on Austria's independence. Joe, like many, did not see this move as a prelude to any battles and wrote in his diary, 'In my mind no general war is visible in the immediate future'. The following day, he went to lunch with Churchill to hear his strenuous objections to Chamberlain's foreign policy. Churchill argued that the German army and air force were growing at a faster rate than in Britain, and that the Government's policy to delay all action until we got stronger was wrong. Futhermore, Hitler's obsession and need for action on '*Lebensraum*' had been made crystal clear when Foreign Minister von Ribbentrop told him, "England must close its eyes to the procedures in the East."[93] Joe reported his lunch with Winston to the State Department, writing, 'Churchill would try to drag America into a war it did not want'.

On 14 March, Winston went to the House of Commons to thunder another of his stirring warnings. "The gravity of the events of 12 March cannot be exaggerated. Europe is confronted with a programme of aggression, nicely calculated and timed, unfolding stage by stage and there is only one option open to us and to other countries, either to submit like Austria, or else to take effective measures while time remains to ward off the danger, and if it cannot be warded off, to cope with it."

Austria's fate did not seem to surprise or overly concern the Government. Six months earlier in a controversial visit to Germany, the Duke and Duchess of Windsor had been entertained by Hermann Goering. The Duke had spotted an unusual map above Goering's fireplace. Pointing to the map and Austria, he asked the field marshal about the mapmaker's novel, "And I might add expansive ideas." Goering could hardly contain himself: "Ho Ho! You refer, sir, to the incorporation of Austria into Germany. Well, I needed a new map and since Austria will soon join Germany – voluntarily of course – it seemed more economical to anticipate the event."[94]

By the middle of March, Hitler was standing on the balcony of the Hofburg addressing a quarter of a million cheering Viennese. He proclaimed it was 'God's will' to bring his homeland back into Germany. (An observer and uncle of the author standing in the crowd in front of the Hofburg that day in 1938 commented that despite the cheering, it was in that moment he first recognised that the proclaimed leader may have 'not got it all together'!) Churchill received an eyewitness report from his cousin Unity Mitford, who was there and who had been infatuated with Hitler since 1935. 'Everybody

looked happy and full of hope for the future', she wrote. After first consulting
the British Ambassador, he wrote back, 'A large majority of the Austrians loathe
the idea of coming under Nazi rule. It was because Herr Hitler feared the free
expression of opinion that we are compelled to witness the present dastardly
outrage'. On this blistering note, he ended forever his correspondence with his
cousin Unity.

On 24 March, Chamberlain made his long-awaited speech on Austria.
To a packed House of Commons he said Britain would not fight over an area,
'where our vital interests are not so concerned as in France or Belgium'. Joe
Kennedy thought it 'a masterpiece' of a speech, 'combining high morals with
politics such as I have never witnessed'. Others disagreed with the greenhorn
ambassador. Churchill rose from his seat and in a low voice told The House,
"After a Boa constrictor has devoured its prey, it often has a considerable
digestive spell and then a pause. Our nation rising in its ancient vigour can
even in this hour, save civilisation."[95] Joe had, by this time, already left the
gallery!

The King invited Rose and the Ambassador to spend Easter at Windsor Castle.
A delighted Rose would describe it as 'one of the most fabulous, fascinating
events in my life'.[96] After being shown to their rooms and taking up their
crystal glasses of sherry, Rose set her eyes on the crested stationery. Moving
towards the writing desk, she turned to Joe. "Why don't we write a letter now,
to all the children on this?" Surveying their regal suite, he exclaimed, "Rose, it's
a helluva long way from East Boston."[97]

Joe sat next to the Queen in the Great Hall and Rose sat alongside the
King. The Prime Minister, his wife and Lord and Lady Halifax completed the
table. Joe opened the conversation and looking at the Queen, said, "When
they remember 1917… they say to themselves never again, and I can't say I
blame them. I feel the same way myself!"

The Queen responded. "I feel that way too, Mr Kennedy," adding delicately,
"but if we had the United States actively on our side, working with us, think
how that would strengthen our position with the dictators." Joe, who had
observed the Queen, 'when fired up by an idea and speaking rapidly, acquiring
a charming animation that never shows in photographs', replied she ought to
visit America, "So that you could charm them as you have me."[98]

Lady Halifax asked Joe about President Roosevelt. The Ambassador
referred to his heroic fight against his disability and said, "If you want him in

one word, it is gallantry. The man is almost paralysed, yet he ignores it and this forces others to ignore it and he dominates a room." Such comments would later rebound against him as the President did not like anyone talking about his disability.[99] That evening at Windsor was the first time Joe had shared a table with sixty-nine-year-old Prime Minister Chamberlain. Although different in style and character, both had been a success in business. Now both shared a pessimistic vision and foreboding of the cost of confronting the growing Nazi menace. From the start they found they had a special relationship.[100] Whilst the State Department had doubts about Joe, it had still been a major coup for an ambassador to be able to strike up a deep rapport with the dour and normally uncommunicative prime minister.

Eighteen-year-old Kick and her mother arrived in London six weeks before the start of the 'summer season' to be 'presented' at Court to the King and Queen. This was the prestigious high point for young 'debutantes' making their arrival into the adult world of 1930's society.

Since arriving at Prince's Gate, Kick had felt a little homesick. Then came an invitation that would change everything – a three-day weekend invitation over Easter from Lady Astor, who invited her to meet other young people about to take part in the 'summer season'. Nancy Astor, an American by birth and Britain's first-ever woman Member of Parliament, was a fabled hostess. She had given legendary parties at Cliveden for many, from Edward VII to Charlie Chaplin and Rudyard Kipling. Cliveden, like the other great houses of England, was in essence a small community with coachmen and carpenters, dairy men, butlers and maids, and over thirty servants, who took care of the seven members of the family and their guests.[101] Kick was understandably nervous when she arrived at Cliveden.

Nancy Astor assigned Jean Ogilvie the bedroom next to Kick's, and told her, "I've got this little American girl. You have to look after her." Kick would have to contend with Lady Astor's two youngest sons, Michael and Jakie, who had inherited their mother's brilliant talent to provoke and amuse, as well as a hyperactive Andrew Cavendish and his cousin David Ormsby-Gore, and Hugh Fraser. The girl assigned to care of Kick, Lady Jean Ogilvie was the nineteen-year-old daughter of the Earl of Airlie (who oversaw the monarch's household). Unsurprisingly, Kick seemed "rather lost at first", Jean recalled, "but it soon became very clear that Kick didn't need any looking after at all!"

When the boys' pranks started, Kick, being used to her brothers' jokes, was up for it. When she discovered all her left shoes had been taken and hidden away, she decided to enter the dining room limping barefoot, declaring simply she had broken her leg! She then joined in gleefully with the boys' conversations, competing on level terms with a fast-talking David, nearly twenty, and his Oxford roommate Hugh. Encouraged by her father to share her opinions and to discuss politics together with her brothers, she sparkled in this atmosphere. Kick's confident chatter came mixed with helpings of self-mockery. The boys were thrilled by this refreshing lack of reserve and her overwhelming vitality. Kick was devoid of the self-consciousness of many seventeen and eighteen-year-olds, watching their own image in the world. She exuded life. Kick had once complained that the boys she met seemed rather dull and humourless. The eager and ebullient boys she saw that weekend, with words and laughter tumbling out so fast from their mouths, changed everything. This was the confident world of the 'aristocratic cousinhood' which she was now entering.

Andrew and David, educated at Eton, were cousins, and grandsons of Lord Salisbury. They shared the same books, manners and habits. They were instantly attracted to Kick and her willingness to join the debates, contributing her own lines of good-natured wit and unafraid of making a fool of herself. Kick emerged from that daunting Easter weekend with flying colours. She wrote, 'Very chummy and much gaiety. Dukes rushing around like mad freshmen.' When she got back to London, she did not wait, as most English ladies might, to phone Jean for lunch – she invited her that afternoon. When Jean replied she was with her father; Kick said her father was at home too; so why didn't she bring him along? The two fathers with the same first name, were soon happily exchanging ideas with their daughters and each other over lunch.

Kick was irreverent by nature but had a scrupulous sense of the appropriate, knowing she could say things a British woman could not say, and knew too the precise point when the naughty became the vulgar. She, like Jack, was uncomfortable with personal emotions and pushed back those who got too close. In upper-class English society, this was not only tolerated, but of course the norm. "She had a raving success, and we all absolutely adored her," said Sissie Lloyd. Deborah Mitford remembers her being 'just a complete star; she was just enchanting'. All were fascinated by this American phenomenon. She was tough and unconventional but above all her shining niceness always came through. 'When she came into a room', her friend Dinah Bridge noted, 'everyone seemed to lighten up. She made everyone feel terribly happy and gay'.

Kick had wavy auburn hair and sparkling blue eyes. Every one of Jack's friends back in America had seemed to want to fall in love with Kick. She wasn't afraid of anyone. It was one of the reasons her father favoured her, because she was not afraid of him either. She was as plucky as her brothers and imbued with the same restless energy and drive.[102] 'All the loneliness I had for America has disappeared because now England seems so very jolly', she wrote on 16 April to Lem Billings.

The press were fascinated by this eighteen-year-old diplomat's daughter Pictures of her featured regularly, delivering baked cookies to Great Ormond Street Hospital for children and riding horseback with her father along Rotten Row in Hyde Park.[103] The whole family attracted interest and even the brusque Ambassador was labelled 'Jolly Joe'. That July, *Vogue* magazine ran a feature on the photogenic family who 'swept in like a conquering horde upon London that had lowered its defenses and admitted itself stormed. The family have taken to life in London', said the American magazine, 'with the ease of the proverbial ducks to a pond'. London newspapers featured the younger Kennedy children watching the Changing of the Guard and Bobby and Teddy starting their first day at school.[104] But it was Kathleen, 'who is about everywhere, at all parties, alert, observant, a merry girl who when she talks to you, makes you feel as if you were seeing it all for the first time.' She was becoming the new Kennedy star.

For debutantes moving from schoolroom to grown-up, Christian Grant describes the regal presentation ritual. "We walked upstairs and down a passage to the Throne Room. I felt marvelous, not a bit frightened, just wonderfully elated and a bit regal. It was the only time in my life I envied the Princesses – for I would have given almost anything to go on living in the fairy tale world in which I found myself. Everything in the Palace was so unexpectedly big – the passages were high and spacious, the Throne Room ceiling seemed somewhere in the clouds. The musicians struck up the national anthem, the people rose and three men in uniform appeared walking backwards and bowing as they walked. It was all so impressive. I shouldn't really have been surprised if the Almighty Himself had appeared. Their Majesties entered slowly, with great dignity, and sat down in front of the canopy. The Queen was wearing a very full white dress, scattered with gold sequins, and two pages so arranged her long train that it looked like a waterfall flowing down the steps of the throne… In the doorway I handed my presentation card to an official and two lackeys spread my train behind me. My card was passed from hand to hand nine times and my name was announced by the Lord Chamberlain by the time I arrived in front of the King. Curtseying was awfully easy and the Queen gave me a sweet smile though the King bowed rather stiffly'.[105]

The press voted Kick 'the most exciting debutante' that year. It was, said Debo Mitford, 'a vintage year for beautiful girls. And then there was Kick, the sister of John Kennedy, not strictly a beauty but by far the most popular of them all'.[106] Amongst the twelve hundred daughters presented that summer were Clarissa Churchill, Veronica Fraser and Sissy Lloyd-Thomas.[107]

The first Monday in May, which marked the start of events opened with the Royal Academy Summer Exhibition and an opera in Covent Garden in the evening. Then followed the Chelsea Flower Show, Trooping the Colour, a week at Ascot and two weeks of Wimbledon. With music at Glyndebourne and racing at Goodwood, the season would slowly draw to an end in early August with sailing at Cowes. The upper classes would then head north to their estates in Scotland to bag grouse, or go south to the glittering beaches of the Riviera.

Three months of entertaining and mixing, meant dances three to four nights a week and sometimes two on the same night. Weekend dances generally took place in the grand country houses. That May, Kick went to a house party at Blenheim Palace where some late arrivals after dinner included her Oxford friends from Easter, all in high and inebriated spirits – Jakie Astor, Hugh Fraser and Robert Cecil.[108] Kick looked on as her Oxford undergraduates managed to break a statue, flinging champagne bottles between themselves under the chandeliers! Kick would record attending a more orderly party at Cliveden later that month seeing 'everyone wearing decorations, and the Queen on a sofa chatting to Charles Lindbergh'.

Kick remained at Cliveden to catch the centerpiece of the season – four days of racing at Ascot. Lady Sarah Churchill described Ascot as a ritual that had for generations helped maintain, through 'proper marriage', one of the longest surviving elites in the world. "Debs too were under starters' orders, just like fillies at a race track, you know being wandered around for sale to the best bidder." Joe and Rose had been invited to the royal box to lunch with the King and Queen, and Rose found herself escorted by the handsome Duke of Kent on one side and a heavily bejewelled Maharaja of Rajpur on the other. Whilst Joe exclaimed, "Well, if that's just not like Hollywood," Rose recorded, 'just the most perfect day… an atmosphere of contentment, of joy, of interest and satisfaction'.[109]

Kick's diary has a summary of her hectic progress in June: 'Cambridge for the annual food fight at Whitsun; two visits to Glyndebourne to see the opera; cocktail party at the Ritz, dinner at David Rockefeller's flat; watching 'Trooping of the Colour'; Cliveden for Ascot week; Hatfield visit – home of the Marquis of Salisbury and grandson Robert Cecil; Wimbledon'. She sat watching tennis in the royal box with Queen Mary, her mother Rose and Grandmother Josie.

Kick joined a thousand guests for Royal Derby night at Buckingham Palace: 'Beautifully bejeweled women. The King and Queen were on a dias at one end with the Dowager, Queen Mary. Daddy was the only man without knee breeches. He looked so funny sitting up with the old Queen Mary trying to get a smile out of her'. A highlight that evening, she added in her diary, was American blonde cabaret singer Evelyn Dall, who appeared in 'blue satin rocking the rafters crooning, "Nice work if you can get it."'

Next morning, Kick was up early and arranging place cards with Rose for her own 'coming out' party. She had invited sixty guests for dinner. She put Prince Frederick of Prussia next to her on the table with Lord Robert Cecil, John Stanley (the grandson of the Earl of Derby), Jean Ogilvy and Deborah Mitford. That evening, after the main meal had been served, another 300 invited guests arrived for the dance party. They filed up a stairway strewn with purple and pink flowers into a French panelled ballroom where they danced to American cabaret singer Harry Rich and 'the Ambrose band'. It was three in the morning before all of Kick's guests joined in a final 'Thanks for the memories'.

'Our brawl went off very well. Tried to get everyone to cut in but it was a most terrific effort. They all acted as if it was absolutely the lowest thing in life to tap someone on the shoulder… but otherwise everything was wonderbar',[110] wrote Kick.

For three months, from May to July, the evenings for the Ambassador's daughter, in that innocent summer of 1938, were filled every night by young men in white tie and tails and gloves joining debutantes in their ball gowns. Kick had her way of adding fun and informality. One night, a friend saw her throw a dinner roll across a dining table, in a provocative gesture that led to another winging its way back up the table. Soon there was one gigantic artillery battle happening with bread whizzing through the air. "If someone else had done that," reflected Lady Lloyd, "it might have been rude or shocking. But she had this way about her that made it seem an absolute liberation."

Britain's upper classes loved the way Kick played up to her Americanness rather than copy a British, or even adopt a phoney accent. Kick sensed the way forward was not to conform but to be utterly and completely herself. Despite all her frolicking and earthy appeal, Kick remained aloof with some sense of destiny, as if she was saving herself for someone special.[111]

In June 1938, Kick's father sailed home on the *Queen Mary* to confer with Roosevelt about the worsening Nazi threat. Jimmy Roosevelt, the President's son, was there to greet him when the ship docked in New York and warned him the press were going to badger him about wanting to run as Democratic candidate to replace his father. Joe spoke to the press with the tactful loyalty of the true politician. "I enlisted under President Roosevelt to do what he wanted me to do… If I had my eye on another job it would be a complete breach of faith with President Roosevelt." Joe knew, if he harboured any intentions of running for the presidency, that publicly he had to proceed with great care. In his memoir, Joe wrote, 'Mr. Roosevelt… had a quality – a failing some have called it – resenting the suggestion that he was to be succeeded'.[112] Joe planned to attend Joe Jnr's graduation ceremony at Harvard and hoped to collect an honorary degree in recognition of his new status as ambassador. But when no degree was forthcoming, he decided not to attend his son's ceremony. "It was a terrible blow," lamented Rose. "Suddenly he felt as if he were once again standing in front of the Porcellian Club, knowing he'd never be admitted."[113]

Ambassador Kennedy as a second-generation Irish Catholic was never secure about his place in the world and had been wounded in youth by the social rejection he suffered at the hands of the Boston Anglo-Saxon protestants. He had laboured hard for thirty years to gain prominence and acceptance. For a while, his new position in London offered his dynamic family the chance of achieving those dreams of social acceptance and security, and to dispel 'his profound sense of being a second-class citizen'.[114] By being close to the centre of action, he could advance his political power – possibly even win the presidency. But it would forever elude him. His siding with Chamberlain, his advocacy of peace at all costs and support for American isolationism, combined with his rebellious behaviour, would eventually cost him the friendship not only of his British hosts, but that of the President and colleagues back home.

The triumphs and failures of Joe, and his tenure in London, would be acutely felt by the Kennedy children. Jack, watching and studying his father's progress, took great care to develop his own independent world outlook and political philosophy. The thousand days as ambassador in London would hover over his son's thousand-day tenure in the White House. Jack learning from his father's mistakes, was in part perhaps the greatest legacy of Joe and Rose Kennedy's tenure in London.[115]

Two days after Joe landed in New York, the *Chicago Tribune* carried the provocative headline, 'Kennedy's 1940 Ambitions Open Roosevelt Rift'. It went on to say, 'Mr. Roosevelt has received positive evidence that Kennedy hopes to use the Court of St James as a stepping stone to the White House in 1940.' The unwelcome article ended: 'The chilling shadow of 1940 has fallen across the friendship of President Roosevelt and his two-fisted troubleshooter Joseph Patrick Kennedy". Roosevelt, who instinctively distrusted Joe, had believed the Ambassador was scheming behind his back. Whilst the President had hoped that an ambassadorship might stop Kennedy inserting himself into the 1940 democratic nomination process, his real concern was that the Ambassador, if not a rival, would become a critic of his faltering 'New Deal' that was vulnerable to business-orientated opposition which Kennedy could mobilise. Interestingly, in sending Kennedy to London, Roosevelt had been 'kind of intrigued with the idea of twisting the lion's tail a little so to speak'.[116]

When Joe dined with the President at the White House on a Friday night in late June, he had no idea his wily boss had been behind the earlier press attack on him. After Joe found out, he was furious: 'It was a true Irish anger that swept over me'. Joe wangled a final meeting with Roosevelt, who denied any involvement. But Joe felt that the President had turned on him. 'In his way he assuaged my feelings… Deep within me I knew that something had happened'.[117]

In Washington, Joe called on the State Department and submitted his report criticising Foreign Service intelligence gathering. He believed 'far too much time was spent by embassy staff in attending teas, receptions and other gala occasions' and 'then picking up chitchat about affairs that was then forwarded to the State Department as if it were verified information'. In the first three months, Kennedy had performed brilliantly, enhancing America's image in Britain. He made all the right contacts to obtain the freshest political and economic information that Washington had seen in years. He had increased embassy efficiency by demanding embassy reports present hard facts. But Kennedy had also dismissed the views of his regular embassy staff on issues like Austria. "I am unable to see that the Central European developments affect our country or my job," he maintained, and would describe London diplomats as adopting 'a semi-hysterical attitude… whenever another unforeseen step occurs'. The economic situation was the key to the whole thing, he felt. Joe was a businessman. He had not read any European history or had experience of international relations. As a businessman, he had made up his mind that Europe's problems would be solved by better cash flow. As he continued to maintain with the State Department, "At the root of the problem… the unemployed man with a hungry family is the same fellow, whether the Swastika or some other flag floats above his head."[118]

After the attacks on him in the American press, Joe was eager to get back to Britain, and now took his two handsome sons with him on the *Normandie*. He was determined that they should gain a greater insight into politics and world affairs.

7

THE 'ARISTOCRATIC COUSINHOOD'

Jack, an instant hit in Kick's circle, and a Mitford says, "That man will be President," Jack meets David, spellbound by Churchill in Parliament, Summer with beautiful people in Cannes and Carinthia, Jack returns to Harvard.

The French SS *Normandie* with its decorated art-deco interior docked at Southampton on 4 July 1938, just in time for Jack to celebrate America's Independence Day in London and join the 'summer season' with Britain's young aristocrats.

The welcome party for Jack at Prince's Gate to meet Kick's new friends was a great success. He was astonished and delighted with Kick's run of young aristocratic suitors. Both laughed heartily at the idea that his reasonably ordinary-looking sister was fast becoming the belle of England![119] Her small exclusive circle, known as the 'aristocratic cousinhood', immediately took to Jack. They accepted him into their circle which did not readily admit outsiders, as rapidly as they had done, three months earlier, his sister. [120]

After this Prince's Gate introduction, Kick and Jack sped off together with the cousinhood at 10pm to get to 4 St James's Square, where Lady Astor was giving a boisterous party for young cricketers returning from the annual Harrow-Eton cricket match. Jack's Boston twang now competed with young men from England's top two public schools, talking exuberantly far into the early morning on politics, books and everything else under the sun!

As a boy, Jack had been drawn to the romantic legends of King Arthur and his Court at Camelot. He read and reread tales of courage and noble deeds, often when he was ill and stuck in bed. Jack was an avid reader and at fifteen, with a keen interest in current affairs was the only boy in his class who had a subscription to *The New Yorker* which he read from cover to cover. He started monitoring Churchill's speeches, became absorbed in his book *Great Contemporaries,* and was fascinated by people whom Churchill had met, like Lawrence of Arabia and Lieutenant Raymond Asquith. The prime minister's son, Raymond, had been killed at the age of twenty-seven at the Battle of the Somme, before he had a chance to fulfil his political promise. Raymond marched to 'his fate cool, poised and resolute'. [121] Given his own often perilous medical condition, Jack seemed to have found inspiration from such wartime courage and *sang-froid*. As a sixteen-year-old, maybe with some sense of destiny, he read Churchill's *World Crises*. In his books, Churchill gave fascinating lessons of courage in high politics, strategy and personal danger – he had taken part in one of the last regimental cavalry charges against the Whirling Dervishes 'with the sun glinting down on many hostile spearpoints'. All this developed in Jack a life-long interest in how wars began – and how they could be stopped.

In London, Kick was introducing Jack to a realm of history that had gripped his imagination as a boy. He was now moving amongst the Ogilvies and the Colquhoons and the likes of his hero Lieutenant Asquith; all debonaire and brilliant. Churchill's *Marlborough*, Cecil's *Young Melbourne* and Buchan's *Pilgrim's Way* – some of his favourite books – were all present in the world of Kick's new circle. Surrounded by Kick's aristocratic cousinhood, Jack seemed truly energised in an England threatened by war.

The prospect of war had propelled this generation of young people entering the 1938 summer season, with intense abandon. Jack and Kick charged headlong into this exciting political and social whirl. Seeming to 'turn up at every party' as a friend remarked, Jack had been an instant hit with Kick's circle, able to see the funny side of life. He would never have a deep political discussion without making some joke at the same time.[122] In contrast to elder brother Joe Jnr. and his abrasive style, Jack and Kick possessed a light-hearted manner and finesse which enabled them to fit readily into British ways. David, Tony, Hugh, Andrew and Billy, together with Sissie, Debo and Jean amongst others, would come together to party and furiously argue the issues of the moment. They would debate questions of honour, principle and compromise in the context of how best to stand up to a dictator. Little did anyone realise, some of them would continue to share such questions with Jack through to his presidency.

Jack strolls across the lawn behind the family home at 14 Prince's Gate, Kensington. As the 'second son' he was not weighed down by the same expectations as had been placed on Joe Jnr. (Courtesy JFK Library)

From the very start, Jack and David Ormsby-Gore seemed to gravitate towards each other. Seeing themselves as part of the 'second sons club', neither was expected to carry the family name to new heights. David and Jack constantly joked when talking history and politics. They shared being spellbound and energised by Churchill when they saw him in the House of Commons and heard his talks on the radio. David was not a natural talker and this was fine with Jack, who was easily bored. There were no long monologues or explanations. This suited Jack's impatience to get to the point of whatever they were discussing. Both liked driving cars fast, and rowdy David was not unknown to throw champagne bottles out of windows, as happened at his graduation party at The George Hotel in Oxford. As Andrew Cavendish put it, they felt it was time to 'drink more and to drive faster!' David boasted a set of false teeth after he had crashed his car at ninety miles an hour on his way back to Oxford College. Under threat of looming war, Jack's generation sensed the need to enjoy and live every moment.

David was exceptionally bright. His ancestors had sat in Parliament for seven generations and his father had been Minister of State for the Colonies in Chamberlain's government. David's mother was descended from the illustrious Cecil family and she seemed to have passed independent-mindedness and liberalism on to her son. David had a marvellously dry sense of humour. The swift repartee which characterised David's back and forth with Jack, set a pattern for their talk and understanding for the next twenty-five years.[123]

British soldiers with fixed bayonets started appearing on the streets of London that summer. In Whitehall, government windows were crisscrossed with white tape. Heavy sandbags were placed around entrances and doorways. The atmosphere was intense with anticipation. There was something in this English setting with its dramatic atmosphere that seemed to suit Jack. His boyhood imagination, excited by Arthurian tales, was meeting a new reality. He was enjoying things immensely. London on the eve of war was turning into the crucible of an education that would serve him in the future. Debo, the Duchess of Devonshire, never forgot how her mother had observed Jack at a party and 'saw something in him which was unlike anybody else. Like Kick, he was an absolute fount of energy, enthusiasm and fun, and intelligence, all the things which make people want to become them'. And her mother said, "That young man will be President of the United States."[124]

As Hitler made preparations for war, British aristocracy continued in that summer of 1938 to follow their regular rituals – either heading north for the grouse season in Scotland or south to the French Riviera. Rose rented a villa half an hour from Cannes, 'Domaine de Ranguin', with the most splendid rose garden in the hills around Cap d'Antibes. The Kennedy family swam regularly at Eden Roc and Hotel du Cap perched high above the shimmering sea. It was set amongst twenty-two acres of pines and tropical garden. It was on this spot that 'the beautiful people' from Scott Fitzgerald's *Tender is the Night* would gather to descend down a hundred steps to the candy-striped cabanas between the boulders below.

The Ambassador and Rose accepted dinner invitations from the wealthy elite, including the Duke and Duchess of Windsor aboard a yacht anchored in the bay. The family made trips inland to country churches and historic sites around St Paul de Vence. Amongst the celebrities on the golden sands that summer were Marlene Dietrich and her daughter. Walking along the beach, the Kennedy children spotted Marlene 'with her hair thrown to the winds and no worry about make up', as Rose noted in her diary.

On 14 August, Jack and Kick left Cannes and headed for Carinthia in Austria, just beyond the Italian border.[125] Jack was curious to see how Austria was coping with Hitler's takeover. They spent ten days with friends at Lake Wörthersee – a picture-perfect resort, visited by royalty and set against a background of mountains. It was Austria's equivalent to Monte Carlo. They stayed at the wooden 'Villa Sekirn', which belonged to a British Major James Foster, nearby the beautiful lakeside church of Maria Worth. Villa staff were quickly taken aback by the lively young Kennedy clan who dived into the warm lake and started playing games from the moment they arrived.[126] Kitchen doors were quickly locked to stop the 'cheeky boys' from disrupting staff!

Kick's diary records her dining with ex-King Alfonso of Spain: 'A small man and rather sallow looking, who wore golf trousers like women's coullettes, and bragged about how much he was doing to direct the Loyalist forces in the Spanish Civil War'. One evening, they visited a bar with Peter, from England, and Rudi, the Jewish son of an Austrian former minister. There, Peter got into an argument with some young Nazis 'over the fact that… [Rudi's] suspenders were showing'. The short argument came to nought but encouraged Kick to record, 'Everyone says Austria has lost its gayness and carefreeness'.[127]

After they returned to Cannes, their mother, worrying mainly about health matters, recorded that Jack was trying to put on the pounds, whilst his elder brother and three sisters were trying to shed what they had put on earlier during the British season.[128] One day, Kick got into trouble swimming out too far. It took her forty-five minutes to get back to shore and recover from her ordeal, in the bedroom of Marlene's young daughter, Maria. When Jack took the opportunity in the evening to dance with Marlene, Lem Billings wrote to Kick asking her to confirm if it was true, as Jack had said, that 'Marlene thinks he's one of the most fascinating and attractive young men she's ever met!'.[129] A home-made film taken by Marlene, records a suntanned Jack moving playfully around a pool in his white bathrobe. Marlene's daughter who idolised Jack, described him as 'the glamorous boy, the charmer of the wicked grin and come-hither look'.[130]

Ambassador Joe joined the family on the Riviera late, having stayed in

London that July to speak to Charles Lindbergh, the US aviator just back from Germany. Lindbergh had seen the Nazi Luftwaffe and claimed it so superior to any other that he thought it would be useless for any foreign power to attempt to stop Germany by force.[131] London had no reliable information to counter Lindbergh's exaggerated claims whilst the Ambassador gleefully relayed the aviator's alarming message far and wide. The German Ambassador probably at this point viewed his American counterpart as being his best friend in London!

In holiday mood and under the influence of the Mediterranean sun, Ambassador Joe started writing a speech he intended to give back in England. Talking about the Nazi threat to Czechoslovakia, he finished by commenting "…but for the life of me I cannot see anything, which could be remotely considered worth shedding blood for." The State Department immediately ordered this part of the speech by the foremost US Representative in Europe to be expunged. To the Ambassador's annoyance, the State Department also informed Roosevelt.[132]

Whilst Jack and Kick were swimming in the Wörthersee and playing on the Riviera, Hitler had by mid-August amassed a million troops on the Czech frontier. Joe, seeing things coming to a climax, quickly left the Riviera, taking Jack with him. They stopped at the Embassy in Paris where Ambassador Bullit agreed to take Joe Jnr on as a temporary aide. Arriving back on 29 August, Jack spent the last hectic days of that summer watching from a ringside seat, Chamberlain dither on how to deal with the Nazi dictator.

Jack boarded the German ship *Bremen* at Southampton on 2 September. His summer in England had been a thrilling education. He had relished seeing history being made. The British upper class, in its last decade of unrivalled power had embraced both him and his beloved sister Kick.

When the *Bremen* docked in New York Harbor, a large crowd of reporters, all anxious to hear about the situation in Europe, were waiting. In his first-ever informal press conference, Jack told the reporters there would be no war and said Americans would not have to be evacuated, adding calmly that "Joe Jnr and the rest of the family will be staying in Europe for the next year."[133]

A few days later, Rose boarded the overnight *Golden Arrow* sleeper train from London to Paris and had a 'heartbreaking' conversation with a Frenchwoman praying that war would not come. "My grandfather was killed in the war in 1870 against the Germans. My husband and brother were killed in the war in 1914. And now they are asking me to send my son to war in 1938. I cannot. I will not."[134]

On 12 September 1938, Hitler fumed and screamed at the Nurnberg Rally about the Czechs and their government. Everybody listened anxiously. But he did not, as expected, declare war.

8

'HE CAME BACK
A DIFFERENT MAN'

*Chamberlain meets Hitler, the 'Teppich Fresser', appeasement
at Munich, relief and shame, First Sea Lord resigns, Churchill
broadcasts to America.*

After he got back to Harvard in late September 1938, Jack's roommate Torby
MacDonald noticed that 'he came back from England a different man'.

Following the huge Nazi Party rally in Nürnberg on 12 September which
had been broadcast live to both America and Britain, Jack's father now made
an increasing number of daily trips to the Foreign Office and Downing
Street. Hitler's ranting speech made clear he intended to 'rescue' the German
minority in the Sudetenland. Joe pressed his support on Chamberlain and
Foreign Secretary Lord Halifax, whose policy of appeasement was reaching
its climax. The Ambassador vainly believed that his warnings, and Lindbergh's
awesome respect for what Hitler could do from the air, had been a decisive
factor in Chamberlain's stand not to call Hitler's bluff.

In a further bid to avert war, Chamberlain now flew to Berchtesgaden.
On that same day on 15 September, Churchill predicted to Lord Moyne, "We
seem to be very near the bleak choice between War and Shame. My feeling is
that we shall choose shame and then have War thrown in a little later."[135]

Travel to Berchtesgaden involved an exhausting early morning flight.
Chamberlain was accompanied by his adviser, Sir Horace Wilson; two
diplomats; two secretaries and a detective. His small team did not surround
themselves with any display or trappings of power. Arriving in Munich, he was
greeted by a crowd of three to four thousand who had turned up in the rain to
get a glimpse of the Prime Minister. Despite the dawn flight, he 'looked fresh

and ruddy, and his eyes were sparkling', recorded Ward Price from the *Daily Mail*. Chamberlain, with 'his stiff wing collar and his tie of heavy grey silk', presented an old-fashioned and unmistakably English note against the sharp line of black-uniformed soldiers beating their drums on the runway. A fleet of fourteen soft-topped black Mercedes, with the hoods up to keep out the rain, was waiting on the tarmac. The tiny British team accompanied by Ribbentrop were then driven five miles to the railway station and saw that lines of people had turned out in force to cheer them. According to Hitler's interpreter, Paul Schmidt, the warmth of the welcome was considerably greater than that which had greeted Mussolini the year before. Hitler had sent his own train of six grey-green coaches for the three-hour journey to Berchtesgarten. More crowds lined the rail route at junctions and crossings for this passing envoy of peace. The Prime Minister enjoyed a lunch of turtle soup in the Fuehrer's maple-lined dining car followed by renken, an Alpine lake fish, roast beef and Yorkshire pudding! Chamberlain seemed restored after his long flight and sufficiently alert, according to Hitler's interpreter, to observe the long troop transports rolling by in the other direction, with soldiers in uniform and gun barrels pointing skywards.[136]

The winding road leading to the Fuehrer's mountain retreat was shrouded in mist. Jackbooted SS troops dressed in crisp and severe black lined the mountain road. Their presence became as foreboding as the day's rainy sky. "We had this tiny delegation and for a great power we looked puny. We didn't know any better," recalled Sir Horace. When the little convoy got to the top, Hitler was standing with General Keitel on the top of the Berghof steps. It was just before 5pm when Chamberlain, who had been travelling since dawn, stepped out in his grey mackintosh with an umbrella over his arm and blinked at the black-uniformed guards surrounding him. A long drum roll came from the 'SS Leibstandarte Adolf Hitler' as the Fuehrer came down the steps to shake Chamberlain's hand. As they climbed up to the door of the Berghof, the tension was palpable. Inside, rain spattered loudly on the windows looking out to the blurred view of the Untersberg Mountains. Invited to sit at a low table set out with teacups, Chamberlain opened the conversation: "I have often heard of this room, but it is much larger than I expected."

"It is you who have the big rooms in England," said Hitler.

"You must come and see them sometime," replied Chamberlain.

"I should be received with demonstrations of disapproval," responded the dictator, allowing himself a dark shadow of a smile.

"Well, perhaps it would be wise to choose the moment," suggested the Prime Minister.[137] Chamberlain took note of the Fuehrer's features. 'His hair is not black, his eyes blue, his expression rather disagreeable, especially in repose and altogether he looks entirely undistinguished'.[138]

After half an hour of platitudes, Hitler abruptly brought the conversation to a halt. With just Herr Schmidt, the translator, he suggested they go upstairs to his private study, a small wood-panelled room with a stove and simple furniture. He let Chamberlain speak first. After a few short exchanges, Hitler started to lose his self-control. He shouted that he had answered the call of seven million Austrians to return the Reich to which they had belonged for a thousand years. Now it was the turn of the three million Sudeten Germans, he declared. "I am ready to face a world war," he said, glaring at Chamberlain. "I am forty-nine years old and I want to be young enough to lead my people to victory."

At this point, Chamberlain intervened: "Hold on a minute. You say that the three million Sudeten Germans must be included in the Reich. Would you be satisfied with that and is there nothing more you want? I ask because there are many people who think that is not all, that you wish to dismember Czechoslovakia." Hitler launched back into a long rambling speech of justification. For the first time, Chamberlain reacted with anger: "If I've understood you correctly and that you're determined in any event to proceed in Czechoslovakia, then why have you had me come to Berchtesgaden at all? Under these circumstances, it is best I leave straightaway." To the astonishment of his interpreter, Hitler backed down and started to speak more quietly. When the meeting came to an end, Chamberlain asked that no military action be taken until they meet again.

"The German military is a mighty instrument," said Hitler, "and once set in motion it cannot be stopped. But I will not set it in motion until our talks are resumed." With this, Chamberlain and his small party left the Berghof, driven back to Munich by Hitler's personal chauffeur along seventy-five miles of impressive new *Autobahn*.

Incredibly, the Prime Minister returned to London convinced, and telling others that he 'had established a certain confidence' with Hitler. Part of the problem was that Chamberlain had never served in the armed forces. Military and naval matters were distant for him. He had never come across anyone back in Birmingham like Hitler! His 'people' had been reasonable and honest and, after customary give-and-take, open to a deal. He believed that dictators could be reasonable men. Eden, who had resigned as Foreign

Secretary, thought otherwise, as did his leading diplomat, Sir Robert Vansitart at the Foreign Office, who had met Hitler a few years earlier. Vansitart was 'acutely aware that villainy was part of the international scene' and according to Lord Home, should clearly have been there at Berchtesgaden instead of Sir Horace, whose career had been spent in the field of industrial conciliation.[139] Vansitart's views, however, lost their force at times because of the violence with which he expressed them. His boss, Lord Halifax, sometimes called 'Holyfox' (reflecting his curious combination of religiosity with wily Yorkshire grit), had met both Hitler and Goering. But, like so many, even he seemed not to have fully grasped the utter ruthlessness of Germany's leaders.

Hitler followed up Berchtesgaden by inviting Chamberlain to Bad Godesburg on 22 September, supposedly to build on the understanding they had reached in the mountains. After landing at the aerodrome at Cologne, Chamberlain was driven in a large black Mercedes, with a Union Jack fluttering alongside a red and black swastika. Cheering crowds lined the road up to the Petersburg Hotel from where long lines of swastika flags could be seen waving in the villages below on the banks of the river. This was the region where the Lorelei and Goth legends were born. Talks were to be held across the Rhine, in Hitler's favourite hotel, the Dreesen, standing on the west bank by the pretty Wagnerian town of Bad Godesberg. This was where Wotan, Thor and gods of the early Teutons were thought to have frolicked. It was where Hitler had stayed every autumn for the last ten years.

A tale had been circulating around the press and diplomatic corps now assembled in Bad Godesberg, that when Hitler was in a rage he would lose control, 'flinging himself to the floor to chew the edge of the carpet'. Some called him the 'Teppich Fresser'. His appearance worried a journalist from the *Daily Express*. 'Hitler had ugly black patches under his eyes. I presumed that Hitler was on the edge of a nervous breakdown'. By calm contrast, when a birdlike Chamberlain appeared, American radio journalist William Shirer described the Prime Minister as looking like 'an owl, smiling and apparently highly pleased in his vain way'.[140] Whenever Hitler walked past, Shirer too observed the Fuehrer's 'very curious walk… it was very ladylike. Dainty little steps… every few steps he cocked his right shoulder nervously, his left leg snapping up as he did so. I watched him closely as he came back past us. The same nervous tick'.[141]

Hitler opened the conference and set out an entirely new list of demands

– occupation by troops with an immediate rather than slow transfer of the Sudetenland which had earlier been promised at Berchtesgaden. The meeting broke up in disarray after a few hours. Early next morning, Hitler then presented his Memorandum declaring Germany would take the Sudetenland by force if the Czechs did not accept the terms set out, by 2pm on 28 September. Chamberlain was appalled. "That's an ultimatum," he exclaimed, with Ambassador Henderson adding a cutting Versailles phrase, "A Diktat!" Hitler replied that the heading on the paper said it was a Memorandum. But as a 'special favour', he said he would agree to delay action on the takeover of Sudetenland by one day to 1 October. It was a gloomy ride across the Rhine and back home for the Prime Minister and his party on 24 September.

When members of the Cabinet were told the details of Hitler's ultimatum, a few offered to resign on the spot. War fever gripped London. A few days earlier, BBC radio announced that thirty-four hospitals had been allocated as clearing stations in London for air-raid casualties. Gas masks were being issued. Long queues of people gathered at town halls, with Chelsea Town Hall looking as if it might have been a church social with everybody – titled girls and telephone girls – queuing. Frantic digging of trenches in parks was taking place all over the city. The council at Hammersmith engaged 2,000 people to dig through the night by the light of flares and headlamps of lorries. Numerous trenches soon cut across Hyde Park and St James's Park adjoining Buckingham Palace and Downing Street.

When the people of Britain awoke on 27 September, war seemed imminent. Chamberlain came on the radio that morning. "How horrible, fantastic and incredible that we should be digging trenches and trying on gas masks here for a quarrel in a faraway country between people of whom we know nothing." The day before, in America, 20,000 people gathered in New York's Madison Square Garden in support of those 'far-away' Czech people. Roosevelt had a little earlier suggested an international conference to Chamberlian but this made little impact. Ambassador Joe then went to the Palace in person to deliver a sealed envelope (he had not been informed about its content) from Roosevelt. The President was inviting the King and Queen to America for a state visit in 1939. On 28 September the Czechs announced they would not accept Hitler's ultimatum. The French Government immediately mobilised 60,000 soldiers and Britain mobilised its Royal Navy.

American-born Chips Channon M.P. recorded the mood at Westminster as Chamberlain addressed the House that day. 'The solemn House… every seat filled, and everyone was aware of the momentous hour and the gravity of the situation, which was beyond anything perhaps the House had ever known'. As Chamberlain started to speak, the House listened in deadly silence as he revealed details of his meeting and final appeals to Hitler and Mussolini the previous night. An audible shudder passed through the House as Chamberlain admitted he was convinced that Hitler was now willing to risk a world war. At 3.15pm, and seated in the Foreign Office, Lord Cadogan received an urgent telephone call from Ambassador Henderson in Berlin. Hitler was inviting Chamberlain to meet him in Munich the next day. A messenger raced across from the Foreign Office and handed over a note in the Peers' Gallery to Lord Dunglass (Alec Douglas-Home), who clambered over his colleagues and passed the note to Sir John Simon,[142] who paused before giving it to the Prime Minister, who had been on his feet for an hour. Chamberlain stopped, adjusted his *pince-nez*, and read the note. 'There was a long pause. Then his whole face, his whole body seemed to change', wrote Harold Nicholson MP. 'He raised his face so that the light from the ceiling fell upon it. All the lines of anxiety and weariness seemed suddenly to have smoothed out. He appeared ten years younger and triumphant'. Chamberlain now continued his address. "That is not all. I have something further to tell the house. Herr Hitler has just agreed to postpone his mobilisation for twenty-four hours and to meet me in conference with Signor Mussolini and Signor Daladier at Munich." Chamberlain paused, "I need not to say what my answer will be."

There was a moment of stunned silence, and then came an extraordinary roar of approval, 'like the biggest thunderstorm you ever heard', Channon remembered. 'We stood on our benches, waved our Order papers, shouted until we went hoarse – a scene of indescribable enthusiasm. Even Queen Mary, normally stoic and undemonstrative, wept and reached out to touch those near to her'. Ambassador Kennedy joined in the shouts of relief. 'I never was so thrilled in my life', he wrote in his diary. Anthony Eden left the Chamber. Churchill stayed glumly in his seat. Afterwards, he told Chamberlain being mobbed by his supporters, "I congratulate you on your good fortune – you were very lucky." The moment Joe Kennedy got back to his embassy he announced, "Well, boys – the war is off."

Chamberlain flew out to Munich for the four-power conference and into what he called 'a prolonged nightmare'. Advisers and diplomats were left to mill around corridors and were excluded from meetings. They were often conducted without formal note-taking, agendas or even a chairman. This suited Hitler. Britain and France succeeded only in extracting from Hitler one single concession – Czech withdrawal from the Sudetenland would occur over a ten-day period and not immediately as originally demanded. While Poland and Hungary were given small areas where their ethnic populations lived, the Germans, not satisfied with just stripping away major resources, also demanded the Czech air force leave 1,350 planes in Sudeten territory.

At the end of the talks, Chamberlain asked to see Hitler privately and went to his small flat at Prinzregentenplatz where he had lived since 1929. Alec Douglas-Home, accompanying the Prime Minister recorded the visit. 'Behind a dark table, was this little, very grey man… dressed in ordinary clothes, in a very dour mood'.[143] As Chamberlain came to the end of his private speech to a disinterested Hitler, he handed the German leader the bit of paper which he had prepared. It declared 'that in future, disputes between Britain and Germany would all be settled through peaceful means'. Lord Home witnessed the signing. 'I was watching Hitler closely when he did so. He gave the text one quick reading and almost perfunctorily he signed. It was somewhat reminiscent of the previous attitude of Germany's leaders to scraps of paper'. But the Prime Minister viewed that scrap of paper as useful. If Hitler broke his word, Chamberlain thought it would 'have its value in mobilizing public opinion against him, particularly in America'.[144]

In his autobiography, *The Way the Wind Blows*, Lord Home records another striking memory from Munich. 'There is only one further impression of the Fuehrer which I took away. Twice I saw him walking down the passage ahead of me. I noticed that his arms hung low, almost to his knees, and they swung not alternately but in unison. I do not know whether this was characteristic of his walk, when alone and in deep thought, but it gave him a curiously animal appearance'.[145] The only person according to Lord Home who 'seemed to be in good boisterous spirits throughout the proceedings at Munich was Goering', who managed to change uniform three times in one day.[146] 'Mussolini strutted about with his chin out, dressed in a uniform that was slightly too tight for him. Daladier looked exhausted and tired, but not Hitler', reported American broadcaster, William Shirer. He observed 'the light of victory in Hitler's eyes as he strutted down the broad steps of the Fuehrerbau'.[147] As Chamberlain and Daladier were driven away from the steps, Hitler turned to Ribbentrop and said, "It is terrible. I always have to deal with non-entities."[148]

Before leaving Munich, Chamberlain and Lord Home were curious to see where the Nazi Party had been 'founded' in the two beer halls of the Sterneckerbraukeller and Burgerbraukeller from where the Fuehrer first marched out to try and seize power in the failed Putsch of 1923. Flags everywhere flapped gently in the soft breeze. The Union Jack and Tricolore flew alongside the swastika. Wherever the Prime Minister and Home turned up, they were greeted by jubilant crowds.[149] It was a warm autumn day – 'Hitler weather' as some people remarked in the huge crowds that day in Munich. As the beer flowed early for Oktoberfest celebrations, many Germans believed Hitler had achieved much – a Reich eliminating unemployment, triumph over the hated peace treaty and the turning of yesterday's enemies, without fighting, into friends!

On 30 September, Chamberlain landed back at Heston Aerodrome. As both Britain and France had agreed the annexation of the Sudetenland, Chamberlain felt he had nothing to show except that 'bit of paper' which Hitler had signed, to lessen the threat of war. Lord Home recalls, 'On our way back to London, Downing Street was packed with people waiting to acclaim the Munich achievement. I was with Chamberlain as we approached the foot of the staircase at No. 10, where Cabinet colleagues and others had assembled. Out of this crowd someone said, "Neville, go up to the window and record history by saying, 'Peace in our time'. I could not identify the voice but Chamberlain turned icily towards the speaker and said, "No. I do not do that kind of thing." He was right because by nature he was the most reticent and the least flamboyant of men. I then lost touch with him on the staircase and the next thing I knew he had spoken those fateful words. Someone in the last few steps to the window must have overtaken and overpersuaded him. He knew at once it was a mistake, and that he could not justify the claim, but it was too late as, leaning out from that open window at No. 10, he waved that bit of paper to the cheering crowd below, calling out, "Peace with honour. Peace for our time."

What price had they paid for peace? How long would it last? For a few days, Chamberlain basked in a huge sense of relief felt by many. The *Telegraph* reported, 'The news will be hailed with profound and universal relief'. The *Daily Express*: 'Millions of happy homes relieved of their burden – to Chamberlain go the laurels'. But this mood was about to change. Over the weekend, the early euphoria evaporated as people had time to work out exactly what had been done at Munich. A sense of disgrace about the morality of Munich –

an agreement to satisfy a dictator – started to emerge. A few days later, on 3 October, Chamberlain faced the House of Commons as Parliament began their examination.

Duff Cooper, who had resigned as First Lord of the Admiralty, opened the debate. "What do those words of the Munich pact mean?" he asked the House. "Do they mean that he [Hitler] will get away with this, as he has got away with everything else, without fighting, by well-timed bluff and bluster and blackmail? The Prime Minister believed in addressing Herr Hitler through the language of sweet reasonableness. I have believed that he was more open to the language of the mailed fist. To give in to Hitler would be to jeopardise the honour and the soul of England."

After forty-five minutes of this full broadside attack, the First Sea Lord concluded: "I have forfeited a great deal. I have given up an Office that I love… I have ruined, perhaps, my political career. But that is of little matter. I have retained something which is to me of great value. I can still walk about the world with my head erect." After he sat down, Churchill passed him a note. It read, 'The speech was one of the finest parliamentary performances I've ever heard. It was admirable in form, massive in argument and shone with courage in public spirit'.

Chamberlain spoke next but did not attempt to answer the points made by the First Sea Lord. He was frequently interrupted by cries of shame from some Members of Parliament. Churchill then spoke, describing Chamberlain's 'total and unmitigated defeat', but he was often drowned out by protesting MPs. At that stage, Winston still did not have that many allies. After four exhausting days, the Government got the Munich Agreement through by a majority of almost two thirds. The Foreign Secretary, Lord Halifax admitted Munich, 'had been a horrid business, it had been humiliating, no use blinking the fact, but better than a European war'.[150] Despite the majority vote, it was the quality of the minority and the individuals who had voted against that would count. They included Churchill, Eden, Amery, Macmillan, Cranbourne and Duff Cooper.

Duff Cooper's statesmanlike address of 3 October was widely broadcast and followed in America. His themes of honour and principle hit their mark. The Prime Minister rapidly lost the confidence of senior ministers and the people, where a poll now showed just eighteen per cent in support of his policies.

Back in America, Jack, like many others from the moment they woke, would turn on his radio to catch the voice of the legendary broadcaster Ed Murrow. He reported from London each morning and his vivid descriptions carried much weight. The arguments which took place across the Atlantic were closely followed. Jack began to sense the change that had taken place that October in England. The new mood was noted in America.

9

KICK FALLS IN LOVE WITH ENGLAND AND BILLY

The Marquess of Hartington, Queen's garden party, Chatsworth and Cambridge, war talk, Kick in St Moritz for Christmas, "Billy – will he, won't he?"

With Jack fully immersed at Harvard again, Kick found herself spending more time with her aristocratic circle of friends and with Billy Cavendish.

Kick had first met the eldest son of the Duke of Devonshire, after returning from a day at Wimbledon watching her favourite sport on 24 June 1938. She had been invited to dinner by her friend Jean Ogilvie. David Ormsby-Gore now introduced his cousin, the pale six-foot-four-tall Marquess of Hartington. He and Billy had been brought up so close together that they looked upon each other as brothers. Both came from ancient families from the heart of Britain's ruling class. Studying History at Trinity College, Cambridge, Billy was considered to be one of Britain's most eligible bachelors. Billy and Kick instantly became so absorbed in each other's company, that it seemed as if the other dinner guests did not exist. When Kick left dinner early for an official photo session for her publicity-conscious father, David offered to drive her to Prince's Gate, only to turn up later with Billy to drive her to a dance hosted by the Speaker of the House of Commons. There, in Westminster Palace, at a party held in honour of the Speaker's granddaughters Ann and Mary Fitzroy, they all danced until dawn. Employing the word *romantic* for the first time, Kick's diary describes the night as 'a romantic spot overlooking the Thames and the bridge'. The first photograph of Billy that she ever placed in her scrapbook was a press picture of him in winged collar and black tie, dancing that first evening with Mary Fitzroy.

Kick and Billy met again when Billy turned up with his Aunt Adele to see Kick selling programmes at a benefits garden party at the Tower of London. He then whisked her away to a dinner at the home of the Duke of Kent,[151] which ended, as Kick wrote in her diary on 13 July, with everyone going to the Belgrave home of Lord and Lady Mountbatten to, 'dance the night away'.

On 18 July, the Kennedys were invited to the Queen's annual summer garden party. Kick, who 'looked most beautiful that afternoon', noted her mother, had Sissy Thomas on her arm, and was accompanied by Jack, wearing his father's top hat. She was on the lookout for Billy and at some point during the garden party they presumably met but there is no mention of him in her terse diary entry: 'A very hot day and very dull procedure. King and Queen stood with the rest of the royal family while different foreign princes came and bowed'. [152]

Billy had been smitten the moment he met vivacious Kick. It was a case of genuine opposites attracting each other. He, the tall, diffident, deeply thoughtful Protestant and scion of the Establishment – she the diminutive Catholic, socially brilliant and flighty. He was "a charmer of great intelligence. He had great presence and he was loved by everybody", recalled Deborah Mitford, adding, "Billy and Kick were about the two most popular people you could imagine."[153] According to his sister Lady Anne Tree, 'Billy was a fairly formed character who would have made a good politician'.[154] Some believed gentle-featured Billy might be an excellent match for Princess Elizabeth before she became attracted to the bold, outspoken Prince Philip.

Billy's Cavendish family were one of the first families in the land, next in line to the royal family, with a history going back to before Henry VIII. Owning 180,000 acres of land, the family had built the magnificent Chatsworth Palladium Mansion. This was the seat of the Devonshire family, along with Lismore Castle in Ireland and Compton Place at Eastbourne on the south coast.

Billy's cousin David Ormsby-Gore was dating Sissy Thomas. Her father had been Private Secretary to the Prince of Wales and had died in a horse-riding accident in February 1938. Joe later agreed that Sissy, who was a Catholic, stay at the residence from time to time. In the months that followed the girls developed a special bond. Sissy, like Kick, was in love with a non-Catholic. That summer, they chatted like sisters endlessly about their suitors,

Picnic at Goodwood Races 26 July 1938. Kick on the right sits next to Debo Mitford while Billy takes something from the hamper basket and younger brother Andrew Cavendish stretches out in the foreground at one of 'the season' events. (Mary Evans Picture Library)

Billy and David. It was at one of the summer events, according to Deborah Mitford, at Goodwood, that Jack really got to know David properly.[155]

When Kick rejoined her 'aristocratic cousinhood', after Jack left for Harvard that September, she went to Scotland to celebrate Jean Ogilvie's twentieth birthday. Billy and David driving from college in Cambridge, arrived at Cortachy Castle late for dinner. The kilted Lord Airlie forbade them to join dinner 'late', so Kick and Jean secretly arranged for the butler to take some food to their room. Usually much loved by the young, the very traditional Lord Airlie had been much irritated by the mood and tension of the moment. He supported the Government's appeasement policy but having met Hitler, abhorred his politics. He had earned a Military Cross in the War and his illustrious father, the 7th Earl of Airlie, had served in the second Afghan war, marching from Kabul to Kandahar with General Roberts in 1880. Five years later, the same earl took part in the heroic Battle of Abu Klea in a bid to rescue Gordon of Khartoum. This illustrious ancestor finally died age forty-four, leading the 10th Hussars in a charge to save the guns at the Battle of Diamond

Hill in the South African Boer War. This Scottish family exemplified Great Britain's role as world policeman during days of Empire. By next morning, the eccentric old soldier had recovered his mood sufficiently to allow the boys to go shooting grouse with him!

Billy and Kick were now very much in love. They would walk the Scottish moors and picnic most days. In the evenings, they would dance to Jean's wind-up gramophone. But talk of war, never far away, kept intruding. Kick wrote on 15 September, 'We listen to the radio for news flashes. The international situation grows increasingly worse. All you can hear or talk about at this point is the future war which is bound to come. Am so darn sick of it'.

Robert Cecil and Debo Mitford then joined them. The group, now assembled at Cortachy, reflected the split in the upper classes. Some, with ties to grand German families like Jean Ogilvie's father supported appeasement. Robert Cecil's father, Lord Cranbourne, was vehemently against it. Unity Mitford was a fanatical supporter of Hitler. Debo Mitford was apolitical but had met Hitler with her sister Unity for a two-hour chat over tea in his Munich flat in June 1937. Diana Mitford married Sir Oswald Mosley, founder of the British Union of Fascists, at a ceremony in the home of Joseph Goebbels, that was attended by Hitler.

It was common between the wars for many aristocratic families to send their daughters to 'finish' an education in Paris, Florence, Vienna or Munich. Their differing experiences would inform their views on Germany. One of these, Daphne Brooke, the daughter of the Admiral of the Fleet, travelled to Vienna in 1937. She met an upper-class Prussian, 'who took me to the Nürnberg Rally when I was just seventeen', to see for herself the threat of Hitler's Germany. 'I'll never forget the sound of the troops, who wore metal soles, goose stepping down roads that had been specially metalled, and the ranting, the "Sieg Heils" – I can hear them still. After the rally the young Prussian took me for a long walk as we felt unable to talk freely in our homes. He said to me, "I took you to Nürnberg so that you can go home and tell your friends about it." He didn't need to say anything more. He came to stay with us in England. He was killed at Stalingrad'.[156]

Unity Mitford was a very unusual devotee of the Fuehrer, joining him and his entourage regularly in Munich. She was treated as an honoured guest at all the rallies. Going to Bayreuth and the Berlin Olympics, they met over a hundred times. A friend Diana Quilter, who spent a year travelling and 'staying at embassy after embassy', described her stay with Unity during the

Winter Olympics. 'She had been given her Munich flat by Hitler. She was enormous fun, very generous and extremely nice to me. Unity dashed in one evening saying, "Do hurry! I've got the whole German Government with me." Outside were streams of black Mercedes – she was in the front one, sitting with Goebbels. I saw Hitler often. Music was what I was chiefly studying and I went to the opera a great deal. We'd find ourselves in seats with Hitler sitting just behind us'.[157] Hitler seemed able to relax with British aristocrats, possibly because they displayed no fear of him. He believed they might be a useful communication line. He once told Unity after a 1935 naval agreement had been signed with Britain, "With the German Army and the English Navy we could rule the world. Oh, if we could only have that!"[158]

On 28 September, a date which became known as Black Wednesday, the young cousinhood at Cortachy Castle in Scotland turned on the radio to listen to Chamberlain describe in Parliament his meeting with Hitler in his mountain retreat. The radio broadcast was sombre and there was a long pause before Chamberlain suddenly announced that Hitler had agreed to postpone mobilisation and had invited him to Munich. The immediate relief and jubilation in the castle caused Kick to remark, "I have never seen such happiness." Three days later, Kick boarded the night train for London, to find everyone still deliriously happy next morning. She went off with Billy and David to celebrate at the theatre and Café de Paris.

More than a hundred million people[159] – the largest radio audience ever – had listened in to the Prime Minister and heard that moment of stunned silence, followed by the burst of wild applause. Only a very few, including Churchill, remained seated, looking glum. Breaking convention, the normally stoic Queen Mary, sitting in the Gallery, 'wept and reached out to touch those near her'.[160] There was normally no question of showing emotion in public.

The euphoria and celebration did not last long. Fiery opposition to the Munich deal and that 'piece of paper' were soon led by Duff Cooper, Winston Churchill and Anthony Eden. They denounced what they saw as Chamberlain's betrayal of the Czechs. They warned that Hitler would not keep his word and that it would not be the last of his territorial demands.[161] Lord Cranbourne (brother to Moucher) would tell the House of Commons, "Peace? But where is honour? I have looked and looked and I cannot see it. It seems to me a wicked mockery to describe so noble a name the agreement which has been reached."[162]

In his autobiography, Lord Home would explain Chamberlain's thinking. 'True, we got war; but also final victory, whereas war in 1938 would have meant not victory but defeat'.[163] An unanticipated side effect of the Munich pact was to thwart a plot by army officers – including the military chief of staff – to topple Hitler if he went to war with the Czechs. No organised opposition to Hitler would exist for another five years'.[164]

Billy Hartington in his long talks with Kick helped her see the hold of his family traditions – honour and duty – traditions which had been betrayed at Munich. Kick had time to absorb Billy's values and ideals unlike anything she had experienced from her father, who believed a war with Nazi Germany was to be avoided at all cost and would be suicidal. In her letters to Jack, she would often tease, 'Billy Hartington wants to know if you think the British are still decadent? Do you?'.[165] Kick's favourite riposte was, "While England lost many battles, she would always win the war."

After Hitler took over the Sudetenland with its three million ethnic Germans, London's mayor opened an appeal fund to help suffering Czech refugees. Britain granted visas to 300 refugees and future Prime Minister Harold Macmillan personally accommodated forty of them on his estate at Birch Grove.[166] On 10 October, in a speech at Saarbrücken, Hitler attacked Churchill as a 'warmonger'. Six days later, Winston broadcast on NBC to America. "The lights are going out, but there is still time for those to whom freedom and parliamentary democracy mean something."

On 19 October, Ambassador Joe went in front of an audience of veteran naval officers who had experienced WWI to give the annual 'Trafalgar Square' dinner speech. Joe first praised Chamberlain over Munich and then proceeded to make a personal pitch for "peaceful co-existence with dictatorships – after all, we have to live together whether we like it or not!" This set off a firestorm in Britain and the American press. New York's *Herald Tribune* pointed out that Kennedy had exceeded his ambassadorial mandate, writing, 'Amateurs and temporary diplomats often take their own speeches seriously. And when they do they often form a mini State Department with its own foreign policy. They do not usually survive long'. The State Department now hung Joe out to dry, stating the speech reflected the Ambassador's own personal view. When 'Kristallnacht' followed a few weeks later on 9 November, the writing was on the wall for Joe. Jewish shops across Germany were broken into, synagogues burnt and over a hundred Jews murdered, with many more beaten. "I could scarcely believe that such things could occur in the twentieth century," Roosevelt said, expressing his horror publicly. If anyone still put their money on Hitler's Germany, Kristallnacht came as a shock. The United States and Germany recalled their ambassadors. Coming six weeks after Munich, it destroyed any residual argument for appeasement. It only took another four months for Hitler's troops to march into Prague and tear up the Munich treaty.

After Kristallnacht, Joe Jnr noted his father seemed tired of his work. He felt he would 'give it up in a minute if it wasn't for the benefits that Jack and I are getting out of it'.[167] The family continued with their daily horse rides down Rotten Row in Hyde Park across from Prince's Gate, and Kick continued with her sparkling social round. She went to the Palace on 16 November for a reception to meet the King's cousin, King Carol of Romania. Kick and sister Rosemary had the distinction of being two of the few young persons amongst 600 guests. Kick found Carol's son Prince Michael, 'good-looking with nice dimples'. This prompted War Secretary Hore Belisha to tell her he was going to announce her engagement to the Romanian prince!

On 23 November, the Cavendish family celebrated with a party at The Savoy, the coming-of-age of Richard Cavendish. He had horrified some by marrying a Catholic, Pamela Lloyd Thomas (a sister to Sissie). Next it would be Billy's turn to brave disapproval. On 9 December, to celebrate his twenty-first birthday, the Duchess seated Kick to Billy's right. By this audacious gesture, Billy's mother had signified her personal family approval of the relationship. Kick defiantly noted the mood of the moment, 'all Billy's relatives sitting around getting an eyeful'.[168]

So very different to each other – Billy languid and relaxed in the extreme and Kick full of boundless energy and vitality – they were growing more attached to each other by the day. As Billy's cousin Fiona Gore noted, 'It was wonderful to see. Here was this lively American girl who through some odd circumstance had become the toast of the town, and she was paying all this attention to Billy. It gave him such confidence. She swept him off his oh-so-steady feet'.[169] Kick, who loved to tease, would call him at Chatsworth and when the butler answered the phone would say: "Hello, is the King perchance in his castle today?"[170] Kick was an Elizabeth Bennet to his Darcy! His two sisters Anne and Elizabeth became devoted to Kick and thought that her teasing irreverence was just what he needed to stop taking himself so seriously. He needed to be laughed at a little. They both shared a love of lively conversation. Billy's mother had once sacked a nanny when the woman announced that she preferred punctuality to conversation.

That October, Billy, resuming his studies at Cambridge, took Kick to see the family castle. Chatsworth was set in a thousand acres of parkland and lawns landscaped by 'Capability' Brown. It had been built in 1547 by Sir William Cavendish. The home held 175 rooms and miles of corridors filled with treasures. Kick saw the beautiful rosary beads made for Henry VIII, given by Catherine of Aragon. She saw the 'Mary Queen of Scots' apartment where the Catholic queen had been held prisoner by Queen Elizabeth. Billy pointed out various ancestral portraits, including that of the attractive Georgiana, Duchess of Devonshire. She had been an influential figure in the eighteenth century, using her popularity to raise support for the Whig Party[171] and had famously turned the drawing rooms of Chatsworth into a hub of political power.

After his intense political work, Joe, exhausted too by attacks on him, boarded the *Queen Mary* on 10 December, to enjoy Christmas with Jack in Palm Beach. Rose decided to take her other children for Christmas to the snowbound Alps around St Moritz. A huge snowstorm delayed the family's arrival as they crossed Europe by train. They did not reach the hotel high in the mountains until late Christmas Eve. Deep snow sparkled around the pointed twin spires of the Grand Suvretta Hotel and its 110 rooms. After quickly exchanging presents, Rose and her children breathed in the fresh night air at a midnight Mass in the church overlooking the skating rink. Next morning, they took 'a sleigh filled with fur rugs looking cosy and luxurious with the tassles bobbing on the horse's head as skiers glided skillfully in and out between the hotel buses and sleighs'.[172] Jack and Joe called them on the phone from the warmth of Palm Beach on Christmas Day.

With typical daredevil recklessness, all of Jack's brothers soon injured themselves. Bobby sprained his ankle, six-year-old Teddy wrenched his knee and Joe Jnr fell and broke his arm. Obliged to set an example to his younger brothers, he ignored the pain and with a scarf as tourniquet, skied back to the hotel. It did not hold back his efforts to find a girl. Eunice wrote, 'He had gone to every hotel in St Moritz', before he was pictured arm in a sling, skating with Megan Taylor, the eighteen-year-old world figure skating champion.[173] A classmate Charlotte MacDonnel, skiing with Kick, teased her about her English beau. She penned a verse: 'Such is Kick! God's gift to Billy!! Will he? Won't he? Won't he? Billy'.[174] On New Year's Eve, the hotel band played *Auld Lang Syne* and Kick and Joe stayed up all night to see in 1939. At 6am, they went out in the snow into the small chapel below where Joe served Mass. Eunice wrote home to Florida, 'It really would have been perfect if you and Jack had been here'.

After three weeks in the sparkling snow, Kick returned to London in mid-January 1939. 'Awful rain and fog, where everyone was sniffling all over the place', her diary records when she met Billy for dinner on her first night back. Over that winter, as Kick grew closer to Billy there were trips to the races at Newmarket, followed by dinner parties in his rooms at Cambridge, where he would serve *pâté de foie gras* from Fortnum & Mason. She teased him about his excessive concern for his appearance and tendency to boss his younger brother. And she laughed at his look of shock when she wanted to snatch up a souvenir ashtray in a Spanish restaurant – something she would have done for fun in the company of her older brothers.

Billy and Kick often stayed at the Mitford family cottage in the village of Swinford near Oxford. Debo did the cooking for them and for Andrew and David and his Catholic girlfriend, Sissy. As barriers to mixed marriages were slowly coming down, Kick and Billy were delighted to go to the wedding of Derek Parker Bowles and Catholic Ann de Trafford – Billy would become godfather to their son Andrew Parker Bowles.

Back in America, Jack was dating with serious intent the rich and beautiful Frances Ann Cannon. She played tennis, skied and had in 1937, been presented at court in London. 'Good-looking, good mind, good wit, and provocative',[175] recalled friend Rip Horton. But the wealthy Cannon family from Carolina did not want their daughter marrying a Catholic and Frances was whisked off by her mother on a four-month cruise, which ended any sudden idea of marriage. Jack was shocked to read her unexpected farewell telegram. 'Great golden tears too plentiful for famous last words, can only say stay away from the hay goodbye darling I love you Frances Ann'.[176]

10

ROVING STUDENT DIPLOMAT, LONDON 1939

Student diplomat races from Danzig to Damascus, Prince's Gate
dinner for King and Queen, Sarah Churchill's floodlit Blenheim
Palace ball, five thousand guests at Billy's party, closing of an era.

'Few years have been so disliked in advance, as 1939',[177] declared London's *Observer* newspaper with great foreboding.

Jack had been desperate to get back to London – to where history was being made. He quickly got approval from Harvard, as part of his course to spend a semester working in London as an embassy aide to his father. On 25 February 1939, the *Queen Mary* set sail for England with Jack aboard.

The Ambassador had left for England on 9 February but only after the President ordered him to end his long vacation! Before his father arrived, Jack's elder brother had dashed off to Spain and reached Madrid weeks after Franco's forces had taken the city. Getting a ride in a British destroyer to Valencia, he saw one of the remaining loyalist strongholds, and buildings which were 'vibrating like drums' as the town and port were bombarded by German Stuka planes.[178] He then headed to the abandoned American Embassy in Madrid to see one skinny Spaniard safeguarding the building with his assortment of refugee cows, sheep, hens and lambs. "Hundreds of people are starving to death every day, and everybody's hungry all the time," reported Joe Jnr. Proud of his son's passion to observe first-hand the front line of conflict, the Ambassador would often read out his son's reports to others.

When Jack arrived in London, newspapers announced he had come to join the Embassy 'as a glorified office boy'! The *Daily Mirror* on 2 March published a picture of Jack sitting behind a huge desk holding a telephone and immaculately dressed in a blue pinstripe suit that he had just been fitted for,[179] not dissimilar to the type Churchill wore. A few days later he wrote, 'Been working every day and going to dinners, etc., with Dad… feeling very important as I go to work in my new cutaway. Met the King this morning at a Court Levee'. Jack relished dressing in white tie and tails at Palace events, which included, as he playfully told Billings, once having tea with thirteen-year-old Princess Elizabeth, 'with whom I made a great deal of time'.[180]

The future remained as fluid and uncertain as ever. On 15 March 1939, German troops marched into Czechoslovakia – Bohemia and Moravia – in violation of the Munich agreement. That evening, Hitler was in Prague. No one in Britain, not even the Prime Minister, could go on pretending that Hitler was to be trusted. Intelligence reports were now confirming Hitler intended invading Poland. Chamberlain's supporters began to abandon him and on 17 March, he delivered a radio address to the nation in which he confessed his foreign policy was in tatters.

At this moment, all the Kennedys including Jack were at the Vatican. The President, as a favour, had allowed them to represent America at the coronation of the new Pope Pacelli, whom Joe knew. Rose, who felt they were America's premier Catholic family, was particularly pleased.[181] As soon as he returned to London, it did not take long for the Ambassador to see how the political climate in Britain had changed. There had been a massive shift in public opinion. Britain seemed united at last in its sense of shame about what Chamberlain had done in pursuit of peace. The country was ready to confront the Germans. In Andrew Cavendish's words, 'Shame had now taken the safety catch off the hunting rifle'.

With this new climate and reality dawning, Rose and Joe joined 180 guests at the Palace for a state banquet for the French President. The King, who suffered from a worrisome stammer now hesitated for several moments before being able to speak, and Joe noted how the Queen felt: '…crimson running down to her throat, and hand absolutely clenched. The poor girl suffers the torment of the damned when he speaks'.[182]

In one of the last great official social events, Joe and Rose went to a reception given by Lord and Lady Halifax on 23 March inside the magnificent Durbar Court at the Foreign Office. They were surrounded by statues and paintings of viceroys, governors and maharajas as they were steered through a seven-course dinner and eight wines, served by waiters wearing scarlet waistcoats and bright blue coats with gold trimmings and dark plush breeches.[183] The glamorous guests, who included the Duchess of Devonshire and Lady Londonderry, wore spectacular family diamonds and jewels. Lilies, azaleas, magnolias and Japanese cherry trees lined the courtyard, and roses climbed the marble Foreign Office pillars.

On 31 March, Chamberlain delivered his one-sentence dramatic reversal in foreign policy: "In the event of any action which threatens Polish independence, His Majesty's government would feel themselves bound at once to lend the Polish Government all support in their power." He had reversed Britain's centuries-old policy of going to war only when it saw fit, and not as a result of a binding alliance. Halifax and Chamberlain had finally decided that only tough limits might avert war. When Kennedy informed the President about Britain's intention to guarantee Poland's western borders, Roosevelt showed his approval of Britain's resolve and willingness to confront Hitler. He understood, "It probably means war."[184]

Hitler, for the first time confronted and blocked by Chamberlain, believed, 'that dastardly Churchill' had pushed the Prime Minister to this point. He had flown into a rage and pounded his fist on the marble surface of his table in Berlin's chancellery. Two days later, Hitler launched another battleship and declared, "He who does not possess power, loses the right to life." On 3 April, the Fuehrer ordered his military commanders to prepare for 'Operation White' – the invasion of Poland for 1 September.[185]

'Everyone thinks war is inevitable before the year is out', wrote Jack to Billings on 23 March from his embassy desk. 'I personally don't, though Dad does'.[186] The Ambassador continued urging Britain to seek terms with Hitler, but it was a very different England six months since Munich, and Joe began to see war as imminent. Meanwhile, Jack was still, 'having a great time… Haven't done much work but have been sporting around in my morning coat, my "Anthony Eden" black Homburg and white gardenia'.[187] Fun, was still Jack's leitmotif. In his increasingly English way, this meant hard work, hard play and hard socialising.

The King invited Joe and Rose to spend another weekend that April in Windsor, taking with them the President's son James. The Queen spoke about their forthcoming tour and joked that if war broke out, she and the King might get stuck in Canada or America! Joe said they 'would love to have her.'[188]

That April, Jack moved to the Embassy in Paris to see events unfolding from a continental perspective. He wrote to his friend Billings, 'Bullit has turned out to be a hell of a good guy. Live like a king up there… Was at lunch today with the Lindberghs and they are the most attractive couple I've ever seen'.[189] In May, he embarked on a rapid and wide-ranging fact-finding tour. Starting in Poland, he met Nazi officials and Polish aristocrats, telling Billings, 'I've been staying this last week with Ambassador Biddle in Warsaw. It's been damn interesting and was up in Danzig for couple of days. Danzig is completely Nazified. Much heiling of Hitler. Talked with the Nazi heads and all the Consuls up there'. Writing about his stays at enormous estates belonging to Polish aristocrats, he told Billings, 'Aside from the political side, have been having a damn good time. Leave for Russia tomorrow. This last bit is very confidential but I have a divorced Romanian princess with whom – however, on second thoughts I will leave this tit-bit till I see you'. [190]

Jack spent several days in Riga and took the train to Leningrad and Moscow. Receiving VIP treatment and staying at embassies along the way, he spoke to diplomats in Bucharest, Istanbul, Jerusalem, Beirut, Damascus and Athens. On 8 June, he turned up at a British High Commission party in Jerusalem to celebrate King George VI's birthday.[191] Staying at the King David Hotel in Jerusalem, he spoke with British military officers and was impressed by the intelligence of the officials he met but was convinced that the policy they were following was doomed to fail. Jack arrived after the British Government had just published its White Paper by Malcolm MacDonald calling for an 'independent Palestine state'. Proposing to reverse the Balfour Declaration, it provoked massive outrage and outbursts of violence. He wrote to his father, the latest MacDonald plan would not work, and that it was 'useless to discuss which side has the 'fairer' claim. The British try to treat each side impartially. But the necessary thing is not a just and fair solution but a solution that will work…' To Jack that meant partition.[192] It was a remarkable analysis already on a par with that of a seasoned diplomat revealing his balanced judgement.[193] Whilst Jack did not have time to interview Jewish and Arab leaders, he felt the people in the area seemed to favour the Arabs, partly because the Jewish people 'have had, at least in some of their leaders, an unfortunately arrogant, uncompromising attitude'. On Jack's last night, the ancient city was rocked by thirteen explosions.

Jack flew back from Paris on 5 May, in time for a farewell dinner his father was holding at Prince's Gate for the King and Queen, about to depart on their state visit to America – the first ever by a British monarch. Jack sat with Kick alongside his younger brothers and sisters, Lady Nancy and Waldorf Astor,

Jack arrives in Jerusalem on a fact-finding tour, briefed by British military and officials on the conflict between Arabs and Jewish inhabitants. 'The necessary thing is not a just and fair solution , but one that will work'. June 1939. (Courtesy JFK Library)

Lord and Lady Halifax, Viscount Cranbourne, the Dukes and Duchesses of Devonshire and Beaufort, and Ambassador Bullit. What Jack said that night in Kensington is not recorded. But it is easy to imagine the King and Queen with gathered guests listening intently to what the young student diplomat had seen on his journey across Europe. That evening at Prince's Gate may have marked the first moment that Jack started shaping views in high places.

For her part, Rose held a brief conversation that night in her bedroom with the Queen, who asked her if she got up in the morning to see the children off. Rose said she had, in what were the good old days, but now rested in the morning. Her diary continues, 'To my astonishment and humiliation, the Queen said she usually got up, half dressed, to see her children and then went back to bed again'. The King and Queen ended the evening with the family watching a Walt Disney cartoon followed by *Goodbye, Mr. Chips*, during which the Queen, 'shed a tear'.[194]

That spring, the social whirl continued apace. Eunice was one of 228 girls who swept down two staircases in pairs and curtsied at the annual ball in aid of Queen Charlotte's Maternity Hospital, hosted by five of Britain's most esteemed duchesses at Grosvenor House. On 9 May, Lady Astor gave a party for debutantes at her town house at 4 St James's Square in honour of her niece Dinah Brand.[195] Rose noted the redolent spring flowers brought up from Cliveden which decorated the ballroom. 'All the representatives of London Society were there. Anthony Eden arrived, dapper as usual. Other guests from other dinner parties began to arrive about 10 o'clock. Kathleen had been to dinner at the Duchess of Buccleuch's and Joe Jnr had been at Lady Airlie's'.

In late spring, Rose and Joe joined the Prime Minister, amid the bluebells at his official retreat at Chequers for the weekend of 13 May. As Chamberlain walked with Joe and pointed out differences between Scottish and English bluebells on the estate, he suddenly turned to Joe and said he believed Hitler had decided to take on Britain – "In August probably, just in time to spoil our vacations!" A week later on 22 May, Italy and Germany signed the so-called 'Pact of Steel'. The next day, Hitler followed up on his secret orders to his generals to prepare in earnest for war with Poland.

The King's seven-week tour, which started in Canada, proved to be a great success. The King and Queen, stepping off their train at Washington's Union Rail Station on 7 June, had been greeted with a handshake on the platform by President Roosevelt. On this first-ever visit by a monarch to the United States, Joe, acting as the monarch's public relations man, declared the handshake as the most important handclasp of modern times, hoping it might serve as a warning to dictators about the 'power of the Anglo-American bond'.

The Queen's 'charm, her kindness and constant smile', Rose noted, 'put everyone at their ease as did the King's straight and almost boyish face and figure, his simplicity, unaffected charm and readiness – even eagerness – to co-operate'. They mingled with crowds, answered reporters' questions and undertook many engagements in that summer's sweltering heat. The President, who had deliberately left Joe out of the visit, had hoped to welcome the monarch with legislation in place to give material support for England, but Congress had thwarted him, despite a Gallup poll in April showing that fifty-seven per cent of people wanted the Neutrality Act changed in order to supply arms to Britain and France. Roosevelt privately now gave the King his personal assurance – America would come to London's aid if the city was bombed by Germany.

King George was welcomed back at Waterloo Station in late June by the British Cabinet and an enthusiastic Joe, who told him, "I knew you would be a tremendous hit." Next day at a Guildhall luncheon, the King spoke with a new confidence and 'without stuttering', Rose noted. Speaking of Empire as a force for protecting peace and goodwill amongst mankind, the King had prompted Joe to tell Lord Halifax, "Your King became a real King of the British Empire today."[196] A few months later, Congress finally amended the Neutrality Act.

The start to the 1939 summer season in Britain was cool; the air heavy with constant talk of war. It was now the turn for another Kennedy, to have a 'coming-out' party – this time for Eunice.[197] British nobility turned out in force for the Kennedys on 22 June. At Prince's Gate that evening, Lady Astor, the Duke of Marlborough and the Duchess of Northumberland and their sons and daughters partied and danced until 2.30am. Jack, who had welcomed the guests standing in line with his father, can be seen enjoying himself immensely when he was being photographed in dinner jacket and white tie dancing with the granddaughter of the Earl of Abercorn, Janey Kenyon Slaney.

On the last day of June, Jack, Eunice and Kick went to the Countess of Sutherland's coming-out party for their daughter Elizabeth. "He didn't make small talk. He wanted to talk about politics," complained Elizabeth. Jack had been energised earlier that day by speeches from Halifax and Churchill, who warned Hitler, "Consider well before you take a plunge into the terrible unknown. Consider whether your life's work – which may even now be famous in the eyes of history – in raising Germany from frustration and defeat to a point where all the world is waiting for her next actions, consider whether all this may irretrievably be thrown away."[198] Chips Channon captured the strange and tense mood at the end of June. 'The whole outlook is appalling. Hitler is a bandit. We are all mad, and Russia is winking slyly – and waiting'.[199]

Jack and Kick then attended two last great English balls before the fabric of Grand Society was to be ripped apart. On 6 July, they went to the coming-out dance for Rosalind Cubitt (mother-to-be of Camilla Shand, who would marry the Prince of Wales). The Ambassador's car joined an excruciatingly long line of traffic as 1,000 guests turned off Kensington High Street into the gates of floodlit Holland House, with its red-brick Jacobean mansion set in seventy-acre grounds – a country estate inside the city which had once been the centre of Whig society. The guests that night were led by the King and Queen, and the Queen of Spain. (Holland House would be destroyed by the Luftwaffe in 1942, underlining the end of an era!)

The next day, on 7 July, the young Kennedys drove to the floodlit grounds of Blenheim Palace to attend a ball for the coming-out of Lady Sarah Spencer Churchill.

That night, 2,500 guests saw the home of the Duchess of Marlborough at Blenheim, in all its grand baroque floodlit beauty. The floodlit terraces shining on the lake and party were described by the American-born Chips Channon: 'All blue and green with Tyroleans walking about singing… it was gay, young, brilliant, in short, perfection… there were literally rivers of champagne', and he wondered 'whether England would ever see the likes of that again'.[200] Eunice Kennedy described coming into the dining room. 'Passing a line of stolid butlers dressed in knee breeches and wigs through a ballroom full of flowers; lilies, pink and white hydrangeas that had taken the place of 20,000 valuable books removed from the library'. After dinner, the American orchestra entertained the glamorous guests with *Big Apple* and the popular *Lambeth Walk*. As Eunice, aged eighteen, recalled, 'Round and round we glided as dawn slowly lit the skies and house guests finished off the party with coffee and hotdogs!' One of the debutantes, Mollie Acland, observed Churchill and Antony Eden on the terrace, 'chatting and smoking', and remembered wondering 'if Jack was shadowing his heroes or if he was too busy charming the ladies'.

Jack clearly enjoyed his floodlit ball at Blenheim, writing to Lem Billings, 'It's really too bad you're not here – it's all darned good fun – never had a better time'.[201] Working away in a suit by day at the Embassy and partying in his tuxedo at night, Jack was in his element, drafting official correspondence, reports and telegrams and attending evening receptions, including one at 10 Downing Street on 27 June. London on the eve of war was providing Jack a special education. For the most part, he was a discreet observer rather than a pontificator. He hid his serious side and fascination with international politics. David Gore recalled, "I mostly saw him at parties and in the family circle at home having a good time. He was very thin, wiry thin with, I don't know how to describe it, this energy exuding from him… I didn't see much of his serious side and indeed, at that date, well, of course he was twenty-one and I was about the same age – probably neither one of us had a serious side to be seen at that moment."[202]

The day after Blenheim, Chips Channon invited Jack and his friend Tony Loughborough for lunch to meet Princess Cecil of Prussia, the Kaiser's granddaughter. The enthusiastic Tony Earl of Rosslyn and Jack had become known as the 'Ross-Kennedy girl-catching team'. Together with the Princess of Prussia, the girl-catching team raced after lunch from 5 Belgrave Square to the House of Commons to hear Chamberlain make his statement on 'Danzig', around which war seemed to hinge. Jack learned to love this type of day and strived to replicate it throughout his life. He was determined to find fun and action wherever he went.

Jack was in tune with, 'English political society with its casual combination of wit, knowledge and unconcern'. It had a careless elegance he had not previously encountered. One of his favourite books, *The Young Melbourne* by David Cecil, published that February, gives insights to his evolving outlook. Jack at twenty seemed attracted by Melbourne and Whig society at a stage in life when books are often read as a guide to conduct, and perhaps, saw in young Melbourne a model. He was fascinated by this Whig society with its confident, detached and light style. The Blenheim weekend had seen young Jack at home in this society and beginning to develop a lifelong affinity for such aristocratic values. Whig aristocracy was a unique product of English civilisation that had dominated government. The Whig nobleman as David Cecil described, had been subjected from his 'earliest years to a careful education, in the classics by a private tutor, then at Eton, then University after which he went for two years abroad on a Grand Tour to learn French and good manners in the best society of the continent. The Whig ideal was the Renaissance idea of the whole man, whose aspiration is to make the most of every advantage, intellectual and sensual that life has to offer'.[203] They all benefitted in 'that spacious freedom so deeply rooted in English soil which allowed personality to flourish and develop'.

In August, Billy Cavendish celebrated his coming-of-age party over two brilliant days of good weather with 5,000 guests. It was to be a final emphatic display of a way of life. As Andrew Cavendish recalled, 'It had something of the Duchess of Richmond's Ball before the Battle of Waterloo'. People sensed it was the closing of an age.

A little earlier on 12 July, when Eunice had taken her turn to be 'presented' at Buckingham Palace, Rose had stood next to the German Ambassador's wife. Rose asked if there was anything comparable to this in Germany. "No," came the reply. "We are too busy with other things."[204]

11

WAR DECLARED

Joe Jnr in Berlin, summer in Cannes, Jack and Torby in Munich, Nazi Stormtroopers, Jack takes secret message to London, German troops stream across Polish border, Jack helps rescued Americans.

Jack and his brother Joe set out from London as the borders of old Europe were closing in that summer of 1939. Joe took off with Kick to see the devastation in Spain, whilst Jack drove with David to France and Germany.

From Spain, with Franco's war now effectively over, Joe Jnr wrote on 10 June reflecting his father's isolationist view, 'Are we going to guarantee liberty in every country in the world… when it is really none of our dammed business but is up to the people in those countries themselves?'[205] Moving on to Danzig and then Berlin, he noted, 'One is immediately impressed here by the lack of talk about war. Hitler is regarded by many people as a God and there is no doubt of the difference between him and the rest. I should think Hitler is backed by 80% of the people'. [206] As anti-aircraft guns were being mounted in Berlin, Joe observed that the population seemed to be in denial, bolstered by the recent alliance with Russia which had given them false hope.

In Munich, Joe met Unity Mitford. 'The city is terribly calm and no one would think there was a prospect of war… Unity Mitford is the most unusual woman I have ever met. She has no interest in other things and thinks only of the Fuehrer and his work. She never refers to him as Hitler but only as the Fuehrer and looked at me rather oddly when I called him Hitler as if I was taking his name in vain. She says the international situation was a complete misunderstanding. She said that Hitler had a tremendous admiration and fondness for the British and would do them no harm unless they forced his hand… She believes him to be more than a genius. Those who know him well consider him as a God. He can make no mistake and has made none. He spends as much time looking after detail, as he does on great things. He can work for weeks without sleep and not show it… She is probably in love with Hitler'.

The Ambassador used Joe Jnr's report, to approach a Cabinet Minister to see if there was still a chance for a deal with Germany. He told Rab Butler, "My son had lunch with Unity Mitford in Berlin the other day and she quoted Hitler as saying that he had great admiration for the British and that he was heartbroken when Chamberlain went home and in one breath talked about peace in our time, and in the other, the necessity for arming against Hitler."[207] The Fuehrer banked rightly on the fact that his conversations with Unity would find their way back to London. Unity was allowed continuous access to British Embassy parties, to be welcomed by the tolerant Ambassador Henderson, standing on his toes to catch her outstretched hand coming down from a Hitler salute! Joe Jnr had noted how Unity was in a state of high nervous tension. Hitler would reassure her a few days later over lunch that Britain would back down over Poland, and he advised her to ignore those who told her to leave Germany.

Jack set off in mid-July to drive across the continent with David Ormsby-Gore and Harvard roommate Torby MacDonald. As they said farewell to Jack's father, the Ambassador cautioned them to stay out of trouble with Germans, 'who were very tough and paid no attention to laws and rules'. He told them if anything happened, just to back away. [208] After renting a car in Paris, they ran into trouble of their own making. Jack was not the world's most conservative driver, and as Torby recalled, 'he was at the wheel and the car gave an uncontrollable lurch to the right and ended upside down with our baggage strewn all over the landscape. In the silence after the crash we were literally standing on our heads in the overturned car. Jack looked sideways at me and said in a casual tone, "Well, pal, we didn't make it, did we?"'[209]

When they finally got to Cannes, they were delighted to see Kick already in their villa. She had just got back from her visit to Spain with Joe and Hugh Fraser, proud of the fact that Joe Jnr had been the only American earlier, walking the streets during the horrible bloody days of the Madrid siege.[210] Kick was now anxious to get back to England to see Billy. However, Rose had finally woken to her daughter's romance with the non-Catholic and now stopped Kick going to Billy's 'coming-of-age' celebrations on 15 August. Torby, who had long fancied himself in love with Kick, realised now she had no serious interest in anyone, but Billy. Kick took some comfort in her house guest Janey Kenyon Slaney, who was tall, beautiful and elegant, and as one of the debutantes presented at court, Janey had invited Kick to her twentieth birthday. Jack had developed a crush on Janey, since dancing with her at Eunice's coming-out party in June. When Jack now failed to get a serious response from Janey, he and Torby both decided to head off on 12 August, for a second helping of the Third Reich.[211] (The elusive granddaughter of the Earl of Abercorn, Janey, would briefly become engaged to David Niven in 1940, and later, joined the staff of Lord Mountbatten's wartime headquarters in the Far East.)

On their arrival in Munich, the cradle of the Nazi Party, Jack and Torby cruised around in their British car. At one point, they slowed and stopped to look at a monument of a Nazi hero. However as soon as their British number plates were spotted, they were heckled. When they both yelled back, stones and bricks were thrown at them by a group of Nazi Troopers. Torby remembered Jack's comment: "You know, how can we avoid having a war with people who think like that?"

They stayed just a night in Munich, seeing the opera *Tannhauser*, and then headed for Vienna. Jack told his father he intended to reach Prague and Berlin. A frustrated Foreign Service officer based in Prague recalls: 'No trains were running, no planes were flying and no frontier stations existed. In the midst of this confusion we received a telegram from the Embassy in London saying one of the Ambassador's sons was on a fact-finding tour around Europe and that it was up to us to help him get across the border into German lines. We were furious he had chosen this time to send his son. Joe Kennedy was not exactly known as a friend of career service officers and many of us from what we had heard about him cordially reciprocated this lack of enthusiasm. His son had no official status and was in our eyes obviously an upstart, an ignoramus'.[212] Overcoming this reluctance from the embassy, Jack interviewed as many people as he could in Prague and then made his way to Berlin, which he reached on 20 August.

Jack bought himself a movie camera and recorded in colour the cheerful crowds he saw in the streets of Berlin, looking relaxed, and seemingly doubtful that any war was coming. Jack reasoned, 'I still don't think there will be a war. But it looks quite bad as the Germans have gone so far internally with their propaganda stories on Danzig + the Corridor that it is hard to see them backing down. England seems firm this time – but as that is not completely understood here the big danger is on Germany counting on another Munich + thus finding themselves in a war when Chamberlain refuses to give in'. Jack was at the Excelsior Hotel when the Russian pact with Germany was abruptly announced. He quickly left his hotel for a final briefing at the Embassy. The American *chargé d'affaires*, handed Jack a secret letter to take to his father in London. Dated 24 August, it predicted the invasion of Poland and war 'within a week'.

Jack Kennedy was one of the last Americans to leave Berlin. With panic breaking out, after Germany announced their non-aggression pact with Russia, Europe's politicians and aristocrats hurriedly left their summer retreats. Joe flew straight back to London. Rose was left to gather up the rest of the family, and Kick and the elusive Janey found themselves travelling in their tennis outfits by train to Paris and then on by plane to Croydon.

Parliament was called into special session on 24 August, and passed the Emergency Powers Act mobilising personnel, resources and industry. On 25 August, Chamberlain asked Joe Kennedy to come to No. 10 to join him, Lord Halifax and Cadogan. Ambassador Henderson in Berlin had just met Hitler. The Fuehrer had worked himself into a frenzy after being presented with the British set of demands over Poland. Hitler told Henderson it was useless for the British to bother about Poland, as he and the Russians had already agreed its fate. (In fact, Hitler had indeed been temporarily stunned, and delayed the order for an attack for five hours after Ribbentrop told him about the Anglo-Polish Alliance.) Dressed in his dinner jacket, Chamberlain now gave each of the three men a copy of Henderson's report which included an assessment of Hitler's state of mind. Chamberlain asked, "What do you make of it?"

Joe replied, "If it weren't for Henderson's additional memorandum about the Germany-Russia cut-up of Poland, I would be convinced that Hitler was disturbed and really wanted to either try some new tactic to drive a wedge between the Poles and England, or he had the wind up. You have to make your solution more attractive to Germany than what she is now trying to get out of Poland. Propose a general settlement that will bring Germany economic benefits more important than the territorial annexation of Danzig." Then Joe went on to suggest, and without prior agreement from Washington, "Get the United States to say now what they would be willing to do in the cause of international peace and prosperity. After all, the United States will be the beneficiary of such a move. To put in a billion or two now will be worth it, for if it works we will get it back and more."[213]

To imagine that Hitler would be swayed by greed or economic incentives did not say much for the Ambassador's diplomatic or political insights. Yet when Joe left Downing Street, he recorded, 'When I left No. 10, I thought to myself that incident has probably been the most important thing that has ever happened to me. Here I was, an American ambassador, called into discussion with the PM and the Foreign Secretary over probably the most important event in the history of the British Empire. I had been called in before the Cabinet and had been trusted not only for my discretion but for my intelligence. It was a moving experience'. Kennedy, clearly moved by his brush with the 'historic' moment, recorded putting his hand on Chamberlain's shoulder. "Don't worry, Neville, I still believe God is working with you."[214]

Until the last, Joe sought to influence Chamberlain and his policy of appeasement without the backing or full knowledge of either the President or State Department.[215] The Prime Minister, who believed that if only he could get the Poles and Germans to start negotiating, that something could be done, remained in secret communication with Goering through a Swedish intermediary. This intermediary, Birger Dahlerus, who had spoken with Hitler and met Chamberlain, told Joe, "It could be done if I could only get the chance. I know these men personally and that is a great advantage. The unfortunate thing is that there is a great body of opinion in England, headed by men like Churchill and Eden, who are telling their peoples to give up nothing… they are wrong. If they persist it will mean war."[216] After sixteen months as Ambassador, Joe, still only understood power in terms of money and economic deals, whilst Hitler did not regard money as the source of power.[217] This left Kennedy and Chamberlain blindsided. On 25 August, the American Embassy issued its first message advising all Americans 'who do not have important reason for remaining, to return to the United States without delay'.

On the day the Nazis invaded Poland, Joe put in a phone call to Ambassador Bullitt in Paris. Bullitt, who maintained that 'peace with honour' could only be achieved by organising a strong front against Germany, was still certain Hitler would back off, 'if the British will only stand as firmly as the French'.

Kennedy now simply retorted, "Nuts! Hitler is not quitting. This is war."[218] Kennedy then records, 'I had hardly hung up the phone when the news came. It came with a rush like a torrent spewing from the wires – German troops had crossed the border. German planes were bombing Polish cities and killing civilians. Secretary Hull called me excitedly at noon. I could confirm little but the one fact. The German Army was on the march'.[219]

Lieutenant Kennedy at the controls of his PT109.
(Courtesy JFK Library)

Jack in front of jungle tents with unidentified friends on Solomon Islands Naval Base, July 1943. (Courtesy JKF Foundation)

Jack with his crew on PT 109 shortly before they were sunk by the Japanese destroyer Amagiri in Blackett Strait on 2 August 1943. (Courtesy JFK Library)

In relaxed mood back at his Naval base, Solomon Islands, 1943. (Courtesy JFK Library)

Kick in Red Cross uniform near Hans Crescent 'personifying the spirit of co-operation between America and Britain' as pictured in 'The Daily Mail.' August 1943. (Courtesy JFK Library)

Kick marries Billy Cavendish on 6 May 1944 at Chelsea Register Office, with Billy's mother the Duchess of Devonshire and Joe Jnr behind. 'Life Magazine' portrayed it as 'The greatest gesture in Anglo American relations since the Atlantic Charter.' (Courtesy JFK Library)

Kick in uniform with Deborah Devonshire and Moucher the Dowager Duchess of Devonshire (mother of Billy) at the Bakewell Fair, Derbyshire on 8 August 1944. (Courtesy JFK Library)

Fifty-seven divisions of Hitler's troops streamed across the Polish border on 1 September.

Early on Sunday morning, 3 September, Joe and his wife went to the Catholic church on Farm Street, and then after dropping her off at the Brompton Oratory, he headed straight to the embassy to wait for Chamberlain's address to the nation at 11.15am. It had taken three days of dithering for Chamberlain to act. Joe, surrounded by his sons, and embassy staff gathered in his office, listened to the Prime Minister. After explaining that the British Ambassador had delivered an ultimatum that morning in Berlin, demanding Germany start withdrawing its troops from Poland by 11am, he told Britons listening intently in homes across the nation, "I regret to say that no such undertaking has been received and consequently this country is now at war with Germany."

The American Ambassador recorded, 'It was terribly moving and when he got to the part of his "efforts have failed", I almost cried. I had participated very closely in this struggle and I saw my hopes crash too. I immediately picked up the telephone and was astounded to be put straight through. "I have just listened to your broadcast. It was terrifically moving. Well, Neville, I feel deeply our failure to save a world war." He said, "We did the best we could have done, but it looks as though we have failed." I hung up. His voice still quivered and he spoke to me with real feeling'.[220]

Joe put a call through to Roosevelt to tell him the contents, at 4am Washington time. Joe, almost hysterical, told the President, "It's the end of the world. The end of everything."[221] The Ambassador conveyed a desperate picture; an impotent Britain that would soon be overrun with a new dark age rolling over Europe. Roosevelt, who carried an immense burden on his shoulders, listened and tried to calm Joe, when it should have been the Ambassador trying to calm the President.

As soon as the morning broadcast ended, Jack along with his brother and Kick headed straight for Parliament. A compelling black and white photograph records them striding purposely forward towards Parliament, passing by the grey-white stone buildings of Whitehall. Kick is wearing a black dress, bright pearls and a wide-brimmed hat. She walks, preoccupied, between her brothers. Jack, in a double-breasted suit looks eager and keen to see history in the making. As soon as the Kennedys took their seats in the cramped strangers' gallery above the green leather benches, the air-raid siren went off at 12.05p.m. They were all hustled into the basement cellar, and resurfaced to hear Chamberlain lamenting, "Everything I have worked for, everything I have believed in, has crashed into ruins." The mournful prime minister sat down.

The solid and stocky figure of Churchill rose. Breathing out a broadside of defiance, he growled aloud, "The storms of war may blow and the lands may be lashed with the fury of its gales but in our own hearts this Sunday morning there is peace." There were shouts of "Hear! Hear!" and the waving of order papers. "This is not a question of fighting to save Danzig or to save Poland. We are fighting to save the whole world from the pestilence of Nazi tyranny… it is a war to establish on impregnable rocks, the rights of the individual, and it is a war to establish the stature of Man." Jack was riveted.

This language may have meant nothing to his father, but Jack was spellbound by Churchill's language. It combined poetry with politics and was delivered in a style to reach the level of that historic moment. Winston called out to a new generation of Britons ready to fight, "Not unworthy of yore and those great men who laid the foundations of our land and shaped the greatness of our country." Churchill's language was now moving the hearts and souls of his countrymen. Storing ideas for the future, Jack felt he wanted to be able to speak like that himself one day.[222]

The Ambassador was exhausted at the end of that first day of war. Rose in her memoires recorded that when they set off on foot to return back to Prince's Gate, 'the air-raid siren began to howl, and we ran for refuge into the nearest shelter we could find'.[223] Later that night, Joe had just got to bed, when the telephone rang. It was 2:30 in the morning and the Foreign Office was on the line. The clipped accent of a night duty officer spelled out a message just received – "*SS Athenia*. Donaldson Line. Torpedoed 200 miles off Malin Head. 1,400 passengers on board. SOS received, ship sinking fast." Joe waited until dawn to tell Jack, and asked him to go to Glasgow to assist around three hundred American survivors. One hundred and twelve people had been killed including twenty eight US citizens. Jack now undertook his first act of public duty which was recorded by the *London Evening News*. 'Ambassador of mercy – 19-year-old Jack Kennedy, son of America's Ambassador, spent one of the busiest days of his young life today, going from hotels to hospitals in Glasgow visiting American survivors. His boyish charm and natural kindliness persuaded those he had come to comfort that America was indeed keeping a benevolent and watchful eye on them… I accompanied young Mr

Kennedy and Lord Provost Dollan... Mr Kennedy displayed a wisdom and sympathy of a man twice his age'. [224] The *Telegraph* newspaper also dubbed Jack 'the schoolboy diplomat', in a report which had mistakenly described him as eighteen years old! Despite his apparent youth Jack had succeeded in his first act of public duty – reassuring Americans that the US Government was genuinely interested in their fate.

In his first public action, Jack had shown genuine concern for others. When three quarters of a million children and teachers were being evacuated from London, Jack, seeing the tearful goodbyes between parents and children at Euston Station, wrote to a friend, 'The big men of Berlin and London sit and confidently give their orders, and it is these kids – so far as I can see – who are the first casualties'.[225]

Kick rapidly arranged a dinner party to say farewell to their young friends. When Billy Cavendish and David Gore arrived in uniform at Prince's Gate, Joe, after dinner, decided to show them a film of the Great War. As soldiers were being mowed down by gunfire, the Ambassador jumped up in front of the screen and startled Kick's young men in their new uniforms. "That's what you'll be looking like in a month or two!" he shouted.

Embarrassed by her father's actions, Kick leaned over to Billy and whispered, "You mustn't pay attention to him. He just doesn't understand the English as I do." She already understood that for Billy and David, imbued with their sense of honour, there was no question other, than to do their duty. They did not need reminding of the price they were likely to pay.

Unity Mitford, when she heard war had been declared, immediately shot herself in the English Garden in Munich. Joe, still pressed on and spoke with the King for an hour on 9 September, trying to convince him to use the American President 'to bring peace to the world without increasing Hitler's prestige'.[226] The King recorded, 'He looked at the war very much from the financial and material viewpoint. He wondered why we did not let Hitler have SE Europe as it was no good from a monetary standpoint. He did not seem to realise that this country was part of Europe, that it was essential for us to act as policeman and to uphold the rights of small nations'.[227]

As the invasion of Poland got underway, Kennedy cabled Roosevelt with his idea to initiate peace proposals. The desperate ambassador saw his president as a new Chamberlain, suggesting, 'the situation may resolve itself to a point where the President may play a role as saviour of the world'. On reading this,

Roosevelt told his staff it was the "silliest message I had ever received. It urged me to do this, and that and the other thing, in a frantic sort of way".[228] He instructed the State Department to rebuke its London Ambassador. 'It is the wish of the President that you be informed, in order that you may thereby be guided… with conditions as exist at present in Europe, the government of the United States see no occasion nor any opportunity for the American President to initiate any peace move… that would make possible a survival of a regime of force and of aggression'.[229]

According to author Brendan Simms, Hitler never wanted to declare war against 'the Anglo-Saxons' of Britain or America. Although he had throughout his political career been against the 'Anglo-American Capitalist world order' and what he saw as the economic stranglehold on Germany after 'Versailles', he understood, and had seen the might of the British Empire in Flanders, and the power of the United States in the battle of the Marne'.[230]

The King, now wrote a 'stinker of a letter' to the Ambassador on 12 September. In his handwritten note covering three or more pages, King George VI, left no doubts about his kingdom's resolve. "My country has no other option, owing to its geographical position in Europe and its place in the Empire… She has been expected to act and has had to act as the world's policeman. As I see it, the USA, France and the British Empire are the three really free peoples of the World and two of these great democracies are now fighting against all that we three countries hate and detest… The Empire's mind is made up, believe me."[231]

Realising that he had strayed into hazardous territory, Joe wrote a subtly apologetic response: 'I was greatly touched by your gracious letter… explaining the British viewpoint. Whatever strength or influence I possess will be used every hour of the day for the preservation of "that life" we all hold dear, and in which you and your gracious Queen help to lead the world'.

The unfortunate ambassador arranged for all his children to leave Britain on separate ships, in case they all be sunk by a German submarine. Joe Jnr left first on *The Mauretania*. Pat, Jean and Teddy sailed with their governess on *The United States*. Rose, Kick, Eunice and Bobby followed on the overcrowded SS *Washington* on 12 September. 'People were sleeping in the lounge, swimming pool, gymnasium, in fact everywhere thinkable. It is all great fun', Eunice wrote. 'Nobody has their bags, and Kick and I wear the same costume for breakfast, lunch and supper but then, so does everybody else'.[232] The student diplomat, now running late for his senior year at Harvard, managed to secure a seat back on the Pan American flying boat, *Yankee Clipper,* on 20 September.

Just before she left, Kick recorded her feelings of wartime London in the blackout: 'England lay in dark silence while smiling moon and twinkling stars shone over her like lights of an anticipated victory. It's an eerie experience walking through a darkened London, and with groping finger make sudden contact with a lamppost. Against which leans a helmeted figure with his gas mask slung at his side… You wander through Kensington Gardens in search of beauty and solitude and find only trenches and groups of ghostly figures working sound machines and searchlights to locate the enemy. One hears the tap, tap, tap, not of machine guns but of umbrellas and canes as Londoners feel their way homeward'. She ends by revealing her love for England. 'May England soon have her midnights changed to midday with lights of victory, and until then may the moon and stars and brilliant lamps of courage and faith shine gloriously in the blackout'.[233]

In love with the land she was leaving, Kick wrote to her father from aboard the SS *Washington*: 'I still can't believe we are actually landing in New York today, this afternoon at 4pm. It can't be eighteen months since we were on this boat going in the opposite direction. It all seems like a beautiful dream. Thanks a lot, Daddy, for giving me one of the greatest experiences anyone could have had. I know it will have a great effect on everything I do from herein'.[234]

12

WHY ENGLAND SLEPT

The British professor, Harvard thesis, gulf between Ambassador and Churchill widens, Jittery Joe moves out of London during the Blitz, Ed Murrow rules airwaves, Ambassador Joe resigns, Jack joins US Navy, Kick introduces Inga Arvad.

"I am taking as my thesis England's foreign policy since 1931 and the class influence in England," Jack told his father in October 1939.

Jack, was the only student in his class to focus on government in Britain. This came as no surprise to Rose, who felt he, 'responded to the British love of culture and literature and all that sort of thing… he was interested in government and of course he did enjoy seeing all the beautiful homes because they were connected with history… and had been there for hundreds of years, like the Devonshires' home'.[235]

By 27 September, the four-week German invasion of Poland was over. An estimated 60,000 Polish and 10,572 German soldiers had been killed. The Harvard University paper, *Crimson,* reported the merciless bombing of civilians in Warsaw. 'A most dreadful bombardment killing more than a thousand civilians in the last 24 hours and leaving half the city in ruins and flames'. Despite this, a Harvard poll of students in the autumn of 1939 showed some ninety-five per cent were still against immediate entry into the war with seventy-eight per cent opposing any United States participation – even if England and France were being defeated. Such pacifism reflected the same mood that prevailed amongst Oxford University students some years earlier.

After Jack got back for his senior year and registered for classes, he went to see Francis Cannon at her New York apartment on Sunday, 1 October.

Kick wrote to her father, 'Jack is taking out Francis this weekend so we can all hardly wait'.[236] When Jack and his Harvard roommate Houghton appeared at her apartment, Francis quickly introduced them to John Hersey, her fiancé! Jack was crushed. He admitted to his father a week later, "Cannon and I have cooled a bit but am looking around sharply for a substitute."[237]

Jack was having a hard time settling down to the humdrum of student life after his exciting recent seven months away in London. A journalist described the student in his college surroundings. 'Jack, handsome, tall, thin and high strung with an ingrained habit of cocking his legs over the arms of his chair. Radios, chairs, laundry and valises scattered everywhere in the three-room suite in Winthrop House'.[238] Student Jack now selected a tutor to help him with his thesis – the thirty-six-year-old British professor, Wheeler Bennet. He had served as a soldier in WWI, and was a close friend to a fellow officer, named Harold Macmillan. The eccentric professor who had a stammer from the effects of a bomb which landed on his school in 1914 was a charming throwback to Edwardian times. He would appear in front of the students, complete with monocle, cane and a carnation in his buttonhole. At the end of a lecture, he would be applauded when putting on his gas mask from the Great War. Jack went up to the front of the room one such time, to introduce himself. Bennet recalls being struck by a 'pleasing open-countenanced, blue-eyed young man'.[239] After talking to Jack and recognising there, an outstanding potential, he agreed to assist him on his Munich thesis.

The British professor undertook to educate Jack in what he liked to call 'the imponderables of the human spirit which would make it possible to defeat Hitler'. They took long walks along the banks of the Charles River, exchanging ideas for his thesis. The professor saw how Jack might have been influenced by his father and soon saw his mission, 'without trying too hard to prejudice him in the opposite direction, to at least to expound the other side'.[240] By being challenged in this way, the student began to exhibit scholarly self-discipline and independent intellectual rigour.

Jack's marks in Government Studies now improved from grades C to B. He took four main courses – Principles of Politics, Elements of International Law, Comparative Politics and Modern Imperialism. Jack made a strong impression on Professor Holcombe, who challenged each student to study a congressman, assessing both his methods of operation and his performance. He urged his class not to substitute objective analysis with personal views. This appealed to Jack, who believed that politics should rest less on opinion than facts. Holcombe reviewed Jack's essay on Bertram Snell, the New York Republican. 'A very superior piece of investigating, and his final report was a masterpiece'. Jack naturally had some advantages, which Holcombe noted. 'When Christmas vacation came, he goes down to Washington, meets some of his father's friends and gets a further line on his congressman and on Congress'.[241]

Jack, was now able to merge theory and analysis with experience from his student diplomat days in London. His imagination had been fired. Biographer Robert Dallek maintains, 'More than anything, Jack's travels encouraged an intellectual skepticism about the limits of human understanding and belief. It was all part of Jack's affinity for skepticism which gave expression to his independence – to his developing impulse to question prevailing wisdom'.

Jack relished grappling with inherent contradictions. He was being stretched with questions about peace treaties in International Law and whether to recognise those treaties signed under duress, such as at Versailles. And how did Great Britain, find itself in another devastating war, only twenty years after escaping the most destructive conflict in history? Was it something peculiar to a democracy that accounted for this failure, or were forces at work here beyond the Government's control? He was being challenged at twenty-two to think through such topics, ones of the moment, balancing questions of honour in foreign policy with pragmatic national self-interest. Ambassador Joe, who often approached these things with a narrow and practical businessman's eye, was not always pleased with his son's broadening views. He would press Jack on the phone: "What's that Limey been telling you now!"

After Christmas 1939, Jack, on his way back to Harvard, stopped off at the invitation of Lord Lothian, the British Ambassador, to talk about his thesis. He later thanked the Ambassador: 'It was our talk that day last January that started me out on the job, and I am most appreciative of the kindness to me at that time'.[242] It was a bold move by him to use his experience in London to explore how the policy of appeasement during the 1930s had led to Munich. It would deepen his understanding of government and democracy. Armed with Lord Lothian's insights into the leading personalities of that time and backed up by material sent in the diplomatic pouch from the Press Secretary in the Embassy in London, Jack set about his work. With only three months to go, and guided by the scintillating historian Professor Wheeler Bennet, Jack now applied the same determination and commitment he had shown in life.

Joe Jnr, who had finished his own thesis on why western democracies had not intervened in the Spanish Civil War, told his father that Jack 'rushed madly around last week with his thesis and finally, with the aid of five stenographers on the last day, got it under the wire. He seemed to have some good ideas, so it ought to be very good'.[243] It was a huge and intensive effort. He had completed 144 pages (compared to the usual seventy for a thesis), with 350 footnotes in a very short time. The excitement of handing it in at the last minute with a furious burst of energy was how Jack liked to work – at speed and racing from one place and project to another.

At twenty-two, the undergraduate had explored the various reasons for Britain's delay in rearming. His aim was to benefit from Britain's experience and provide warning to America. Had the fault been something that lay with Britain's leaders or was it something inherent in the principles of a democratic system based on a capitalist economy? Demonstrating his fresh approach, he wrote, 'In the calm acceptance of the theory that the democratic way is the best, lies a danger. Why exactly is the democratic system better? It is better because it allows for the full development of man as an individual'. The undergraduate continued: 'While things indicate that democracy is a "pleasanter" form of government – it did not indicate that it is the best form of government for meeting the present world problem. It may be a great system of government… but its weaknesses are great. We wish to preserve it here. But if we are to do so, we must look at situations much more realistically than we do now'.[244]

The wife of the Winthrop House janitor remembered, 'Jack used to come home that spring his hands full of books… and we'd be in bed with the window open about that much, and he'd have his window wide open, and then you would hear him. His typewriter would go a mile a minute. He used to come home at eleven o'clock, twelve o'clock at night. It would be all quiet around here and you'd hear his typewriter going a mile a minute'.[245]

Jack's study of the 'isms… fascism, communism, militarism, nationalism, imperialism, gave him a valuable perspective on political creeds. He was exploring basic assumptions about liberty and the real world. It appealed to his intellect and engaged detachment.[246] Exploring the differences between idealism and realism, helped Jack become what Ted Sorensen described as a 'profound realist' with an unsparing honesty in dealing with facts. Jack ended his thesis on England on a theme of sacrifice: 'If you decide the democratic form of government is the best, be prepared to make certain great sacrifices…

With this new spirit alive in England, my story ends. England is now awake'.
The academics were satisfied, but were not unduly impressed. He was awarded
a *magna cum laude* – the lowest of three honour grades – when he graduated
on 20 June 1940. Whatever his views, right or wrong on this complex subject,
Jack had shown that he was willing to work very hard in trying to unravel
important issues.

New York Journalist and friend Arthur Krock viewed the work as 'an
excellent job'. He agreed with Joe that it could be a commercial success,
and taking his cue from Churchill's book, *While England Slept*, suggested a
new title for Jack: *Why England Slept*. Joe suggested surprising amendments,
including apportioning greater blame on leaders like Chamberlain for Britain's
slow rearmament. He wrote, 'The Leader is supposed to look after the national
welfare, and to educate people when, in his opinion they are off base. It may
not be good politics, but it is something that is vastly more important – good
patriotism'.

Jack's thesis was timely. Released just after the fall of France in July, it
became a runaway success. It sold 3,500 copies in two weeks. Joe sent a copy to
Churchill who, when he read it, said to his young aide at lunch, "You slept too,
didn't you!" Roosevelt sent a personal letter of congratulation. The *Boston Herald*
praised the 'rather modest youth' and his 'intelligence which goes far beyond
his years for his book which offers a capable diagnosis of the ills of democracy
facing international danger'. Joe told his son, "You would be surprised how a
book that really makes the grade with high-class people stands you in good
stead for years to come."[247] The 'modest youth', treated himself that September,
to a bright green Buick convertible with red leather seats, as soon as he arrived
in the sunshine state of California.

Back in London, Churchill became First Sea Lord. The Ambassador, now very
much out of touch in his views, was becoming further isolated. The First Sea
Lord called him to his new offices on 5 October, to make clear England's new
mood. As Joe records, 'We were shown into his office. Churchill was sitting
in a big chair in front of its fireplace reading the afternoon paper, smoking a
cigar with a highball at his side. He offered us a drink that we declined. He
said there could be no peace without the military destruction of Germany.
More than this after her defeat Germany had to be disarmed... All this will
cost us dear. He said we will of course win the war and that is the only hope
for civilisation'. The Ambassador's note continued: 'He characterised the Nazi

government as a monster born of hatred and of fear. Of England and the last war he said, the victor forgot, the vanquished plotted on'.[248]

Wary of Winston's determination to get the USA involved in the war, Joe wrote in his diary, 'Maybe I do him an injustice, but I just don't trust him. He always impressed me that he was willing to blow up the American Embassy and say it was the Germans, if it would get the United States in'.[249] Joe was disturbed when Churchill told him, "If Britain was bombed into subjection the Germans would insist on taking over the Fleet. And if we hand it over, their superiority over you becomes overwhelming."[250] Joe felt it amounted to blackmail.

In Washington, the British Ambassador, Lord Lothian, was irritating the President about the increasing dangers of the situation in Europe. His early approaches had made an unfortunate impression. Roosevelt wrote to a friend, 'I wish the British would stop this we who are about to die salute thee… attitude. Lord Lothian was here the other day… and went on to say that the British for a thousand years had been the guardians of Anglo Saxon civilization – and that the scepter or sword or something… the USA must snatch up… only FDR could save the world! I got mad clear through and told him that just as long as Britishers like him took the attitude of complete despair, the British would not be worth saving anyway. What the British need is a good stiff Grog, inducing not only the desire to save civilization but the confident belief that they can do it'.[251]

The President's view and letter found its way to the Foreign Office and whether Lord Halifax took a stiff Grog on reading it or not, Lord Lothian was soon taking a more robust and effective line with the President.[252] He reported to the Foreign Office, 'There is a rising feeling here that the US is playing an unworthy role in one of the greatest dramas of history and is in danger of losing her soul unless she shoulders her share of the burden'. Roosevelt now sent one of his long-time friends, Under-Secretary Welles, on a 'fact-finding mission' to check out Churchill, and his ambassador's reports. Welles returned mightily impressed with Winston, and his 'cascade of oratory, brilliant and always effective'.[253]

The gulf between Joe Kennedy and Churchill was huge. When Churchill first heard of Joe's defeatist views, he remarked sharply, "Supposing, as I do not for one moment suppose, Mr Kennedy were correct in his tragic utterances, then I for one would willingly lay down my life in combat rather than, in fear of defeat, surrender to the menaces of these most sinister men."[254] Joe considered it a foolish and futile fight. But few of his embassy staff, mirrored Joe's gloomy view. Seymour, the Press Secretary who had won a Croix de Guerre in the First World War and had been supplying Jack with material for his thesis, wrote to the student, 'We have had our share of cold and fog which has not improved our lovely Black Out. London is a different and almost incredibly beautiful place in these conditions. I get a kick out of walking these empty streets – moonlight makes it especially lovely… The spirit of the people is marvellous – firm, serious and courageous, ready I feel to face any sacrifice or privation to achieve the one and only end they are willing to accept'. Seymour, who would remain in London, not just throughout the Blitz but for the rest of his life, signed off his letter to Jack with, 'You may not know one thing, that your cheery presence is really missed here. I mean it. Good luck'.[255]

Joe's status was fading fast. During a call on Winston that October, Churchill, 'read me a letter that had been sent to him in a sealed envelope from Roosevelt. It said I am delighted you are back at the Admiralty. Takes me back to last war when I was with the US Navy. Want you to feel if there is anything you want to send me, anything personal, just drop me a line and send it by pouch'.[256] Nothing could have been better designed, to show the Ambassador he was now being sidelined. Joe recorded, 'A rotten way to treat his Ambassador and I think it shows him up to other people'. It was unprecedented for a president to be sending secret letters to the Lord of the Admiralty. But Roosevelt and Churchill saw themselves as allied in a great and noble struggle against Nazism and took whatever means they deemed appropriate. Both had to fight the tide of pacifism in their countries, following the tragedy of the First World War. Unlike most politicians, who were inclined to follow, rather than lead public opinion, they felt a special calling. As biographer, Laurence Leamer put it, 'While politics is the art of the possible, at the very highest levels in which Churchill and Roosevelt operated, politics was also an alchemy that transformed the impossible to the possible'.[257]

After taking a long Christmas break, extended by doctor's notes to nearly three months home leave, Joe was ordered to return to his post. Because of his public announcements in America, that Britain would be beaten, he was very unwelcome back in London. Foreign Office files record top official Vansitart, commenting on 29 February 1940, 'Very worried by the return of the American Ambassador'. When an official suggested, 'It would be useful if Kennedy would no longer be treated like an honorary member of the Cabinet', Lord Cadogan responded, 'I should think it is a diminishing temptation'.[258] Britain's *Spectator* magazine wrote, 'He will be welcomed by the shiver sisters of Mayfair and the wobble boys of Whitehall… few envoys, on returning to their post, can have received a welcome of such embarrassing variety'.[259] Churchill was now weeks away from greatness as Prime Minister. Ambassador Kennedy was months away from the end of his public career.[260]

When German soldiers streamed into Holland and Belgium, Chamberlain resigned. The King asked Churchill to form a new government. King George was privately concerned about Churchill's reputation as a volatile and impetuous adventurer and had written in his diary the night before, 'I cannot yet think of Winston as PM'. In the event, they were to go on to form an extraordinary wartime partnership which would exemplify British courage and resolve. On 10 May, age sixty-five, Winston went to the Palace with Clementine to accept his king's offer to form a government After years of unheeded warnings and sacrifices, he relished the moment. 'I felt as if I were walking with destiny and all my past life had been as a preparation for this hour and this trial'.[261]

On 13 May, three days after taking office, Churchill appeared in Parliament for the first time as Prime Minister. That same day, the Germans crashed through France's Maginot Line. Churchill now gave a speech that brought his audience to its feet. "I have nothing to offer but blood, toil, tears and sweat… You ask, what is our policy? It is to wage war by sea, by land and air with all our might… against a monstrous tyranny, never surpassed in the dark lamentable catalogue of human crime… You ask what is our aim? It is victory at all costs, victory in spite of all terror, victory, however long and hard the road may be; for without victory there is no survival."

A dejected Joe Kennedy wrote to Rose, 'The English will fight to the end, but I just don't think they can stand up to the bombing indefinitely. What will happen is probably a dictated peace with Hitler probably getting the British Navy, and we will find ourselves in a terrible mess. My God how right I've been on my predictions. I wish I'd been wrong'. Lord Halifax called Joe to the Foreign Office on 14 May, and told him Britain would, 'need every airplane the United States could muster'. Joe was later summoned at midnight to the Old Admiralty Building, now heavily guarded by soldiers. Churchill and Lord

Beaverbrook (who had just accepted the crucial role as Minister for Aircraft Production), asked what help America could provide. Joe replied, "Right now our Navy is in the Pacific, our Army is not up to requirements and we haven't enough airplanes for our own use." Churchill pressed on, until Joe said, "If we wanted to help all we can, what could we do?" Churchill asked for more airplanes and for older destroyers.

On 16 May, Roosevelt went before Congress. He gave a galvanising speech calling for America to produce the unimaginable number of 50,000 warplanes during the next year and twenty-five times the number built in 1939. Demanding a new 'toughness of moral and physical fibre', he asked for a budget of $1.2 billion for national defence. The President got one of the longest ovations Congress had ever given him. 'Overnight', Joe Jnr wrote to his father, 'the people turned strongly sympathetic to the Allies, and now many people are saying they would just as soon go to war'.

On 4 June, after the 'miracle' of Dunkirk, Churchill delivered a singularly defiant radio broadcast to the nation. "We shall fight on the beaches, we shall fight in the hills. We shall never surrender! …until in God's good time the new world with all its power and might steps forward to the rescue and the liberation of the Old." The last line which is not often quoted, revealed Churchill's passionate belief in the power of and need for American involvement.

The world was stunned when German troops entered Paris and marched down the Champs-Élysées just ten days later on 14 June. After the fall of France, Churchill addressed the wider world. "Upon this battle depends the survival of the Christian civilisation," adding hopefully, "if the British Empire and its Commonwealth last for a thousand years, men will say this was their finest hour."

Joe Kennedy obtained two copies of the Empire speech. "I had them all signed for the children," he told Rose, "as I think they will be important historical documents."[262] He knew that Jack, an admirer of Churchill, would be especially pleased. He was the Kennedy, that had been able to recognise Churchill's masterful magnanimity and greatness. Winston, mystified Joe, by maintaining his personable and courteous manner towards the Ambassador. He had badly misjudged Churchill before, reporting after Britain's evacuation of Norway in April, 'I have never, since I have been in this country, seen the undercurrent of discontent which exists at present. Mr Churchill's sun has been caused to set very rapidly by the situation in Norway which some people are already characterising as the second Gallipoli'.[263]

The Battle of Britain raged over the fields and skies of England that summer. On 7 September at 4pm, a force of 350 bombers escorted by 600 fighters, advanced on a twenty-mile front down the Thames, virtually unopposed, and turned London's docklands with 337 tons of bombs alight, with smoke so intense that it obliterated the evening sun. It decimated the East End slums, setting the warehouses and docks ablaze. That night, the American broadcaster Ed Murrow, broadcasting his daily, *This is London,* conveyed to millions of Americans in their homes, the sounds of the German bombers that evening, and told his audience, 'The fires up river had turned the moon blood red'.[264] Some days later, a bomb managed to land on the grounds of Buckingham Palace and blew out the windows of the King's study and demolished the swimming pool.[265]

Joe described his own ordeal in a letter to Rose, on 10 September. 'The last three nights in London have been simply hell. Last night I put on my steel helmet and went up on the roof of the Chancery and stayed up there until two o'clock in the morning watching the Germans come over in relays every ten minutes and drop bombs setting off terrific fires. You could see the dome of St Paul's silhouetted against a blazing inferno. No. 14 Prince's Gate just missed being hit. One of the bombs hit the barracks, you know, facing Rotten Row. One last night, dropped in the bridle path facing the house… the Natural History Museum they finally got Sunday night setting fire to it'. (Interestingly, the deep explosive bomb scars from that night can still be seen on the walls of the Victoria and Albert Museum today along Exhibition Road.) Kennedy told Hull back in America, "There's been hell to pay here tonight."[266] In the very first raid on London, nearly 400 people were killed. This was hell indeed. It was the first of fifty-seven straight days of bombing, in what became known as the Blitz. Three hundred thousand people would lose their homes and about 8,500 would die.[267]

Joe, estimated that the Germans dropped ten bombs within 200 yards of the American Embassy. He was nearly killed when a delayed time bomb exploded fifty yards from his car, tossing it up on the pavement in Mayfair. He was unhurt.[268] Billy Cavendish had a lucky escape the following spring. After a period of relative quiet, London had one of its heaviest attacks for weeks on a moonlit night on Saturday 8 March. At Café de Paris, where Snakehips Johnson and his band were playing, at 9.40pm, a fifty-pound bomb had penetrated eighty feet underground, landing straight on the band below. Sarah Norton, who Billy was escorting that night, describes how after dinner at the Mirabelle, they emerged into a silent Curzon Street and, finding one of the few taxis braving the bombs, set off for the 400 Club. On the way, they spotted an incendiary bomb, stopped the taxi and helped firemen put it out with a bucket of sand from the pavement. 'That bomb actually saved our lives', recalled Sarah. 'Stopping for it, we just missed the devastating one that landed on the Café de Paris by Leicester Square'. They saw the building in smouldering ruins, Billy and another man went inside to help bring out the wounded. After a while Billy returned. And I said, "Well then, let's go to the 400!" We felt we shouldn't let ourselves be daunted by anything the enemy did, and that we had to continue. So feeling very shaken we went on to the 400. While we were dancing another raid started and we soon had to stop – it was like trying to balance on a ship's deck in a storm. Sitting down was almost as difficult as the seats rose up and then crashed down again as bombs fell. The bottles and glasses fell off people's tables and rats came out from behind the red curtains round the walls. By this time I was motionless with terror – I couldn't eat, speak, drink or smoke. It seemed to go on for ages and then suddenly there was an enormous explosion right beside us and an air-raid warden staggered in to say the building was on fire and we must leave. Outside, the pavement was so hot that it scorched through the thin soles of my shoes and the broken glass cut me round the ankles. Suddenly it was all quiet again and all you could hear was the roar of burning buildings and the crackling of smaller fires'.[269]

Like many young people at that time, whenever Billy got a pass the couple would brave the bombs and fires. "You had to go out," said Lady Ford, remembering that night. "Life had to go on. You had to behave in what to a later generation would have seemed an uncaring manner. But dear heavens, if you didn't do that you would have gone mad."[270]

The Ambassador soon moved out of London, explaining to Rose, 'Because they are working against Kensington I have moved out of there completely. When I have to stay in town I am planning to sleep in the Chancery building and the rest of the time go out to Windsor'. [271] But even Windsor was no escape, as Joe described a Messerschmitt pilot that flew close. 'I could almost count his buttons and I thought he was going to land on the home'. The townspeople of Windsor had benefitted by one of Rose's last acts in England, raising money for an American ambulance, which Joe presented to the Mayor on 2 September. In another gesture of his own, Joe later arranged for royalties from Jack's book, to be given to the severely damaged town of Coventry.

The Blitz produced a surprising effect on many. As one Mayfair housewife described it, 'An extraordinary mood of exaltation sweetened the air of London...The combined sense of danger and unity was exhilarating'.[272] And now the tide was beginning to turn. The energetic Beaverbrook had managed to hugely increase the output of fighter and other planes. On 15 October, an immense force of 700 German fighters and 250 bombers targeted London and five other cities. Fifty-six German planes were destroyed that day whilst the Royal Air Force lost just twenty-eight. Lord Beaverbrook's factories had produced over 700 fighters since the beginning of July, far more than the Germans had calculated. On May 9 1941, one of the last and worst of the bombing raids took place, leaving a record 1,400 people dead and reducing to rubble the Chamber of the House of Commons. Though a few sporadic raids continued, Hitler postponed his planned invasion of England, named Sea Lion, and started to turn his attention on the east. On 22 June, the Germans launched their military might against Russia. The much-feared prospect of an invasion of Britain that summer, was over.

'Jittery Joe', as some called him, was suffering from nerves and lonely without his family. He now pleaded with Roosevelt to be allowed a break. Taking a night flight to Portugal on 22 October, to board a sea plane for New York, Ambassador Kennedy gave his final interview, in which he praised Londoners for their grit and determination. "I did not know London would take it," he declared. "I did not think any city could take it. I am bowed in reverence."[273] He got home a week before the presidential elections in November. He would not return to his post in London.

The Ambassador now posed a danger to the President. He carried a large number of potential Catholic votes with him. As soon as he landed, a worried Roosevelt immediately asked Joe and Rose, to spend a night at the White House. Rose, implored Joe to behave. "Remember the President sent you, a Catholic, as Ambassador to London which probably no other President would have done." Roosevelt repeatedly assured Joe he had no intention of sending American boys into the European conflict, and promised Joe, over dinner of scrambled eggs and sausages, to help his sons if they ever ran for elective office.[274]

On 29 October, Joe now publicly endorsed Roosevelt on 114 radio stations belonging to the CBS network. He argued for the need to send armaments to England now as a way of keeping the war away from America. He cited Jack's book as a lesson to follow. 'Those of us who know the stuff of which Churchill and the British leaders are made, those of us who know the courage and the calibre of the officers and men of the Royal Navy, know that surrendering the fleet to Hitler is beyond the basis of belief'.[275] Jack wrote to his father, 'Proud to have sponsored you. Thanks for the plug. Love Jack'.[276] A few days later on 4 November, Kick went to see Roosevelt campaigning in Boston with both Honey Fitz and Joe at his side. She was thrilled by the scene, writing to her dad, 'It's great to be famous – goodnight from your 4th hostage'.[277] The next day, on 5 November, Roosevelt beat Willkie by a slim majority. The Kennedys felt they had been king makers.

A few days later, an exhausted Chamberlain died and his friend Joe recorded in his diary, 'I had hard work trying to keep from crying. He was noble. He was kind and fair and brave'.[278]

Later that day, Joe was in the Ritz-Carlton in shirtsleeves, eating apple pie and cheese in his room,[279] and gave an off-the-record interview to two reporters from the *Boston Globe*. To Joe's annoyance, they promptly published. 'Democracy Dies if US Enters War – Kennedy', became the startling headline in the *Washington Times* on 12 November. It recorded the Ambassador claiming, 'Democracy is finished in England… and probably in America as well'.[280] At a luncheon in Los Angeles, Joe repeated these views, fuming that he 'knew more about Europe than anyone else'. The British Council office reported that he caused 'something tantamount to a panic amongst the luncheon audience'. Joe told his Los Angeles audience, "The Queen has more brains than the Cabinet put together," thereby putting himself back in the position of being on the outside again, and effectively ending his public career.

Joe's 'appeaser image', which had angered so many Americans, now spurred Jack to take the initiative. At the young age of twenty-three, showing deep care and independence, he wrote an extraordinary letter to help out his father. 'You might explain with some vigour your ideas on how vital it is for us to supply England. You might work in how hard it is for a democracy to get things done unless it is scared… England may fall through lack of support. Therefore you are gloomy in the hope you can get the country stirred up'. [281] Jack was trying to create an image for his father, akin to a Churchill; a patriot willing to speak his mind whatever the cost to his prospects and popularity.

Jack flew out of San Francisco leaving behind his college girlfriend, Harriet Price, who had shared fun times driving around with him in his Buick convertible. She would wonder, as she missed him, who amongst her friends could change in the space of a few minutes from a cheerful young man whose greatest attribute was his charm, to an adult pondering the big questions of his time, and then back again to his happy carefree self.

Christmas 1940, saw Kick still pining over Billy. She sent a telegram: 'Miss you. Hope New Year brings us together again. God bless you always. Love Kick'. [282] She was trying to adjust to being a student at Finch College, New York, but in love with Billy she desperately wanted to return to England and do her part. [283] She had told her father back in the summer of 1940 that her college had held a vote on America joining the war. "I and one other girl were the only two yeses. It looks like the Germans will be in England before you receive this letter. In fact from reports here they are just about to take over Claridge's now. I still keep telling everyone the British lose the battles but they win the wars'.

In the summer of 1941, Kick got a 'paying job', as her father put it, working for Frank Waldrop, the editor of the *Washington Times-Herald*. Three weeks later that September, Jack joined her in Washington. He lived in Dorchester House on Sixteenth Street, ten blocks away. Most evenings now, they were in and out of each other's apartments, and going to cocktail parties, dinners and the cinema together. Jack's newfound literary fame got them invites to all the best parties. Known affectionately as the 'Kennedy Kids', they became popular dinner guests, as they handed out signed copies of *Why England Slept*. Jack's friends now, for the first time began to speak, usually playfully, about how he might one day run for President.

Kick then introduced Jack to yet another person fated to play a role in his life – this time to the stunningly beautiful Inga Arvad. She had been born into a well-to-do Danish family. She was well travelled, witty, clever and sophisticated, and at twenty-eight possessed a subtle style. Working at the *Times-Herald* with Kick, they had become best friends. Inga recalled the moment she heard Jack was coming. 'Kick curled up like a kitten, her long tawny hair fell over her face as she read a letter, jumped up, her Irish blue eyes flashing and began a whirling dance like some delightful Dervish. He's coming to Washington! I'm going to give a party at the F street club. You will just love him'. After this build-up, when the blue-eyed Inga met Jack, she wrote, 'He came. She hadn't exaggerated. He had the charm that makes the birds come out of their trees. He looked like her twin, the same thick mop of hair, the same blue eyes, natural, engaging, ambitious, warm and when he walked into a room you knew he was there, not pushing, not domineering, but exuding animal magnetism.' [284]

For a Dane who had only reached the United States a year earlier, her English was astonishing, as was her understanding of Jack. 'He hates only one subject – himself. He is the best listener I have come across. Elder men like to hear his views which are sound and astonishingly objective for so young a man'. Inga went to parties and movies with Kick's group and enjoyed talking the hours away. 'Most evenings', Inga recorded, 'Jack, Kick, Torby MacDonald, Chuck Spalding and a few others would have dinner, always the same menu: steak, mash potatoes, peas, carrots and ice cream. Touch football was played in Kick's living room. Everything was discussed, mainly politics, but somehow it always got back to Jack. He was all of twenty-four and torn between a life of service to his country and teaching at some college. We planned half-heartedly and in some fun that he should someday be President. He laughed and said, "If I ever decide to run for office, you can be my manager."[285]

That November, Inga, who was becoming the great love in Jack's life, became the focus of FBI interest. When working as a Danish journalist, she had gained access to leading Nazis in Berlin, and using her wit and beauty, became friends with Goering and his wife, and even Hitler, it appeared. Because she had been photographed in a ringside seat in the Fuehrer's box at the Olympic Games, the President personally agreed to Hoover's FBI investigation. "I think it would be just as well to have her specially watched." The FBI were worried how she had secured a long interview with Hitler, who had given her a signed and framed photograph. Inga herself, had been puzzled that Hitler had happily spent two hours being interviewed by her, 'as if he had nothing more important in this world than to convince me that in National socialism lay the future of the world'.[286]

With a job in Naval Intelligence, Jack, would have been advised to leave Inga. But neither Jack nor Inga were conventional people. She was the most intriguing woman Jack had ever met. She wrote many heartfelt and eloquent love letters. 'You said to me last Sunday that, "To you I need not pretend – you know me too well." I do, not because I have put you on a pedestal – you don't belong there nobody does – but because I know where you are weak and that is what I like. A man or woman who thinks and makes others believe he has no weaknesses in him or her, well, they are like diamonds cut from an unskilled hand'.[287]

Inga was able to observe and encourage Jack's great potential. 'Go and defend your country. I say the same but somehow the pride is not there, only a hope that God will keep his hand safely over you. And more important than returning with your handsome young body intact, to let you come back with the wishes to be White House man', she wrote on Valentine's Day 1942. 'If you feel anything beautiful in your life… do not hesitate to say so, don't (sic) hesitate to make the little bird sing. It costs so little, a word or a smile, a slight touch of the hand… life is going to be tough, and doubly hard for the people who have ideals, who have hopes, who have someone they really love, who understand humanity'.[288] Inga had no doubts that Jack was destined to do great things and exhorted, 'Plan your life as you want it. Go up the steps of fame. But – pause now and then to make sure you are accompanied by happiness. Stop and ask yourself, "Does it sing inside me today?"'. Later, she would write, 'I obviously have a tiny weakness for you – that is because you are the kind of person the world ought to swarm with. You have just sufficient meanness in you to get along and enough brains and goodness to give to the world and not only take… I can't wait to see you on top of the world. That is a very good reason why [this] war should stop so that it may give you a chance to show the world and yourself that here is a man of the future…'[289]

Kick, who always believed in Jack, revelled in his reputation in Washington, as a rising man. At the end of a social evening, she would put on a bathrobe and sit up late with her brother, discussing the various people they had met. John White, an admirer of Kick, recalled, 'Their speech with one another was always elliptical and telegraphic; darting from point to point and they rarely finished a sentence'. 'Everything was discussed, mainly politics', as Inga remembered, 'but somehow it always got back to Jack'. The tone was always light and amusing.

Although Inga was finally cleared of FBI suspicion, the constant phone tapping did not stop until well after Jack had been transferred to a naval backwater base at Charleston, in January 1942. "They moved me down to South Carolina because I was going round with a Scandinavian blonde, and they thought she was a spy," Jack fumed to a friend years later. It is likely that Joe too, had exerted his influence as soon as Inga, twice married, started gaining unhelpful newspaper attention.

After Jack's departure for Palm Springs, Inga wrote, 'Is the sun shining, the pool tempting and your family spoiling you? I do hope, dearest Jack, you are having all the fun in the world. You should. Why? I don't know except you seem to be one of the very rare people born to sunshine and happiness'.[290] But, by now the grand affair that had rocked Washington was largely over. [291]

Jack finally left the backwater at Charleston and was accepted fit for sea duty, despite back problems, on 22 July 1942. Inga saw him off and told a friend, "But you know his back – he looks like a limping monkey from behind. He can't walk at all. That's ridiculous sending him off to sea duty."

The war was not going well for Britain in 1942. After the fall of Tobruk, Singapore, and a relentless catalogue of disasters and misfortunes which included the sinking of the *Prince of Wales* and *Repulse*, a furious Churchill confined himself to saying, the conduct of the large army in Singapore, 'does not seem to have been in harmony with the past or present spirit of our forces'.[292] Harold Nicholson's diary entry of 27 February outlined the mood. 'This Singapore surrender has been a terrible blow to us all. It is not the immediate danger but the dread that we are only half-hearted in fighting the wholehearted. We intellectuals must feel that in all those years we have derided the principles of force upon which our Empire was built, we undermined confidence in our own formula'.[293]

Britain's first victory and a turning point before direct American participation, came at the Battle of El Alamein, in October 1942. Amongst the injured was the son of the British Ambassador, Lord Halifax. The President offered to fly Lord Halifax, out from Washington to the hospital in Cairo, but he declined his help, on account of the fact that other boys in hospital could not have similar visits. Twenty-two-year-old Richard Wood recovering in Washington went about in a wheelchair, and it was Kick who took him out to his first baseball game.

Billy and his battalion during the miracle of Dunkirk had been one of the last to be evacuated. Back in England, Billy had felt ashamed that "We ran and ran!" He was determined to get back and recover England's honour and fight for freedom. Knowing that Billy could not get Kick out of his mind, Lady Astor wrote to her. 'Stop all this foolishness, come over right away and marry Billy!' Kick would return to England, at the same time as Jack was about to face his test of duty in the fight for freedom.

13

'YOU'VE GOT TO HAND IT TO THE BRITISH' – JACK RESCUED

Popular skipper, message on a coconut, Jack and crew rescued after five days, Jack 'disdains hero stuff', Kick returns to England and marries Billy, Joe Jnr in Cornwall volunteers for secret mission and Billy leads troops into Brussels. Two sons killed within weeks of each other, Jack's bond with Devonshire family deepens.

Arriving on 25 April 1943, at his Pacific island base, Lieutenant John F Kennedy was made skipper of an eighty-foot wooden boat, PT 109, tasked with patrolling the Solomon Islands. He was at home in these small daring PT boats, often captained by men like him from wealthy backgrounds who had learned to sail on family yachts.[294] The freedom that came from skippering such small boats, called 'bucking broncos', appealed to Jack with his fundamental dislike of authoritarianism, cheekily thumbing his nose at discipline in Choate, and his mother's mania for rules.

Jack's role was to intercept Japanese destroyers and troop transports, firing his torpedoes quickly before darting back out again. On the island of Tulagi, he found a thatched hut by the side of a bank of huge refrigerator units on the edge of the jungle. "Let you and me clean it up and go live there," he suggested to his executive officer Lenny Thom. It was not the Waldorf, but it was tolerably clean and not too close to the latrines. Jack installed his portable Victrola and his favourite songs, *Old Black Magic* and *All or Nothing at All*, were soon playing along with tropical birdsong high in the trees above their thatched world. Jack surprised his crew by adding a 37mm anti-tank gun which he found and fitted, secured by an additional log to the deck of his

PT 109.[295] He then picked up the nickname 'Crash Kennedy' after he raced another PT boat and went streaking 'into the dock like an eighty foot missile on the loose!'[296] There were a lot of laughs, recalled crew member Barney Ross. Enlisted men do not always like officers much, but they instinctively warmed to Jack, who was popular too with his brother officers. He was discovering – not that he'd ever doubted it – his talent for leadership.

Night after night, Jack's crew went out in patrols from Russell and Rendova Islands at low speed in rough water, trying as best as they could to find enemy ships. Despite five mentions in 'after action reports' and thirty patrols, Jack and his crew had not seen a single destroyer. On a moonless night on 1 August, after being attached to another squadron things were about to change. At eleven that night, PT 109 sailed into the Blackett Strait along with fourteen torpedo boats to intercept the 'Tokyo Express' – a convoy of Japanese ships supplying their forces.

Jack was at the wheel wearing his Mae West. He carried a lucky gold coin given to him by Clare Luce, next to his identification tag hanging from his neck. A sheath knife was fixed to his belt and a Smith and Weston revolver into his waistband. He took off his helmet from time to time, too heavy to be worn for long. In order to escape the glare of searchlights, he ordered his boat to cut one of its engines; propellers that left shimmering a white trail in the blackness would expose his position. At this point the silhouette of a ship appeared out of the dark, bearing rapidly down on them. The crew thought at first it was another PT boat, but with no time to restart both engines, *Amagiri,* a Japanese destroyer, sliced through the plywood hull of PT 109, immediately killing two of Jack's crew as gasoline tanks exploded and flames shot in the sky.

Jack and ten men were thrown clear in the water and clung on to the boat's wreckage all that night. When dawn came and no sign of any PT boats coming to rescue them, Jack, seeing an island three or four miles away, decided they should head there. With his men paddling alongside the coconut log – the one fitted by him – he led the way. McMahon was too injured to paddle, so Jack, taking the lead from his lifejacket, put it in between his teeth and pulled his crewman along. It took them five hours to reach the island. Hoping not to be spotted by Japanese aircraft, they lay exhausted after their epic swim under the few palm trees shading Plum Pudding Island. That night, Jack swam out to James Foster Passage to a point where standing on a reef, he could wave the lantern he had swum with. With no sign of any passing PT boat and seeing only flares flashing in the distant horizon, he swam back, exhausted. After Barney Ross tried the same the next night, Jack decided they would stand a better chance if they could swim to a bigger island closer to the Passage. They set out with him pulling the injured McMahon again for three hours. The new island, Olasana, had plenty of fallen coconuts to quench their thirst, and Jack and Ross swam to a large atoll where Jack had seen flashes of gunfire. Here, on this island named Nauru, they discovered a canoe with a barrel of water and a tin of shipwrecked Japanese crackers and candy.[297] They also saw two natives running away. When they got back with their cargo of water and candy, to their astonishment, they saw the two natives who had run away chatting to their crew. By good fortune, Biuku and Eroni were coast-watching scouts working for His Majesty's Royal Australian Navy. A relieved Jack took out his pocket knife, and inscribed his famous message on the husk of a green coconut that Biuki handed him: 'NAURO ISL NATIVE KNOWS POSIT HE CAN PILOT 11 ALIVE NEED SMALL BOAT KENNEDY'.[298]

Lt. A R Evans, Royal Australian Navy, scrutinised Jack's message on the coconut husk and after loading Biuki and Eroni with food supplies he wrote out a note he put in a brown 'On His Majesty's Service' envelope: From 'Senior Officer, Naru Is'. 'Friday 11pm. Have just learnt of your presence on Nauru Is. Two natives have taken your news to Rendova. I strongly advise you to return to here with this canoe… by the time you arrive here I will be in Radio communication with authorities in Rendova + we can finalise plans to collect rest of party'.

When the two scouts handed Jack the unexpected envelope, he looked over to Ross exclaiming, "You've got to hand it to the British!"[299] Out of sight from Japanese planes which sometimes buzzed his canoe and covered over in green palm fronds, Jack arrived at Komu Island, forty miles within enemy lines. As he stepped out from the boat and splashed through the shallow water, his legs blotched with coral wounds and six days' growth of beard, he put out his hand: "Hello, I'm Kennedy," he smiled, as Lt. Evans approached him. Pointing to a tent under palm trees, the Royal Australian Naval Officer invited him to 'a cup of tea'.[300]

Jack's squadron of PT boats going out that fatal night had seen hundred-foot-high flames and heard the roar of gasoline set alight on impact, and assumed all on PT 109 had been lost. They were unaware that a wind had blown the flames on the water away from the crew. Just a single PT boat went to look for survivors an hour later, as the rest returned to base at Rendova at

4am. No further rescue attempts were made, despite an order from Admiral Halsey in Washington under pressure from Joe.

Twenty-six-year-old Lt Kennedy had become a near legendary figure amongst his fellow PT officers. This despite a certain nonchalance possibly contributing to his being the only PT boat almost sliced in two in the Pacific. He impressed not by bravado or chumminess but by his confident friendliness and courage. Despite his back problems, the oppressive steamy heat, and food in limited supply, Jack never complained. Camaraderie was one of the things that made miserable conditions bearable. What was remarkable too was his ability to relate to different people from different backgrounds without, in any way, distorting or being untrue to his own character. For some, this absence of phoniness precluded him from a possible political career. "I didn't think he had any more chance of being President of the United States than the man on the moon," recalled Lt. Woods. "He was simply not bullish, forceful or opinionated enough."

Another naval colleague, Al Custer, whose father was a Republican politician, recalled, "We often talked about what we were going to do after the war. You've got to remember that Kennedy – he wasn't an introvert, but he was a writer. Kennedy, I think, wanted to be a writer."

James Reed remembers, "Jack was very embarrassed by the fact that his father had not served in WWI; the things that Mr Kennedy said when he was Ambassador must have also spurred on Jack, to do a lot of things. He always had that sense of leadership; quietly assertive. Not at all flamboyant. And that magical quality that everybody liked him."

All his life, Jack had been a rich boy amongst rich boys. And now he was amongst men that might have ridiculed his accent and his seemingly affected ways. These men knew life, the way that rich boys never could. But when they sailed out together in danger, depending on each other, they would look up to Jack. As crewman Ted Guthrie said, they "gained strength by the courage" shown by Jack.[301] Those men on the Pacific islands who shared a close-up view of character, were certain about Jack's potential. Johnny Isles: "It was written all over the sky that he was going to be something big. He just had that charisma. You could tell that just by his nature, by the way people would stop by and visit with him."[302]

James Reed: "He never tried to dominate the conversation. There was an aura about him that I've never seen duplicated in anybody else. He was an extraordinary fellow. First of all, he had such a broad interest. He was several steps ahead of all of us. He'd had the opportunity to be exposed to people in high places. He had first-hand experience of foreign affairs plus the fact that he had such a marvelous sense of humor. He had a light touch, and a serious side."[303]

In *Pilgrim's Way*, his favourite book he took to the Pacific, about a generation of upper-class Englishmen in World War I,[304] Jack had made a mark against a description of T. E. Lawrence. 'It is simplest to say that he was a mixture of contradictions which were never – perhaps could never have been – harmonised. He had... immense self-confidence and immense diffidence. The gentlest and most lovable of beings with his chivalry and considerateness, he could also be ruthless'.[305]

As skipper of PT 59, Jack received an overall 4.0, the very top marks for leadership and performance which included his performance in a leading role of a daring rescue, of fifty marines evacuated from one of the nearby islands. Al Custer, his commanding officer in December 1943, recommended promotion. 'This officer has demonstrated a cool effectiveness under fire and exhibited good judgement and determination in entirely strange conditions. His cheerful attitude and initiative qualify him to be the executive officer of a PT Squadron'. But before any promotion could be effected, an X-ray on Jack's worsening back and stomach ensured that he was soon sailing home on the USS *Breton*, arriving on 7 January 1944, at San Francisco's Golden Gate Bridge.[306]

Kick was in London when she first heard about the *New York Times* headline, 'Kennedy's son is a hero'. She had just finished reading his good-humoured letter of 24 June, sent to his parents, saying 'Kathleen reports that even a fortune teller says that I'm coming back in one piece. I hope it won't be taken as a sign in a lack of confidence in you all or the Church if I continue to duck.'[307] Later, she wrote to her war hero brother , 'Goodness I was pleased to get your letter. Ever since reading about it in the newspapers over here, I have been worried to death about you'.[308]

Jack stayed with Inga who now lived in San Francisco, for a week. Discovering she had found a new partner, he left, but not before she had written up his exploits, in the way he knew she could best express his close brush with death. Jack spent the winter recuperating at home in Palm Beach. He was in precarious health, prone to bouts of fever when his skin would turn a yellowy brown in the way he had suffered as a schoolboy. A friend recalled, "There were days when we go to St. Mary's hospital after he came back from the Solomons, he'd go into a fever and he'd be shivering with cold and his face would be yellow. We all thought he might die. We'd call the ambulance and I'd go with him. But in three or four days he'd snap out of it."[309] When Jack recovered, he was back at the Stork Club in New York with his old flame Frances Cannon and her husband, writer, John Hersey. His Navy service adventures on PT 109 were written by Hersey and appeared in June 1944 in the *New Yorker* and *Reader's Digest*.[310] They reflected his outlook. 'Nothing heroic or historic but a web of blind chance that allowed life to assert itself'.

That previous summer, Kick had arrived in Glasgow on 28 June 1943, aboard a heavily camouflaged grey *Queen Mary*. Dressed in a Red Cross uniform carrying a canteen, gas mask and first aid kit strapped to her belt, she arrived with 18,000 American soldiers who had slept on decks and hallways and anywhere they could be squeezed aboard! She had shared a cabin with seven girls, part of a group of 160 nurses which she described as 'a lot of tough babies'.[311] Her diary records her shock and surprise at how openly the girls talked about themselves, sitting up every night until 1.30am. Kick had quit her job at the newspaper after seeing an advertisement to join the American Red Cross, setting up recreation clubs for US servicemen overseas. American papers reported her going, 'heart-whole and fancy free, and determined to make her own mark in the world sans her famous father's influence'.[312]

After four years and many false starts, Kick wanted to keep her arrival a surprise for Billy. After reporting in at the Hans Crescent Club, barely a mile from her original Prince's Gate home, the first person she went to see was Sissie Ormsby-Gore, now married to David. "First day back in London and I can't believe I am really here. It is all like a dream from which I shall awaken quite soon." In Sissie's garden, she caught up with Jack's letters from his Pacific island about his own dream awakening. 'That bubble I had about lying on a cool Pacific island with a warm Pacific maiden hunting bananas for me is definitely a bubble that has burst', he wrote.

After David phoned with the news, Billy raced down as soon as he got leave from his training camp with the Guards Armoured Division in Scotland. Meeting on a Saturday night at the Mayfair hotel, they celebrated dinner with a bottle of champagne before going to the 400 Dance Club near Leicester Square. They danced until 3.30am, and decided to walk back home in London's romantic rain. She was eighteen and Billy twenty when they had first met. Now five years later, Kick wrote to Jack, 'Billy is just the same. A bit older, a bit more ducal but we get on as well as ever. It is queer as he is so unlike anyone I have known at home or any place really'.[313]

All Kick's old friends rejoiced at her return. To her relief, no one in England directly 'mentioned a thing about Pop'.[314] She told Jack, 'I feel that my devotion to the British over a period of years has not been without foundation and I feel this is a second home more than ever. I'm still recovering from a rather hectic trip over', adding, 'food is very good – blitzed areas are not obvious'.[315] Kick's new hectic life was challenging. 'I am here recuperating after five and a half days of jitter bugging, gin rummy, ping pong, bridge and just being an American girl amongst 1500 dough boys a long way from home!'.[316] She wrote to her old boss Frank Waldrop, 'You will be glad to hear that I am more pro-British than ever and spend my days telling the GI's about that great institution, the British Empire, and that there'll always be an England!'

Everyone saw how much Kick meant to Billy. They would talk and talk with each other at parties until dawn. They were genuine opposites, powerfully attracted to each other. She the diminutive Catholic-American heiress, socially

Kick dines with Billy Cavendish soon after her return to London in June 1943.
(Mary Evans Picture Library)

brilliant and flighty. He the tall, diffident and deeply thoughtful Protestant and scion of the British Establishment. Many considered the softly spoken Billy to have been a fine match for Princess Elizabeth, had she not grown up to be attracted to bold, outspoken men like Prince Philip of Greece. Billy "was a charmer of great intelligence. He had great presence", the Duchess of Devonshire would say. "He was loved by everybody and he and Kick were about the two most popular people you could imagine".

Joe was always sentimental about his absent daughter. "Kick is the steadiest battler there is for England. She seems to be very happy and while we miss her like the devil, whatever she wants is always right by me." He advised Tony Rosslyn, "I wish you would say to her sometimes as I've said to Jack – that he doesn't have to win this war all by himself, any more than she has to entertain the entire American army, or be the focal point for British-American relations!" A newspaper clipping which Rose had kept reported Kick 'was a more effective envoy to the people of Britain than her father, our pre-war Ambassador'.[317] A *Daily Mail* photograph taken in August 1943, of her smiling on a bike in her Red Cross uniform, had helped Kick become a joyful symbol of America helping Britain win the war.

Kick missed her 'wee brothers and sisters' and begged them to keep writing letters. 'I love their letters and read parts of them to the gang here. They all get a terrific kick out of them'. She was tickled pink to find that she was accused of having an English accent but quickly reassured her family, 'the boys keep me from going too Limey!' Joe Jnr now joined her in England with his VB-110 naval squadron, and coming up from his Coastal Command base in Cornwall, arrived at the Hans Crescent club with a crate of eggs from Virginia and a package from home full of ham, brownies, cookies, candy, oranges, lemons and apples. Joe visited often, playing bridge with the officers and his sister. If he was losing, he would lecture Kick: "Everyone makes mistakes, Kick. But you make too darn many… Gee, Kick, aren't you ever going to learn?"

Kick was trying new things. She arranged a party for her brother's entire naval air squadron when they played Irving Berlin's latest song: 'My British Buddy, we're as different as can be. He thinks he's winning the war, and I think it's me!

British-American relations had been rebooted when the new ambassador, John Winant, took over from Joe. Relatively shy and quietly spoken, the one-time Governor of New Hampshire made a favourable impression on Churchill. Spending weekends at the Chequers retreat, the new ambassador was invited into the family circle. The Ambassador's wife had remained in America, and Winant soon became very close to Sarah Churchill, whose own marriage to an American citizen, Vic Oliver, originally from Austria, was falling apart. The Prime Minister made no effort to interfere with the wartime "love affair which my father suspected but about which we did not speak", Sarah recalled. In the stressed conditions of war, such relationships were seen to be more like companionship than cheating.

In late 1943, the two leaders of America and Britain headed to Tehran to meet Stalin. Sarah, who accompanied them, witnessed her father's caring fondness for the President in the wheelchair. Sailing out to Cairo on the battleship *Renown* via Gibraltar, she records, 'The Rock rose from the sea in solitary splendor surrounded by a necklace of lights, the first I had seen since the blackout had begun in 1939. We stopped at Gibraltar long enough to pick up Harold Macmillan who was Resident Minister in Algeria. It was a wonderful night, one night after full moon; the *Renown* never looked more magnificent as I stood on her moon-silvered decks, A and B turrets and then the Bridge rose to grand echelon to the stars. We arrived at Malta on November 17th at about 6pm. Generals Eisenhower and Alexander were there to join us'. In Cairo, she met the President. 'This was my first meeting with him; I found him immensely impressive. One knew, of course, of his physical handicap, but after two minutes one never thought of it again. He was a vivid personality with a disarming air of simplicity. A great warmth emanated from him. One day after lunch with the President my father called me aside and said, "Please arrange a car as I want to go and have a look at the Sphinx and Pyramids. I want to see how close you can get in a car, because if it is possible, I want to take the President, but I don't want to raise his hopes if we can't get close enough."[318]

'We set out and found it was possible to get quite close, so we drove straight back and my father bounded out into the room and said, "Mr. President, you simply must come and see the Sphinx and the Pyramids. I've arranged it all." Such was my father's enthusiasm that the President leaned forward on the arms of his chair and seemed about to rise, when he remembered that he could not and sank back again. It was a painful moment. My father turned abruptly away and called over his shoulder, "We'll wait for you in the car." Outside in the shimmering sun, I saw that his eyes were bright with tears. "I love that man," he said. The visit to the Pyramids was a great success'.

On their last night in Cairo on 26 November 1943, Sarah says her father was, 'in terrific spirits at dinner where he talked, despite a tired, husky voice from 8.30 until 1.30am. He talked everybody into the ground except Anthony Eden. Mountbatten went to sleep on the sofa and I did not know how to keep my eyes open. On the way home that night my father talked lovingly about my mother. Then he fell silent and presently said, "War is a game played with a smiling face. But do you think there is laughter in my heart? We travel in style and round us there is great luxury and seeming security, but I never forget the man at the front, the bitter struggles, and the fact that men are dying in the air, on the land, and at sea."'[319]

Back in London, Kick's days were long. She had taken on extra work with lectures to the Women's Voluntary Service and of course still found time to stop off, 'at the Dorchester for a dance or two'. Together with Jean Ogilvy, she went to visit Lady Nancy Astor. As before, the butler, Arthur, served them tea on the spacious terrace looking over the steep bank down to the Thames. But now they shared tea with some Canadian doctors. Like Blenheim, Cliveden was being used as part military hospital. Nancy, energetic as ever, told them a telling tale about Stalin from her visit to Russia in 1933. She had asked Stalin why his enemies were shot without benefit of a trial. Before the interpreter turning white with shock fully recovered, Stalin replied without pausing, "This is war against the capitalist system and I am simply killing off my enemies."

The Soviet leader then talked about Great Britain. What made it special, he asked?

"I believe," Nancy said, "that when they translated the Bible and kindled it into the common language, and read it, and studied it, they became an uncommon people, because they had a measuring rod, and they thought for themselves, and they had a sense of justice, and mercy, and a sort of generosity and bigness."[320]

Leaving Cliveden, Nancy told Kick, "You must marry over here. You will never be happy in America now that England is in your blood."[321]

Kick and Billy spent many weekends that summer at Compton Place, often hearing the drone of the Luftwaffe bombers flying on to London, when the south coast was not being bombed.[322] But she loved it there. Once, managing to get hold of some peaches, they took a walk on the beach and 'for twenty-four hours', she wrote to Jack on 29 July, 'I forgot about the war'.[323] She told him about the surprising absence of criticism of their father. 'Of course a lot of it, I can put down to British reserve, which feels that some things are better left unsaid… but most of it I blame on their ability to make friends, which last all their lives. They are slow about it at first, but once made then it's lasting – wholly and completely'.[324]

When Jack finally got home after his Solomon Islands ordeal and rescue by the Royal Australian Navy, his mother wrote just before Christmas, 'He really is at home – the boy for whom you prayed so hard – at the mention of his name your eyes would become dimmed… what a joy to see him… to feel his coat and to press his arms… to look at his bronze face which is thin and drawn'.[325]

The early months of 1944 were stressful for both Kick and Billy. They adored each other but, at opposite ends of a religious divide, felt trapped in a 'Romeo and Juliet' situation. Kick wrote to Jack, 'I know he will never give in about the religion and he knows I never would. It's all rather difficult as he is very, very fond of me and as long as I'm about he'll never marry. It's really too bad because I'm sure I would be a most efficient Duchess of Devonshire in the post-war world and as I'd have a castle in Ireland, one in Scotland, one in Yorkshire and one in Sussex, I could keep my old nautical brothers in their old age', she joked.[326]

In January 1944, Billy resigned his Captain's Commission to follow his father's wish to stand in the local West Derbyshire by-election. Kick, who loved politics, went around canvassing with his mother, Moucher, handing out leaflets headed, 'A vote for Hartington is a vote for Churchill'. Mary Churchill with her 'lovely blue eyes'[327] took part in a campaign dinner with Kick. The rising tide of popularity emerging then for the Labour Party, stopped Billy from winning. "He was just too nice. He never should have come back. He should have stayed with his Regiment," remarked a family friend. Kick had impressed Moucher with the way she involved herself in Billy's campaign. If he were unable to win back the traditional family seat, Kick could be counted on to win it for him, she said! In a final speech, Billy told his audience, "I am going out now to fight for you on the front. After all, unless we win the war, there can be no home front."[328]

Later that spring and in uniform, carrying a sack of oranges over his shoulder, Billy stood at the front door of Jean Lloyd's house in Scarborough. Pushing the door open and seeing Kick cooking bacon and eggs for breakfast, he tossed the sack of oranges in her direction and announced with a beaming smile, "We're off!" With the invasion of France at the front of their minds, they feasted on champagne and lobster and talked till dawn. Three days later, Kick had made up her mind. They married at the Chelsea Register Office on 6 May.[329] It was the first time since 1694 that the heir to the dukedom of Devonshire had been married outside the family chapel.

To have captured the heart of Britain's most eligible heir was a tribute to Jack's sister and to her extraordinary gifts and personality. Her grandfather Honey Fitz proudly told Boston reporters, "She's all quality, and that boy must have been quality to have won her."[330] America's *Life* magazine described the marriage as, 'The greatest gesture for Anglo-American relations since the Atlantic Charter'![331]

Joe Jnr, flying submarine patrols from Cornwall, was the only Kennedy to join the small wedding party with Billy's sister Elizabeth and parents and Nancy Astor. 'Kick handled herself like a champion', telegraphed Joe Jnr, trying to comfort his mother and her religious concerns. She had gone into a health clinic with stress and to avoid making any public comment. 'As far as Kick's soul is concerned, I wish I had half her chance of seeing the Pearly Gates. I do know how you feel, Mother, but I do think it'll be all right',[332] Joe Jnr told Rose. He had warmed to Billy and the Duchess, telling his family, 'I like her very much. She is the one who is so much in favor of it. Billy is crazy about Kick, and I know they are both very much in love… I think he is ideal for Kick'. After some delay, Kick's father wrote, 'With your faith in God, you can't make a mistake. Remember you are still and will always be tops with me'.[333]

Kick spent a week honeymooning in the spring sunshine by the sea at Compton Place, wearing the ring Billy had inscribed with, 'I love you more than anything in the world'.[334] They moved to the Swan hotel at Alton near Billy's army base, and she spent hours roaming the countryside on her bicycle and listening each evening for the 'putt putt' of Billy's motorbike coming down the country lane. On 6 June: 'When we woke this morning, Billy said he was sure the Second Front had started. Planes had gone over unceasingly for two hours', wrote Kick. They had only been together for five weeks when D-Day began. When she moved to London as Billy marched off to war, she wrote, 'This is the saddest evening. Ever since May 6, I have had a wonderful sense of contentment. B is the most perfect husband'.

That July, pilot Joe Jnr had been due to return to Boston. But wishing to prove himself to his father and following Jack's award of a naval medal, he extended his tour. All that the elder brother wanted in family life was to be first; a condition that he thought was his natural right. Rose understood this. 'In their long brotherly friendly rivalry, I expect this was the first time Jack had won by such a clear "advantage", by such a clear margin. And I dare say it must have rankled Joe'.[335] Lack of news worried Jack. 'Heard from Joe a while back – they have had heavy casualties in his squadron – I hope to hell he gets through OK'.

On 12 August, Joe Jnr set out on a secret volunteer mission to fly his B17 plane carrying a new and massive ten-ton bomb towards a heavily bunkered coastal gun site. Following some distance behind, Elliot Roosevelt (son of the President), in a reconnaissance plane, saw Joe's B17 suddenly disappear in a huge flash over the Kent coast.

The family had just finished eating Sunday lunch and Joe had gone upstairs to take his nap when two priests arrived with the awful news, in Hyannis Port. For the Ambassador, the loss of his eldest son on whom he had placed such great ambition was a massive shock. Concealing his pain, he instructed the family, "We must carry on like everyone else… and take care of the living because there is much work to be done," before he withdrew into a silence of his own. Whilst the rest of the family carried on as instructed, with plans to sail, Jack could not simply 'carry on'. He spent the rest of the day walking on the beach by himself, lost in memories.[336] His brother gained the Navy's highest decoration for his volunteer mission.

When Kick arrived at Boston's Logan Airport in a military plane three days later wearing her Red Cross uniform, she hugged Jack in a tearful embrace. His back operation had been a failure and Kathleen was shocked by his appearance, with cheek and jaw bones jutting out. In a family where feelings were unmentionable and constant activity was the order of the day, the little clapboard church of St Francis Xavier provided them a place of solace that first evening. Over the next few days, Kick's presence, as she talked of Joe Jnr's last few months did much good for the shocked Kennedy family. Despite the awful tragedy, her joyfulness at having just married Billy came through and seemed to have had a positive healing effect on the family. 'It even shone through her sadness over Joe's death', wrote Jack to Billy's mother.

On 20 June, Captain Billy Cavendish waded ashore in the rain onto the beaches of Normandy with his battalion, the 5th Coldstream Guards. Soon engaged in heavy fighting around Caen, his company commander standing not far from

Billy, was struck by shrapnel. Major Howard, aged twenty-six, died instantly. When another of his commanding officers, Lt Colonel the Lord Stratheden, was wounded, Billy found himself leading a battalion. He had been fighting for a month in France before he finally found a peaceful moment on 26 July, to write to Kick, 'I have been spending a lovely hour on the ground and thinking in a nice vague sleepy way about you and what a lot I've got to look forward to if I come through this all right'. He continued, 'I feel I may talk about it for the moment as I'm not in any danger so I'll just say if anything should happen to me I shall be wanting you to try and isolate our life together, to face its finish, and to start a new one as soon as you can. I hope that you will marry again, quite soon – someone good and nice'.[337]

Billy was promoted to Major, and with the German army in fast retreat, his battalion quickly advanced 430 miles in six days. His was one of the first units to enter and liberate Brussels. He rode atop his tank, as cheering Belgian crowds flung flowers and garlands onto him and his vehicle. He told Kick a few days later, on 4 September, from the Chateau Frontenac, 'I have a permanent lump in my throat and long for you to be here as it is an experience which few can have and which I would love to share with you'.

Sleeping often in trenches and bombed-out villages, Billy always took care to look smart. Out in the field each morning, he would pull out a small mirror from his breast pocket to give himself a proper shave and order his batman, Ingles, to bring out the rum to toast in proper glasses.[338] Resuming their advance in a northward direction to support 82nd US Airborne Division at Nijmegen, his battalion was ordered to take the villages of Beverloo and Heppen. Here, on 9 September, the Coldstream Guards met fierce resistance. The area had been the training ground for the maniacal 12th SS Panzer Division, Hitlerjugend. Soon, a quarter of Billy's company had perished. He was the last officer left alive and unwounded. The next day, his company found themselves pinned down by concentrated fire from the elite Hermann Göring Parachute Division at Heppen. With fire being directed at him and needing to inspire his troops, a sense of calm took over. Leading the Infantry ahead of the tanks and carrying his beret 'as calmly as if he had been in the gardens at Compton Place', he gave his last languid order: "Come on, you fellows, buck up."[339] At that moment, he died instantly, targeted by a German sniper. He was wearing his pale corduroy trousers, white mackintosh and no helmet. In this fierce and fatal engagement at Heppen, Staff Sergeant Jim Cowley then took over command and would receive the Victoria Cross.

Shopping in Bonwit Teller's elegant department store in New York, Kick sensed something was wrong when her sister Eunice arrived for lunch. Eunice simply said, "Why don't you go talk to Daddy." She rushed to the former ambassador's suite at the Waldorf Astoria, where Joe handed Kick the telegram with the devastating message from the War Office. When Kick returned to Hyannis Port, Jack stayed up all night to comfort his beloved sister. She talked and talked until dawn about Billy and why she loved him so. Nothing could lessen her pain. Jack told a friend, it was the worst night of his life.

The two eldest sons of both families on whom so much promise centred, had died in battle within weeks of each other. Three days after his death, Billy's mother sent Kick a moving letter. 'All your life I shall love you – not only for yourself but that you gave such perfect happiness to my son whom I loved above anything in the world'. Thinking of Kick in her sorrow and not herself, the Duchess finished, 'My heart breaks for you when I think of how much you have gone through in your young life'. Jack sent back a heartfelt and elegant letter dated 21 September, that revealed the special bond that now existed between the Kennedy and Devonshire families.

Dear Duchess,

The news of the death of Billy was about the saddest I have ever had. I have always been so fond of Kick that I could not help but feel her sorrow.

Her great happiness when she came home, which even shone through her sadness over Joe's death, was so manifest and so infectious, that it did much to ease the grief of our mother and father. It was obvious what he meant to Kick and what a wonderful fellow he must have been that we all became devoted to him and now know what a great loss he is. When I read Waterhouse's letter about the cool and gallant way Billy died I couldn't help but think of what John Buchan had written about Raymond Asquith, 'Our Roll of honour is long, but it holds no nobler figure. He will stand to those of us who are left, as an incarnation of the spirit of the land he loved… He loved his youth and his youth has become eternal. Debonair and brilliant and brave, he is now part of that immortal England which knows not age or weariness or defeat'. I think these words could be so well applied to Billy. I feel extremely proud that he was my sister's husband.

Please accept my deepest sympathy. I know how you loved him and I feel so deeply for you all,

Sincerely

Jack did not often show his emotions. Not because he did not care; but because he felt deeply. He paid Billy the highest compliment – comparing his qualities to those of his hero, Lt. Asquith – qualities which he thought no longer existed in Britain. When Roosevelt asked Churchill what sort of boy Billy was, the Prime Minister replied, "He was one of the most promising lads in England."[340] President Roosevelt wrote to Joe, 'Please tell Kathleen, I and Mrs Roosevelt are thinking of her in her crushing sorrow'.

Ambassador Lord Halifax arranged for Kick to fly to Britain in the Royal Air Force plane taking back General Sir Alan Brooke, Chief of Imperial Staff, who had been Billy's commander at the time of the Dunkirk evacuation. As she waited alone for the aircraft at Quebec, she wrote to her parents. 'Tell Jack… not to marry for a long time', as she promised to keep house for him. 'I don't mind feeling sad because why should I mind? If Eunice, Pat and Jean marry nice guys for fifty years they'll be lucky to have five weeks like I did'.[341]

The war had tested Kick's aristocratic circle. Hugh Fraser was parachuted into the Ardennes as liaison officer of the Special Armed Services (SAS) and awarded the Belgian Croix de Guerre. David Mitford, Debo's only brother, was killed in Burma fighting the Japanese. William Douglas-Home took part in the invasion of Normandy but faced a court-martial and was imprisoned shortly after for disobeying orders. He had refused to lead an assault on Le Havre, before civilians, as requested by the German commander, had been allowed to evacuate. (Two thousand French civilians and nineteen German soldiers died in the subsequent shelling – weeks later, civilian evacuations were being agreed. Kick would often visit William in prison.) Captain Andrew Cavendish narrowly escaped death when taking the village of Montecatini Alto. He was awarded the Military Cross and then his war ended when his uncle, Harold Macmillan, Political Minister at Allied Headquarters, intervened to ensure the Dukedom. He sent him home with his father, the Duke, returning from an inspection of colonial troops in Burma.

When Kick arrived back at Waterloo on the General's private train, the Duke was there to meet her. But he was never the same again after his eldest son's death. At home in Compton Hall, Kick read the many letters written to her by Billy's soldiers. They had clearly held him in huge regard. One soldier wrote that they were so furious when they saw their commanding officer shot, that no prisoners were taken that day. Another told Kick that her husband 'was brave and fearless... just and fair... and admired and respected by all whom he commanded'.[342] Kick treasured these memories and made a point of copying paragraphs from these soldiers' letters, to send home, so that her brothers and sisters who 'did not know Billy very well, might like to know how well he did'.[343] Rose wrote to Kick with newfound grace. 'I have been thinking about you day and night ever since you left... After I heard you talk about him and I began to hear about his likes and dislikes, his ideas and ideals, I realise what a wonderful man he was and what happiness would have been yours'.[344]

A dispirited Kick told Jack, she felt like she had no purpose and felt like 'a small cork that is tossing around', adding, 'there are hundreds like me, but it doesn't help heal the wound'.[345] That September, Kick could not be left to sleep alone and Billy's sister Elizabeth would sleep on a mattress on the floor in her room at Compton Place. Kick parted with some of Billy's possessions, giving them as gifts, such as a pair of diamond and sapphire cufflinks that Billy received on his twenty-first birthday which went to his godson Andrew Parker Bowles.

Recovering his fragile health in Arizona and thinking about his brother, Jack decided to gather recollections from twenty people who had known him. Trying to make sure he kept dispirited Kick busy, he tasked her with putting together tributes from London friends. Jack was in awe of the heroic aspect to his brother of probably knowing he did not have it in him to achieve all his father's aspirations. But he *had tried!* In '*As we remember him*', Jack wrote, 'Though at a glance Joe's record shows that he had great success, things did not come particularly easy for him. I think his accomplishments were due chiefly to the amazing intensity with which he applied himself to the job in hand. I do not think I can ever remember him sit back in a chair and relax'. Joe remained an enigma. 'I suppose I knew Joe as well as anyone and yet I sometimes wonder whether I ever really knew him... He had always a slight detachment... a wall of reserve which few people ever succeeded in penetrating'.[346]

After two minor operations, one for a hernia, Jack spent Christmas with his family in Palm Beach. It was then, that he felt the pressure from his father to fit into his brother's shoes. He told a friend staying with them, "I can feel Pappy's eyes on the back of my neck." He seemed unable to escape that brotherly rivalry which in a way had helped define him. "I'm shadow boxing in a match where the shadow is always going to win,"[347] he told Billings. A fresh sense of purpose and duty, which had so attracted Kick to Billy, now emerged in Jack. Close to New Year's Day 1945, he decided he would try to become America's first Catholic President.[348]

As the war started coming to a close, Jack spelt out his future ambition in a surprising letter to his teacher at Choate: 'The war makes less sense to me now than it ever made… and I should really like – as my life's goal in some way and some time – to do something to help prevent another'. It seemed that the life and death realism of foreign policy were needed to fire Jack's intellect and imagination. Preventing a war was to ensure his future place in history.

When the war in Europe ended, standing in a huge crowd, together with David and Sissie and Hugh Fraser, was Kick cheering with them, arm in arm and looking up to the balcony of Buckingham Palace. There stood Winston Churchill, giving his familiar 'V' sign salute, surrounded by the King and Queen and their daughters. It was an exceptionally warm evening. Bonfires and fireworks lit up Green Park. Hundreds of searchlights swept the London night sky. People everywhere were celebrating, climbing lamp posts, waving flags and dancing in the streets. The next night, Kick sat alone with Billy's mother at dinner; both trying to steel themselves to face life without the ones, 'who would never come back'.[349]

14

JACK PREDICTS CHURCHILL WILL LOSE ELECTION

Jack reports founding of United Nations and on UK elections, sees ruins of Berlin, Kick joins Churchill in Florida, Winston warns of 'Iron Curtain' and need for a 'special relationship'.

Two weeks before Victory in Europe (VE) Day, Jack went to San Francisco for Hearst newspapers. He was to report on the conference with delegates from fifty countries gathered there to set up the United Nations.

Jack was skeptical about the new UN organisation, worried it might be 'the product of the same passions and selfishness that produced the Treaty of Versailles'.[350] Roosevelt's ambition had been to create an international structure for world peace, 'based on the just and sound principles of the Atlantic Charter'. This charter had in fact emerged at sea aboard HMS *Prince of Wales* and the USS *Augusta* when the two wartime leaders met and issued a press statement on 14 August, setting out American and British goals for the world after the end of the war. It became known as the Atlantic Charter, where Roosevelt looked forward, 'to the beginnings of a permanent structure upon which we can build, under God, that better world for our children and grandchildren'.

In his first dispatch on 28 April to *The Herald American,* the twenty-seven-year-old journalist wrote: 'The average GI in the street, and the streets of San Francisco are crowded with them, doesn't seem to have a very clear-cut conception of what this meeting is about. But one bemedalled marine sergeant gave the general reaction when he said: "I don't know much about what's going on – but if they fix it so that we don't have to fight any more – they can count me in." "Me, too, Sarge," added Jack.

But Jack did not hide his disappointment. With a wry serviceman's perspective, he wrote to a PT-boat friend: 'When I think how much this war has cost us, of the deaths of Cy and Peter... Joe and Billy and all those thousands and millions who have died with them – when I think of all those gallant acts that I have seen or anyone who has been to war – it would be a very easy thing for me to feel disappointed and somewhat betrayed... You have seen battlefields where sacrifice was the order of the day and can compare that sacrifice, to the timidity and selfishness of the nations gathered at San Francisco'.[351]

At the conference, Jack had the chance to see David, Antony Eden and Lord Halifax. Soviet power had just been permitted to establish itself in the heart of Europe, despite Churchill having tried to persuade Roosevelt in early April of his wish that the Allies should advance as far as possible and, 'if circumstances allow, enter Berlin'. But Roosevelt was nervous about losing Soviet commitment to the Pacific war and the San Francisco Conference, which had been his brainchild. Churchill then pushed the new President Harry Truman, to retain the ground they had won but this too was rejected. 'It was a fateful milestone for mankind', declared Churchill,[352] as Allied Forces withdrew to allotted zones. As Jack talked with Antony Eden and David about the emerging Russian threat, they will have recalled Jack's first night in London when Eden had pressed his father about Britain and America needing to stand together then.

Jack's next job took him back to London to cover the surprise 1945 election. Keen to spur her brother's ambition, Kick wrote, 'All the boys you knew here have been adopted by the various constituencies for the General Election. What about you...?'. When he arrived in June, Kick wrote, 'Everyone here thinks he is only about 18. I think he is getting a little bored with being thought so young'. Her circle – Andrew Cavendish, Hugh Fraser, Robert Cecil, Michael Astor and Julian Amery – were all fascinated to see what had become of the young Kennedy. Back in 1939, he had seemed less formidable and promising; now, just twenty-eight, he was a celebrated war hero and author of a successful book, not dissimilar to a young Winston.

Cramped alongside Kick in her tiny car, Jack would follow Churchill's campaign and that of Hugh Fraser. Every afternoon, the young aristocrats, who had known each other so well before the war, would meet for drinks at around five to discuss politics in the Grosvenor Hotel. The great wartime leader now seemed surprisingly out of tune with the country's new mood.[353]

He had made a calamitous start to his campaign in a radio broadcast on 5 June, when he told voters, that Socialism in Britain would lead to political repression and Gestapo-like tactics. Jack was also fascinated by Hugh's campaign, and bombarded him daily with questions about his speeches. They agreed to make a recording so that Jack could study the speaking style when he was back in America. Hugh's sister describes Jack at a party fundraising ball. 'He was charming and debonair and quick-witted as ever and danced beautifully with all the right ladies... and flirted with all the wrong ones whenever our backs turned. If anyone had said to me 15 years from now, Jack will be President of the United States, I would have thought them barmy'.

At the end of June, Kick took Jack down to Compton Place. There he was warmly welcomed and made to feel completely at home by the Duke and Duchess. Jack wrote a sympathetic portrait for Hearst newspapers. 'The head of the Devonshire family is an eighteenth-century story book Duke in his beliefs – if not in his appearance. He believes in the divine right of dukes and in fairness, he is fully conscious of his obligations – most of which consist of furnishing the people of England with a statesman of mediocre ability and outstanding integrity... He has a high sense of *noblesse oblige*, and it comes sincerely from him. It was by their contribution of integrity, that such figures as the Duke earned their keep. His wife, the granddaughter of Lord Salisbury, Prime Minister of England, is a woman of intense personal charm and complete selflessness'.[354]

Jack noted in his dairy, 'The Duke believes Labour will win an overwhelming victory. He is the only Conservative that I have heard state this view'. The Duke warned him, 'Free enterprise is a losing cause at the moment and capitalism is on the way out even though it might not be applicable to England with its great democratic tradition and dislike of interference by the individual'.

Since Billy's death, David and Sissie had grown ever closer to Kick, and now joined them at Compton Place. A deep intimacy of shared family experience connected them all to each other. Jack saw that Kick had been made to feel part of the Devonshire family; 'It had become her family'.[355] Jack was accepted as part of their aristocratic world.

Anticipating working for Billy's future, Kick dedicated herself now to helping her brother, and spent as much time as possible taking him about in her little Austin Seven. She wrote to her parents, 'It ran like hell – the windshield wipers didn't work and a lot of things like that, but we were grateful to have it because in following Churchill around, he was delivering speeches at racecourses, dog tracks and what have you'. Benefitting from 'family' insight, Jack correctly forecast the oncoming tide of socialism. His first report to the American public carried the eye-watering title, 'Churchill may lose election!'[356] Just two young aristocrats from Kick's circle, Hugh Fraser and Michael Astor, would escape the rout of Churchill's Conservative Party. The two would often celebrate with Tony Rosslyn (now in the House of Lords) in Kick's Westminster Gardens flat, which became a hive of activity and political gossip. Winston Churchill was living in a flat just above Kick's (which she shared with Billy's aunt). When she heard he had a shortage of eggs and milk, Kick once left some outside his door!

Jack flew to Berlin on 15 July and accompanied US Navy Secretary James Forrestal.[357] They were greeted by the Soviet Guard of Honour that had turned out for Churchill days earlier, and drove past miles of lines of rugged and unsmiling Russian soldiers on their way to Potsdam. Flying over Germany, Jack saw that 'all the city centers had an ash grey colour... like churned-up and powdered stone and brick'.[358] After seeing the shocking cost of war, he visited Hitler's Eagle's Nest in the Bavarian Alps where he wrote a poorly worded note in his diary about Hitler: 'He had boundless ambition for his country which rendered him a menace to the world... and had in him the stuff of which legends are made'.

The first atomic bomb fell as Jack was flying home from heavily destroyed Europe. After the second bomb destroyed Nagasaki on 14 August, the Japanese surrendered. Viewed by Churchill as a 'miracle of deliverance', the bomb was the start of much sombre reflection. David Ormsby-Gore wrote, 'I think for any intelligent young man living in the period 1938–1945, your mind turned to thinking of what ought to be done about this world. Clearly our elders and betters had not made a great success of conducting the affairs of the world. You had a strong feeling that somehow after 1945, an effort must be made to see that human affairs were conducted in a more responsible and sensible way than they had in the past, in that you could not afford another world war with nuclear weapons around'.[359]

Having witnessed the founding of the United Nations, seen Churchill swept away in elections, and Russian soldiers standing in the streets of Berlin, Jack saw the new world order taking shape; one with nuclear weapons. Jack at this stage seems to have been unclear about any deeper sense of political mission. John Buchan's idea that 'politics is still the greatest and the most honorable adventure' was still to be tested alongside a need to prove to himself, and to his family, especially Kick, that he could do it.

Whilst Joe Jnr had been groomed to become President, others had spotted Jack's comparative strength. Angela Laycock, wife of a British Commando leader, who knew Joe Jnr, said, "I had the feeling Joe was in awe of Jack's intelligence and believed that his own was no match for it, particularly since his younger brother's recent triumphs (PT 109). He was sure it was his brother Jack who would ultimately be President."[360] Those friends who shared the Pacific huts of Tulagi, such as Red Faye and Jim Reid, were convinced and had seen that Jack had it in him to achieve the highest office.[361]

Winston Churchill took a long American vacation following his surprise election defeat. The United States was a land where he found deep personal meaning and received much adulation. Travelling with family, he went to a fashionable resort in Florida, famed for its many lakes and pink flamingos. There, in Hialea, he met Joe Kennedy, who invited him to his grandstand box at the racetrack. They had a short discussion, before sharp wartime memories raced to the fore. Joe asked, "After all, what did we accomplish by this war?"

Winston replied, "Well, at least we have our lives," and Joe shot back, "Not all of us!"

Kick had invited Pamela Churchill to stay with her in Palm Beach. The divorced wife of Winston's son remained popular for her spirited devil-may-care approach to life, much admired by Kick who now joined the Churchill entourage, riding in cars escorted by police on motorbikes and cheered by crowds. In the early morning, Winston, who liked painting, could be seen sitting under a cabana getting out his oils to compose a view of the blue-green Atlantic giving way to daylight with distant clouds on the horizon. Kick watched him swim. 'Winston presented a very comical sight, bobbing around in the surf', she wrote in her diary. In her polka dot summer dress with pearls, Kick looked less girlish than when riding her bike in London, as she laughed, throwing back her auburn hair with Winston in Florida.

On 5 March 1946, Churchill presented his dramatic new world view, in a speech delivered in the small town of Fulton. "From Stetin in the Baltic to Trieste in the Adriatic, an iron curtain has descended across the Continent. From what I have seen of our Russian friends and Allies in the war, I am convinced there is nothing they admire so much as strength, and there is nothing for which they have less respect than for weakness, especially military

Kick accompanies Winston Churchill with Clementine on his Florida vacation, after his surprise election defeat. 'Winston presented a very comical sight bobbing around in the surf.' 27 February 1946. (Courtesy JFK Foundation)

weakness." President Truman had read his visionary speech on the train with Winston down to Missouri, with its main message . "Western democracies might still control their own fortunes… if only they confronted Moscow with overwhelming strength and if only Britain and the United States are united in a special relationship." This vision shaped the way that Jack would look at the post-war world.

15

KICK MAKES WESTMINSTER HOME

Kick buys a home, Jack becomes Congressman, David and Sissy warn Kick, 'No American ever loved England more', Churchill sends wreath, Jack does not attend funeral.

Kick decided to remain with her friends and make her life in England. She now bought a charming Georgian townhouse with a small garden at 4 Smith Square, a stone's throw from Parliament. Her father could not understand what attracted her to life in war-scarred Britain. But, as her mother once said, "It was as if everything that made Kathleen what she was, had come together in London."

Kick wrote to her parents about the pre-war grandeur, tradition and strength, still being very much part of England. "I know my little brothers will think Kick has gone more British than ever and my persecuted Irish ancestors would be turning over in their graves to hear talk of England in this way. You'd better not let Grandpa Fitz see the above!"[362]

The whole Kennedy clan back in Boston were working fervently for Jack's election to Congress. Rose and her daughters started hosting numerous tea parties in the style they had seen in London, to the delight of New England women voters. This was both new and effective. In response, Jack's opponents now focused on those British links, highlighting, that Kick had married a descendant of Cromwell and scourge of the Irish. Pictures appeared in Boston's papers describing her as 'Lady Hartington', and Jack took to reminding Kick to be mindful, joking, "Let's not forget that I'm running for Congress, not Parliament."[363] He was fighting for the seat once held by 'Honey Fitz'. He had inherited his grandfather's weapon; his love of people, and charm which appealed especially to women voters. Jack's appeal was best described, according to Jim Reed's wife, in a poem by E Robinson:

'He was a gentleman from sole to crown,
Clean favored and imperially slim…
And he was always human when he talked;
But still he fluttered pulses when he said,
Good morning and glittered when he walked'.

In one of his first public appearances on 4 July in the City Hall of Boston, Jack chose to speak about American character and idealism. "Our idealism will be a steadfast thing. A constant flame, a torch held aloft, conceived in Grecian thought and strengthened by Christian morality." He emphasized, that stamped indelibly into American political thought, was the right of the individual against the State. "Each man is free. He is free in thought. He is free in worship." Impressed, the *Boston Globe* predicted, 'Could be he'll yet outshine his dynamic and famous dad'.[364]

Tony Gallucio, a friend, observed Jack's political base was full of young people who had no political affiliations and that this suited the young amateurish mood. 'He was not forceful. He was a lousy speaker when he started. The only thing was, he was quick, he was relaxed up there… His big asset was that he was relaxed and smiling and informal,[365] even if a bit on the shy side and often reluctant to meet people.[366] It was difficult for Jack to overcome his natural shyness. When Jack went out one day to introduce himself to a group of Longshoremen in East Boston, an astonished Joe said, "I would give odds of five thousand to one that this thing we were seeing could never have happened. I never thought he had it in him."[367]

Kick followed every detail of her brother's campaign from across the Atlantic, collecting all the press clippings. When she stayed a week at the home of Lord Halifax and his son Richard, she told Jack 'there was nothing that her hosts did not know now, about the 11th Congressional District'. In this mainly blue-collar and one of the poorest districts in New England, he would go into bars and drugstores and pool halls, stopping people in the street. It must not have been easy for the diffident candidate. When his agent Mulherne whispered to him, "The hard way is the best way," he responded lightly, "I don't know about the best way, but I know it's the hard way!"[368]

As the campaign rolled on, the young candidate, dressed in a navy blue pinstripe suit tailored for him in London, could be seen working his way along two car trolleys saying… "Hello… I'm Jack Kennedy, nice to meet you," whilst his assistant, Tom Broderick, shuffled behind, explaining to puzzled faces, "He's running for Congress…This fellow's running for Congress."

Jack's campaign style on the road was a four or five-minute speech, sometimes delivered haltingly, followed by a few questions, answered briefly. It was a British style of campaigning, ending simply with a reminder for people to vote. The few long speeches he gave were about his war experience and even then he avoided talking much about himself. His team had to work very hard to dispel any notion that a congressional seat was being 'purchased'. (Joe Kennedy had once joked that for all the money he spent, he could easily have elected his chauffeur!) Every week, Jack would spend a whole day in each of the district communities and wards of downtown Boston. He shook workers' hands at factory entrances and at the docks. He knocked on doors, visited barber shops and bars, post offices and pool halls – anywhere he could meet and speak to people. He used his deadpan humour to often deflect hostility aimed towards 'the tycoon's son from Harvard'. One such time, Jack was entering an auditorium in Cambridge when his rival candidate Mike Neville paused to sneer, "Here comes the opposition. Maybe he's going to talk to you about money, or how to manage a bank!"

Jack shot back, "I'm not going to talk about banking, Mike. I'm going to talk about you!" The audience exploded in laughter and unavoidably so did Neville. Another time, a moderator tried to disparage Jack, by introducing all the other speakers as having come up the 'hard way'. Facing the audience, Jack said, "I seem to be the only person here tonight who did not come up the hard way. I hope you won't hold it against me."

Along with the whole Kennedy family and his old friends – Torby MacDonald, Lem Billings and Red Fay – his campaign continued attracting a big team of young unpaid volunteers. Inexperienced Jack was showing himself to be way ahead of other politicians; in rewriting the rules; courting the power of the young; and targeting the female vote.

Jack did not speak or act like his father. His speeches were not assertive or threatening. They were personal, informative and infused with a questioning sincerity that evoked not hostility but goodwill.[369] He was able to make an audience, men and women, feel comfortable about themselves. Gene Tierney, the actress, recalled, "I turned and found myself staring into the most perfect blue eyes I had ever seen on a man… He smiled at me. My reaction was right out of a ladies' romance novel. Literally my heart skipped... Jack told me how he was going to conquer the world. He was so sure of himself, but there was also this wonderful little boy quality about him." She added, "I am not sure I can explain the nature of Jack's charm, but he took life as it came. He never worried about making an impression. Gifts and flowers were not his style. He gave you his time, his interest."[370] Jack won a decisive forty-two per cent of the vote in East Boston. At twenty-nine, he was one of the youngest in Congress.

For his first day in office, Jack showed up late in tennis shoes, open-collar shirt and no jacket. During the first week, the doorkeeper mistook the congressman with his youthful look, for one of the page boys. Another time, Jack told his staff, "How do you like that? Some people got into the elevator and asked me for the fourth floor!"[371] The war hero and author continued to wear his accomplishments lightly. As his naval friend Jack Reed recalls, "He had what I thought was the common touch despite his wealthy background. He had an ability to communicate with people of all levels."[372]

Many who knew him only casually, mistook his refusal to display emotion as a lack of concern or commitment.[373] He displayed a lightness of touch, together with a strong streak of liberalism and optimism. Special Counsel, Ted Sorensen saw in Jack, 'the truest kind of liberal: the free man with the free mind'. But Jack was 'a practical Liberal'. He did not like the all-posturing never-get-anything-done liberalism. His father had no time for liberals, appealing to the working class with guarantees of ever-rising wages when it 'was sheer gumption that pulled a man out of poverty!'[374]

Jack was proud of his academic training but did not believe that all wisdom resided in Harvard or other colleges.[375] When he called on Professor Laski at the LSE in London, he was surprised to see 'great venom and bitterness' and came away unimpressed. "I think that unquestionably from my talk with Laski, he and others like him, smart not so much from the economic inequality but from the social. He being a Jew said he could understand what it is to be an Irishman in Boston. That last remark reveals the fundamental activating force of Laski's life – a powerful spirit doomed to an inferior position because of his race – a position that all his economic and intellectual superiority cannot raise him out of."

In January 1947, the new congressman rented a small three-storey townhouse in 31st Street, Georgetown, with sister Eunice. They had chosen a quaint area of narrow streets and historic buildings and neither seemed to have time to keep the house tidy. Their rooms looked like students' college rooms after a riotous weekend, as Joe Alsop remarked, when he arrived early for dinner to see, 'the complete disorder of the living room'.[376] Jack did not care about such matters. In his Congress office there was always a golf club propped up in a corner and he would often stand close by the desk practising his swing whilst dictating a letter. He wore mismatched socks, rumpled pants, and his ties were spotted with food. With his weak stomach, he lived mainly on cream of tomato soup, creamed chicken and bland foods.[377] His small apartment and office in Bowdoin in Boston had a wobbly table and broken chairs. His desk was always clear and tidy, but visitors would be shocked that someone with his wealth would live like that.[378]

Back in London, Kick was redecorating her new home and told Jack, 'The folks here think you're madly British, so don't be destroying that illusion until I get my house fixed. The painters may not just like your attitude'.[379] Her circle of friends would stop by on their way to Parliament, a short walk away, for a talk, like David and Hugh Fraser, 'nose to nose'. Kick held a salon every night from six to eight and was never short of invitations to the best parties. Men, young and old, fell in love with her. Friends admired her courage and dignity and her enduring vivacity. As one sympathetic friend said, "Gaiety like honesty is a kind of social courage. It is not easy to be unfailingly charming, lively and original. It requires energy and generosity always to make the effort to be on one's form."

Kick often stayed with the Devonshires at Compton Hall, who kept her busy and in good humour. On 20 October 1946, she wrote to Jack, 'The two Princesses arrived last night just before tea. They are very sweet but Princess Elizabeth is very hard to talk to. We were all exhausted by the time the Princesses left this morning, as we could never sit down when we wanted to and every time they moved, we had to leap to our feet and of course, we had to get downstairs to all meals before they arrived'.[380]

Kick was trying hard to move on. When during the war, people had lived for the moment, they were now planning their future. Kick's friends were encouraging her to see herself as someone in a position to 'straighten out Anglo-American relations' in the post-war world.[381] 'She longed to play an important part in this country', explained her friend Richard Wood, 'which she would have done, I am quite convinced, if Billy had not been killed'. In his last letter, Billy had told Kick that if anything should happen to him, he wanted her to marry again 'someone nice and good'. In early 1946, it seemed as if that person might be Lord Halifax's son, her friend Richard Wood. He had by his own account fallen in love with her even before she married Billy. Richard had brilliantly overcome his war injuries and managed to drive, ride, shoot and swim. He wanted a life in politics and Kick wanted that as well. He was brave, kind and learned, and had stayed in close touch, ever since they first met when in his wheelchair at the Embassy in Washington. All of Kick's friends thought it would be an excellent match. But then in June 1946 she bumped into Peter Fitzwilliam at a Victory Ball.

Fitzwilliam was rich and owned the best stud farm in England. He was a married man with a reputation as a lady's man. Though a brave and daring wartime soldier, he had no interest in public duty or politics. One evening at Smith Square, Jean Lloyd heard the phone ring in the middle of dinner and asked Kick, "Is that Peter Cazelet?"

"No," Kick replied. "Peter Fitzwilliam." It was her old friend's first inkling of Kick's romantic involvement with the older married aristocrat who moved in 'a rather more racy group'.[382] Fitzwilliam started taking Kick to horse racing events and to France.

Jack came on a fact-finding visit with Congressmen to Europe the following summer. His beloved sister invited him to see her in her Irish castle estate in Lismore – the same castle, she told him, where Billy's ancestor had been brought in dying when shot by Irish patriots in 1882![383] Kick had invited Pamela Churchill and Antony Eden to join them, anticipating that 'Antony... and Jack will have fixed up the state of the world by the end of the week'. Eden had made an early impression since that night in London when he called on America to join in a stand against the Nazi threat. Eden now told his friends about his meeting with Hitler. At the age of thirty-six and number two in the Foreign Office, he met the German Chancellor at an embassy lunch, arranged in Berlin in 1934. Eden, who had been awarded the Military Cross and become the youngest Brigade Major, had seen some of the worst fighting on the Western Front. Hitler was keen to reminisce about his experience in the trenches and they both drew up a map of their front lines on the back of a menu card, which they both signed after they discovered they had once directly faced each other. The French Ambassador later asked Eden if this was true. "And you missed him – you should be shot,"[384] cried the diplomat!

Before Jack left Ireland, he went to search out his ancestral home. It was in the teeth of the potato famine in 1848 that his great-grandfather Patrick had walked out of a thatched-roof cottage on his thirty-acre tenanted farm in Dunganston to sail to Boston. It took Jack and Pamela four hours to reach that old homestead. They found a relative, Mary Ryan, and they took her for a ride in Kick's shiny station wagon together with a number of Mary's cousins. Surrounded by farm chickens and pigs, Jack left two hours later 'in a flow of nostalgia and sentiment'.[385] Before he left Lismore, Kick told him – the only family member she could tell to keep her secret[386] – that she was in love with Peter Fitzwilliam. At the same time, Eden, whose wife Beatrice had decided to go and live in America (following the death of their beloved fighter pilot son in Burma in July 1945), was showing an interest in Kick, despite the age difference. He wrote, after he left Lismore: 'I long to see you. I love your letters, especially when you write as you talk.'

Almost immediately on leaving Ireland, arriving at Claridge's Hotel, Jack was suddenly struck down with his recurring health problem. He called Pamela, who urgently sent for her doctor. "That American friend of yours," Sir Daniel Davies told Pamela, "he hasn't got a year to live."[387] He had diagnosed symptoms of Addison's disease of the adrenal glands and Jack now received lifesaving cortisone injections in hospital. Sir Daniel was the first to make a correct diagnosis of his condition. Four weeks later, Jack sailed home, confined to the sick bay on the *Queen Elizabeth*. In New York, a charter plane took him straight to Boston from where he was carried on a stretcher, drawn and pale, that October into the New England Baptist Hospital to recover.

In February 1948, Kick felt ready to go to America to tell her parents about her intention to marry Fitzwilliam. She asked Pamela Churchill first, and then Billy's sister, Elizabeth, to go with her to Florida because she was 'terrified of confronting her mother'.[388] On her last night in London, her friends David and Sissy told her over dinner she would feel out of place in his world and would eventually find it irritating, and strongly advised against marriage. Kick burst out crying.

For two months in Florida, Kick never mentioned Fitzwilliam. As the end of her holiday approached, the Kennedy family gathered together for a celebrity gala at White Sulphur Springs. After listening to Bing Crosby, Kick went up to the band and cajoled them into playing her favourite song from the new Broadway show: *How Are Things in Glocca Morra?* She now finally summoned the will to tell her mother about her intention to marry and Kick was stunned by the response. The religious matriarch told her, she would have nothing to do with her if she ever married 'that man and divorcee'! Joe kept his silence. Despite Rose's explosion, Kick at lunch the next day 'looked really alive. She was all revved up and ready to go', recalled Tom Schreiber. 'She had written off her mother, but not the old man', and she told Schreiber, "I'd like to get Dad's consent. He matters. But I'm getting married."

But it was not to be easy. A few days after Kick got back to London, Rose appeared at the front door of her home in Smith Square. She stayed for four days, insisting her daughter return to America. Kick stood firm. The Hungarian housekeeper, Ilona, was shocked by Kick's tearful state and the bullying. Kick knew she was her father's favourite, and knowing he was on an official visit in Paris with a team reporting on the Marshall Plan, phoned him, hoping he might give his blessing. Joe agreed to meet Peter, in Paris at the Ritz Hotel on Saturday, 16 May. Ilona recalled never having seen Kick, look so ecstatic as after that call. With Joe on her side, she believed her mother might eventually forgive her, as she had done before with Billy.

Fitzwilliam chartered a private plane for the Whitsun holiday to take them to the beach at Cannes before going on to meet Joe in Paris. Stopping on the way down to refuel in Paris, Fitzwilliam called some friends to gather for a last-minute lunch. They got back to the airfield late, and the pilot, a Royal Air Force veteran, now told them they faced heavy storms over the Rhone, and as all commercial flights had been grounded, advised them against travel. But Fitzwilliam, used to getting his way, insisted. It was a reckless decision. The storms were to prove the worst anyone in the area could remember. The small private plane, in the middle of the violence of the storm and just fifty miles north of Avignon, had its wing broken off and crashed into the side of a mountain, killing all aboard. When Joe Kennedy raced down from Paris, he scribbled a note: 'No one who ever met her didn't feel that life was much better… we must not feel sorry for her but for ourselves'.[389]

She had been much loved in England since first arriving in March 1938. The Catholic church in Farm Street was filled with friends young and old. She had enchanted all, with what *The Times* described that morning as 'her infectious gaiety'. Randolf Churchill asked one young woman why she had come to the service in a hat so flamboyant and gay. "Because I thought it's exactly what Kick would have wanted me to wear!" A huge sadness, however, overwhelmed many. Passing Kick's coffin, Sissie Ormsby-Gore dropped to her knees and, laying her head sideways on the casket, began to wail.[390]

A special train was laid on to transport 200 mourners from London to Chatsworth, where Duchess Moucher organised a joint Protestant and Roman Catholic service, unprecedented at Chatsworth.

Much of Kick's life – flawed but always vividly intense – had been spent in England. She had radiated a sunshine that made everybody feel very happy and had been cut off in the prime of her life at twenty-eight. It caused enormous shock – especially to Jack. Kick had been the only Kennedy to break out of the family and take hold of her own life and destiny.

Lady Anderson, who had loved Kick like a daughter, reflected, 'It is not always a compliment to say that a woman or man has no enemies, but the fact that everyone loved her came from no weakness in her nature, but from the sheer worth of her character... In what lay her unusual charm? Her evident goodness, her most attractive sense of humour... her radiant blue eyes, her smile in which was reflected the beauty of her spirit. It is difficult to say, but no one could have been more richly endowed for friendship'.[391]

England's leading paper, *The Times*, printed a friend's letter.[392] 'No American man or woman who has ever settled in England was so much loved as she, and no American ever loved England more'.

Back in America, The *Washington Times-Herald* staff were so heartbroken, that when trying to write a tribute, they gave up and decided instead to leave a white space as being more eloquent.[393]

Ambassador Joe, the only Kennedy present, stood alone and lost in a blue crumpled suit. Winston Churchill sent a wreath. It was a terrible shock for all.

Jack was on his way to the airport when he turned back before reaching New York, too grief-stricken to attend the funeral. She had been the one who had always believed in him, the one who instinctively knew all his feelings. Overwhelmed by memories, he found it difficult to fall asleep at night. He told Lem Billings that as soon as he shut his eyes, he would start to think about all the nights when he and Kick had stayed up talking.[394] The stifled romantic in Jack admired her courage to express, and follow her own instincts and emotions. She was the one who perceived who Jack really was. She had been the sister to whom he could tell everything. Jack knew he had to become the man she had always believed in.

Kick in Red Cross uniform, August 1944 (Courtesy JFK Library)

16

'THOSE DAMN TEA PARTIES!' – SENATOR LODGE

Cold War starts, David becomes MP, 'Young Melbourne' role model, Jack wins stunning Senate victory, weds Jackie, TV recognition in 1956, presidential campaign, runs on 'Churchill ticket', TV debates, Jack wins by 118,00 votes.

President Truman took the first decisive steps in the Cold War when the Russians blockaded Berlin on 24 June 1948. He launched a Berlin airlift to supply two and a half million Berliners with food to keep the city alive. The crisis had been sparked by Britain and America suggesting they merge occupation zones and introduce a new currency. Truman's quick action contrasted favourably with 'Munich', 1938.

Jack arrived in London at the start of the Berlin crisis, just six weeks after Kick's funeral. Moucher Devonshire, who had come to regard Kick like her own daughter, did her best to console Jack. David Ormsby-Gore saw the anguish in Jack's eyes at the loss of his beloved sister, whom he persisted in calling his best friend. But when the time came to travel to the Edensor village church at Chatsworth, again he could not bring himself to go.

Jack had been present with Kick at 'the closing of an age'. He had seen the debates, the momentum and the miscalculations that led to war. Now in June 1948, a decade since that Prince's Gate dinner party when Kick had introduced him to the aristocratic cousinhood, Jack was again feeling deep ties of family and friendship, bound up with his much-loved sister, that was to serve him well.

The Berlin question and how best to combat dictators – the theme which would dominate his presidency – was discussed with the same intensity as once before on the eve of the Second World War. After a week with his circle in London, Jack flew to Paris, and following his 1939 credo that 'the only way you can really know what is going on, is to go to all the countries', he flew on to Berlin. Despite having no official foreign policy role, he had meetings with military leaders and a briefing by General Lucius Clay. On returning to America, he was starting to feel a bit frustrated with his limited role as a congressman.

In the following year, Jack jumped at the chance to accompany President Eisenhower on a tour of Europe, and stopped off in London to exchange ideas with David, who to his own surprise had won a seat in Parliament. Churchill won the next general election in October 1951, and he appointed Antony Eden as Foreign Secretary and Selwyn Lloyd as Minister for Disarmament, for whom David worked. David at the Foreign Office now led the British delegation at the Geneva talks on disarmament and nuclear weapons, and started plunging headlong into the complex subject that would become the focus of his political life.

Jack watched Churchill as Prime Minister, address a joint Session of Congress, in January 1952. The great statesman, now seventy, called for a more flexible and sophisticated approach to the Soviets. Churchill believed that if the 'Iron Curtain' were lifted to allow free commercial and cultural links between people, the power of leaders in Moscow would be broken. This would become a central tenet of the Kennedy-Macmillan strategy.

Jack began to present Russia as 'a slave State, run by a small clique of ruthless, powerful and selfish men', with people 'literally chained to the Hammer and Sickle'.[395] The theme of personal freedom had always been central to Jack. It was the thing that aroused real and powerful feelings in him. Jack's abhorrence of tyranny probably stemmed in part from his experience of oppression at home with the 'Stalinesque overbearing figure of a father', whom he adored and resented at the same time.[396] But one element in Kennedy's life, that more than anything else influenced his later leadership, 'would be a horror of war'.[397] As his diary records, the Duchess of Devonshire had told Jack that out of seventy-five young men she had known in 1914, seventeen had been killed in the Great War. In the Second World War, over six hundred Harvard men died. After the death of his brother, and his beloved sister's husband, taking bold practical steps to strive for a safer world, starting now with an arms agreement, would become Jack's focus as President.

In 1952, aged thirty-five, Jack ran for the Senate. He was up against Cabot

Lodge, hailing from a prominent 'Brahmin' Boston family who had dominated Massachusetts politics for decades. Cabot's grandfather had beaten Honey Fitz in 1906. Jack now put to good use his family's well-honed campaigning skills, backed yet again by an army of young volunteers and innovative round of tea parties. Rose or one of her daughters was present at every one of thirty-three tea parties.[398] Jack achieved a stunning victory. Running against a national landslide swing towards Eisenhower, he beat the supposedly invincible favourite by a margin of 71,000 votes. He had run a near-perfect campaign. He had worked very hard, visiting 351 towns and 175 factories. He had to. The 'first Irish Brahmin' to beat a 'Yankee blue blood' left the loser Lodge complaining, "Those damn tea parties beat me!"

Jack had displayed his golden touch in politics just as Joe had in making money. He was developing acute observation and good judgement. His interest in reading meant he knew where and how to find facts quickly and fully. And it was on this basis he usually made up his mind. Throughout his life, he saw himself as a free agent, picking and choosing his own course. With his quick wit, cool head and sophisticated presence, he began to impress many.

Jack had grown into a handsome and complicated man with many sides to his winning personality. An admirer and friend, Kay Halle, compared Jack's 'reserved' style to that of an English squire.[399] She had witnessed his steely determination at a Washington party when he leaned against a chair and it suddenly moved. As he collapsed on the floor, landing on his spine, "He turned white as a sheet," Halle recalled. "He rose, righted himself and went right on talking to me. I knew that he must have been in desperate pain, but he just went straight on with the conversation. I thought that was the most remarkable demonstration of his iron courage and power to dominate the physical with his will." This admirer added, "Jack brought that remarkable will to politics in his own unique way. I always had a curious feeling about him that he had a sense of his own destiny and in a curious way, that, perhaps he was not going to have a long time as he might wish, to do all he wanted to do. There was some curious sense in him that every moment seemed keenly important and was not to be wasted."[400]

To understand Jack's approach to life, we might examine again his fascination with Cecil's book on the young Melbourne and the Whigs. They had directed England's destiny with a self-confident vigour that had made William Pitt prime minister at twenty-four.[401] Melbourne had a grace and relaxed style, 'light and learned, civilized and spontaneous'. Melbourne refused to take anything too seriously. His favourite remark: why not leave it alone? Important to Jack, was that Melbourne looked as if he enjoyed himself and 'reaped the rewards of his courage'. Abrupt and casual, Melbourne 'seemed to saunter through life, but got closer to truth, and pierced far deeper onto the significance of things, than the majority. Like other young men he was attracted to the idealistic and the daring, all likely to send a shiver down the spine of the timid and the conventional'.[402] Melbourne, Cecil wrote, was 'that rare phenomenon, a genuinely independent personality – his every opinion the honest conclusion of his own experience'. This appealed to Jack.[403]

Melbourne's evolving character, as Cecil noted, was subject to the influence exerted on his spirit by others and 'to understand him, we must understand them'. Cecil includes here the influence of the Devonshire family 'and their privileged position which had always allowed them to express their naturally refined temperaments',[404] and Lord Byron with his noble struggle to liberate Greece, which had 'shaken the nineteenth century from end to end and shown how life might be lived given enough talent and courage'.

The seriousness of purpose, once shown by Billy and Joe Jnr, was now emerging in Jack. There was also a certain essence in Jack's style, that people sensed and respected, even if not known in detail by those who would see and hear him.[405] Beneath that style and glamour, they could sense the energy and romantic conviction of 'a serious man on a serious mission'.[406] And Jack, growing as a leader, would continue to ask questions and to listen rather than talk.

The young senator found little difficulty in maintaining the colourful life of an eligible bachelor. "He was the golden boy… every girl from Massachusetts wanted to date him and I wasn't any exception,"[407] remembered Margaret Coit, winner of a Pulitzer Prize. But in January 1953, a new symmetry entered his life. The newly elected senator escorted Miss Jacqueline Bouvier to Eisenhower's Inaugural Ball. Some of Jack's friends were surprised he had been attracted to her – she was not then the epitome of style she would later become, and seemed almost homely. But they recognised they were kindred spirits in certain ways. As children, they found solace and sustenance in books and in part invented themselves out of their reading. Both were preoccupied with history – he with Britain, she with France – and they enjoyed memorising each other's poems.

Jackie was employed as a reporter, like Kick once before, for the *Washington*

Times-Herald. In June 1953, she was asked to cover Queen Elizabeth's Coronation. Once in London, she was immediately taken up by Jack's aristocratic circle; David and Sissie and Andrew and Deborah Devonshire and others of Kick's pre-war set. They would get together and call Jack over the phone. Jackie's witty and exuberant accounts of her adventures evoked immediate memories of youthful times, once shared with his beloved sister. As soon as Jackie's plane landed back in Boston, with her suitcase stuffed with books on British history and politics, Jack went aboard, and there and then proposed to her.[408] They married three months later on Rhode Island, Newport.

Betty Cox believed that Jack was drawn to Jackie precisely because he associated her with his late sister whom he had called 'his best friend'.[409] "Jackie helped fill a hole in Jack's heart left by his sister's death," maintained Chuck Spalding's wife.[410] Jackie had 'allure and composure, and a voice that was a perfect wedding of innocence and steel' according to Betty Cox.[411] As far as Joe was concerned, Jack couldn't have found a better wife. "He found her a bright and spirited girl that he could laugh with and tease as a substitute for Kick," said Betty Cox.

In late 1954, Jack's back worsened so much, that he found it difficult to walk even with crutches. He entered hospital for a serious operation with a predicted 50:50 chance of survival. Joe had advised against surgery, but Jack, pounding on his crutches with his fists, said he would rather die than spend the rest of his life on them.[412] David Ormsby-Gore visited him after the operation on 21 October. Jack had been close to death and a priest had to be called, after he developed an infection. But as often before, Jack pulled through, with Joe standing vigil at his bedside. Whilst recovering, Jackie famously arranged a visit by Grace Kelly, dressed up as a nurse. When she entered his room and whispered, "I'm the new night nurse," the sedatives stopped the patient from appreciating the film-star-as-a-nurse moment! With his wife at his side, Jack left hospital on a stretcher that December to spend Christmas at Palm Beach. He did not get back on his feet properly until Spring, to return to the Senate, in May 1955, not fully cured of his back problem but a more determined man than ever.

During his recovery, Jack had read books by the political philosopher Edmund Burke, and decided to write a book about senators who had been prepared to take political risks. He had seen the gap between what a leader ought to do on behalf of his country, and what he did in the light of public opinion to win votes. He had already made a name for himself in early 1954, after boldly voting to support the St Lawrence Seaway Bill and putting national interest ahead of 'local' interests which might have benefitted the Boston Port authority. This caused a friend to remark, "If ever I ever saw a person make a decision on conscience and on its merits, it was that decision made by Jack Kennedy." Jack believed in quoting Senator Taft and the right of others to think differently from one's self. It was only 'with a free mind, open to new ideas', Jack recorded in *Profiles in Courage*, 'that the very courageous would be able to keep alive the spirit of individualism and dissent which gave birth to our Nation'. His book won the Pulitzer Prize in 1956.[413]

That year, Jack made his big breakthrough on television. The Democrats had chosen him to be the voice behind the film that would promote the Party at their Convention in Chicago. This was the first time Jack and his clipped accent was heard and seen by many Americans watching television, estimated at forty million. Overnight, Jack Kennedy became the Democrats' young star. The *New York Times* wrote, 'Kennedy came before the Convention tonight as a movie star'.[414]

Jack worked hard and travelled widely, making the Kennedy name, Kennedy smile and Kennedy charm, known across the country. In one five-week period of the campaign he covered 30,000 miles and made 150 speeches in twenty-six states.[415] Dwight Eisenhower and his Republican Vice-President, Richard Nixon, won that 1956 election, beating the Democrats that Jack had worked for. With the family gathered in Hyannis Port for Thanksgiving dinner a week or two later, Jack announced he had made up his mind. From 1957 onwards, every Kennedy family move would be concentrated towards the presidency. He was going to seek his party's presidential nomination in 1960.

Jack had become more and more convinced of his own fitness to hold high office. He had sensed the public's response to him and he reacted to that. The image that Jack and Jackie projected of sophistication and intelligence offered something new, that satisfied the American desire for change.[416] Jackie was a refreshing change from the usual candidates' wives. She would not bother with a phony show of enthusiasm about everything and everyone she met. The crowds saw that, and it impressed them.[417] With that gift for publicity, which was half instinct and half intelligence, Jackie knew part of her allure was also her inaccessibility, and her family life which she kept private as best she could, especially following the birth of Caroline in 1957 and John Jnr in 1959.

In 1958, Jack was returned to the Senate, winning by a margin of 73.6 per cent of the vote, the largest majority won by a senatorial candidate that year. He was now the best-known figure of any political party. Meanwhile, in London, Macmillan was forming a new government. Amongst those taking up new duties were David Ormsby-Gore, Hugh Fraser and Richard Wood. When Jack publicly announced his candidacy for the Presidency on 2 January 1960, he set out his primary role as he saw it. From all his travels and service in World War II and fourteen years in Congress, he explained 'I have developed an image of America as fulfilling a noble and historic role as the defender of freedom in a time of maximum peril – and of the American people as confident, courageous and persevering. It is with this image that I begin this campaign'.

The United Nations meeting in 1960, when David Ormsby-Gore accompanied the Prime Minister, was fraught with Cold War tension. The Soviets had shot down America's U2 spy plane over Russia, and their leader was now attacking America and Britain at the Assembly. In one encounter, Macmillan responded from the podium, telling the Soviet leader he was "ignoring his own Empire, the one he knew best, the one consisting of East European countries under the domination of Moscow".[418] Khrushchev exploded! In full view of live television, the Soviet leader leapt to his feet from behind his table and, taking off his shoe, banged it repeatedly on his desk. The Prime Minister looked at Khrushchev, and waited. After a pause and a flicker of a smile, Macmillan asked, "Mr President, perhaps we could have a translation. I could not quite follow."

Macmillan's words flew around the world's television and radio stations as UN delegates, broke out in loud and spontaneous laughter. It was a memorable moment – 'British phlegm' versus 'Russian excitability'. Drumming on his table to the beat of Soviet antics, David knew his friend was seeing something worldly and sophisticated that he would come to admire in the Prime Minister.

Macmillan, who had also listened to Eisenhower deliver his United Nations speech, was concerned. "The President made a good enough speech but it had no fire in it nor was it especially adroit… The most powerful country in the world has, at the moment, weak leadership."

Jack had run his presidential campaign on a 'Churchill ticket'. Happy to identify himself with the man who had warned the world about Hitler, Jack's main theme had been to ask whether the United States was militarily ahead of Russia. He warned there was a missile gap and it was growing alarmingly. He told television audiences that his opponent, Vice-President Nixon, had once told Khrushchev, "You may be ahead of us in rocket thrust but we are ahead of you in colour television." Jack would now tell voters, that if Nixon, "really believed in the things he says about this, then in my opinion he disqualifies himself. I will take my television in black and white. I want to be ahead in rocket thrust".[419]

For most of Eisenhower's time in office, the nation had enjoyed an era of peace and prosperity. Kennedy's team now portrayed it as one of sleepwalking complacency, with an economy sliding into recession and unemployment at seven percent. The Soviet Union had become a full-blown nuclear power. It cast a military shadow over Europe and over third-world countries where Khrushchev had advocated 'wars of national liberation'. In Cuba, Fidel Castro had taken control, heading a communist revolution.[420]

Kennedy hammered away in his campaign at the communist threat, with references to Britain in the 1930s. He told voters in Grand Rapids, Michigan, "the best way to understand the present was to study the history of the thirties. I know what happens to a nation that sleeps too long… I saw how Winston Churchill tried in vain to awaken the British people, and while England slept, Hitler rearmed. If we sleep too long in the sixties, Mr Khrushchev will bury us yet".[421] But would the American people be willing to put their faith in such a young candidate at this dangerous time? Jack had a subtle, sophisticated understanding of America's role in the world, but he was asking to be elected by people who largely did not have his insights, or share his views.[422] Jack believed individuals could make a difference to history, and within limits could make a great difference – Churchill and Roosevelt being the clear examples. "He thought, he would like to be like that too," said Arthur Schlesinger.[423]

American politics was racing into the visual age. Within a single decade, television made that quantum leap to rival that of school and church in shaping the North American mind. Television ownership in 1950 had jumped from just eleven per cent, to eighty-eight per cent of all homes by 1959.[424] Jack took readily to this new political tool, conveying his abundance of personality and ideas via black and white television.

Harold Macmillan and David watched the first of the four Kennedy-Nixon television debates in a suite at the Waldorf Astoria. Rather to his surprise,

Senator Kennedy besieged by crowds during his Presidential campaign, Carbondale, Illinois, 3 October 1960. (Alamy)

President elect leaves his snow-covered Georgetown home early, to attend Mass before delivering his Inaugural speech in Washington, 20 January 1961. (Jacques Lowe Estate)

Jack without top hat leaving Capitol Hill in a convertible presidential limousine after taking his oath of Office, 20 January 1961. (Alamy)

Greeting Harold Macmillan at Key West for their unscheduled first meeting because of the alarming situation in Laos, 26 March 1961. (Courtesy JFK Library)

Checking watches, Key West Naval Base on 26 March 1961. (Alamy)

A belligerent Soviet Leader Nikita Khrushchev meets the President in Vienna on 4 June 1961 believing the 'soft and indecisive young man did not have it in him to fight.' (Courtesy JFK Library)

Jack, after leaving Vienna, is met by Prime Minister Macmillan at Heathrow and notices the anti nuclear campaign demonstrators holding, "Portsmouth Youth Demand to Live," banner, 4 June 1961. (Alamy)

Leaving the London home of Jackie's sister Princess Lee Radziwill at 4 Buckingham Place, after attending christening ceremony for niece Anna Christina, at Westminster Cathedral. (Alamy)

First Lady and President about to be driven to Buckingham Palace for a 'private dinner.' 5 June 1961. (Alamy)

Prime Minister Macmillan, leads the President with hat in hand (at the end of his visit and dinner with the Queen) ahead of Foreign Secretary Sir Alec Douglas Home and Ken Bruce the American Ambassador, at Heathrow, 5 June 1961. (Alamy)

The Duke of Edinburgh laughs with Jacqueline as Jack and the Queen engage with each other before proceeding to dinner. 5 June 1961. (Courtesy JFK Library)

the Prime Minister found himself admiring Jack's powerful performance. He initially favoured Nixon, but by next morning, sharing breakfast in the Waldorf with his wartime friend, he said to Eisenhower, only half joking, "Your chap's beat!"

Macmillan worried about getting on with a future president so young and relatively inexperienced. After Eisenhower left office, Macmillan sent his friend a note. 'I will try my best to keep our Governments and countries on the same course. But I cannot of course hope to have anything to replace the sort of relations that we have had'.[425]

The Ambassador reported to the Foreign Office that many viewers had seen Kennedy answering questions at least as aggressively, maturely and responsibly as Mr Nixon, and with an even greater wealth of information and statistics at his command. By the time of the third TV debate, Walter Lippman, the leading columnist for the *New York Herald Tribune*, wrote on 19 October 1960, 'It has been truly impressive to see the precision of Mr Kennedy's mind, his immense command of the facts, his instinct for the crucial point, his singular lack of demagoguery and sloganeering… the stability and steadfastness of his nerves, and his coolness and his courage. And through it all have transpired the recognisable marks of the man who, besides being highly trained, is a natural leader, organiser and ruler of men'.[426]

As the last votes were being counted, Jack went over to Bobby's house in the Kennedy compound. At 3am, there was a television broadcast from Los Angeles. With wife, Pat, close to tears, Richard Nixon indicated that if the present trend continued, Kennedy would win. Jack stood up and said he was calling it a night. He walked back to his own home, ate a sandwich and drank a glass of milk before climbing into bed.

At half past eight, there was a gentle knock on his bedroom door. It was Caroline's English nanny, Maud Shaw. She opened the door and according to biographer Geoffrey Perret, Caroline then rushed in, jumped on the bed and pulled the blanket that covered her father's head. He groaned and gave her a kiss.

"Good morning, Mr President."

"Well now. Is that right?" said Jack, suddenly awake. He glanced at Maud Shaw, standing in the doorway. "Am I in, Miss Shaw?"

"Of course you are, Mr President."

John Fitzgerald Kennedy won the United States election that November night in 1960, by just 118,574 votes. Yet he had won it. He was the youngest president, at forty-three, ever to be elected to office.

On Armistice Day, 11 November 1960, Jack received a telegram from the statesman he had been following since he was a boy: 'On the occasion of your election to your great office I salute you. The thoughts of the free world will be with you. May I add my own warm good wishes. Winston S Churchill'.

Jack, looking to the future, wrote to Harold Macmillan, 'Thank you for your warm personal message. I formed a warm affection for the British people when my father was Ambassador to the Court of St James and it has continued to this day. I know that our two great countries will work together in the future – as they have in the past – to further the cause of freedom throughout the world'.[427]

17

YOUNGEST PRESIDENT –
MACMILLAN POINTS THE WAY
(1961)

*Snow-covered White House, Jack greets Debo and Andrew
Devonshire at Inauguration, David resumes 25-year
conversation, Macmillan clicks with President, Yuri Gagarin stuns
America, Jack asks Congress to fund $7bn programme to send man
to the moon.*

Eight inches of snow fell overnight. Washington sparkled in the morning sun as Jack stood in front of the White House to take his oath of office.

The young president presented a fresh picture to the world. Speaking with his breath visible in the crisp air, he delivered those stirring and memorable lines: "The torch has passed to a new generation… ask not what my country can do for me, but ask what I can do for my country."

With family looking on, it took Jack just sixteen minutes to read his short speech. In under sixteen hundred words he created a fresh sense of purpose and idealism. America, the youthful outward-looking nation was ready to help men everywhere solve their problems and search for peace.

The *New York Times* drew a comparison with Henry V's summons to his troops before Agincourt. 'Remarkable… a revival of the beauty of the English language'.[428] Andrew and Deborah Devonshire were seated in the first few rows behind Jack – the first members of British nobility to attend a president's Inauguration. Ambassador Joe sat with Rose, dressed in the gown she had worn when presented to the King and Queen. Jack now reached out to a new generation. A worldwide audience listened and was spellbound.

Jackie Kennedy recalled the moment: "Jack's speech was so pure and beautiful and soaring that I knew I was hearing something great." She predicted it would 'go down in history as one of the most moving speeches ever uttered – with Pericles' funeral oration and the Gettysburg address'. "I was so proud of Jack. He looked so happy. I could scarcely embrace him in front of all those people, so I remember I just put my hand on his cheek and said, 'Jack, you were so wonderful!' And he was smiling in the most touching and most vulnerable way."[429]

She describes their excitement. "On the night before Inauguration day... well, it was like children waiting for Christmas or something that night. I couldn't go to sleep. I was awake when Jack came home... then the next morning getting up and getting dressed, and the snowstorm – all the excitement, leaving our house. I was just so proud of him... there's a picture where I have my hand on his chin and he's just looking at me and there really were tears in his eyes."[430]

"Jack was just so happy. We got in the car for that parade, sort of not knowing quite how to wave. And then we got to the White House, I guess we went in for a minute and walked out to the stand. Oh, Jack was just so happy. They had hot soup or something in that stand and he wanted to see every single bit of that parade. I left after a couple of hours because again I was really so tired that day." Jackie recorded going to the many reception balls. "And there's that wonderful picture of him sort of pointing. Then we went to one at the Mayflower where Lyndon was right next to us at that one. And then we went to a third one at the Wardman Park and just on the way, it was like Cinderella and the clock striking midnight... so Jack just said, 'You go home now,' and he sent me home with that aide. And I guess he went on to all the other balls, and then to Joe Alsop's. And I was so happy. Sometimes I thought later I wish I'd been able to sort of share all the night with him. But he had such a wonderful time, then he must have gotten home about three or four, but he came in and woke me up. And – well, he was just so happy. Then the next morning when he woke up, very early, well, I was awake too, and... you know, we both sat on the bed. I mean, you did again feel like two children. Think of yourselves sitting in Lincoln's bed! And then he went off with that wonderful springing step to his office."[431]

Andrew and Deborah Devonshire were seated under warm leg blankets just a few yards from Jack that day, and had also been thrilled by the words of the president along with millions listening in the warmth of their homes across the globe. 'Jack's Inaugural was wonderful, the words were so good, almost biblical', [432] recorded Deborah. They had been personally invited by Jack and were staying with Ambassador Sir Harold Caccia; the warmth of the welcome of the Kennedy family was something she and Andrew would never forget. 'We were given the best seats at all events, far above anything we expected, and the bitter cold and unrelenting snow made it all the more dramatic'. The Capitol that day, she wrote in her diary '…was all gleaming white marble… against the blue sky and snow'. But the bracing air quickly made everyone 'thankful to get up and move when the ceremony was over, as we could only think of getting out of the cold and wind'. Despite the cold, the Duchess sat alongside Jack as he had requested for three quarters of an hour to watch the passing parade. 'Jack has got an aura all right and he was obviously enjoying it all so much'.[433] In her diary, she records another moment at a ball held that night. 'Waiting for Jack to appear. When he did, he got terrific applause. He didn't go down to the dance floor but spoke to various people along his row. Sitting in the top row in the presidential box, with Jack fenced in as usual by humans and coming along the first row, he saw us, broke away and climbed over seven rows of seats to say goodbye, to the utter astonishment of the people sitting either side of us. I then told Jack of Unity's letter of twenty-one years ago saying how he was going to have a terrific future'.[434]

Newspaper columnist and friend Joe Alsop invited Jack home at the end of Inauguration night. 'I heard very hard knocking on my door. I rushed to open it. The scene in the open doorway was unforgettable. Dumbarton Avenue was solidly blocked by a vast Secret Service cortege of black cars and limousines. Every one of my neighbours' windows were open and lighted and in every window, people in their dressing gowns were clapping and cheering. I can still summon the picture of the new President standing on my doorstep in my mind's eye. He looked as though he was still in his thirties, with snowflakes scattered about his thick reddish hair'.[435] The Secret Service eventually clocked Jack back in the White House at 3.45am.

The President saw his chief task as a statesman, would be to avoid war and ensure peace between America, Britain and the Soviet Union. His greatest fear, he told Pierre Salinger, was that he would be the president that would be called to start a nuclear war. The clear theme of Jack's presidency, the control of arms, had been spelt out at the end of his inaugural speech: "Let both sides

for the first time formulate serious and precise proposals for the inspection and
control of arms and bring the absolute power to destroy other nations under
the absolute control of all nations. It will not be finished in the first 100 days
nor in the life of this administration… but let us begin."

On 25 January 1961, Harold Macmillan sent his first letter to the new
President. 'I have just seen my nephew Andrew Devonshire on his return from
Washington. He has given me a vivid account of all the ceremonies connected
with your Inauguration… All this has touched us very much. May I add what
a great impression your speech has made in this country. Everyone has been
struck by its content as well as its form'.[436]

Ambassador Harold Caccia had also been impressed. He reported,
'Kennedy's speech has been widely acclaimed. It is what the man would like to
be. In many ways it would pay us if he were to live up to this first enunciation of
his aims'.[437] Could Jack become the man he wanted to be?[438] The Ambassador
was cheered to see the President had 'taken care to surround himself with
learned men who knew the limits and consequences of power'.[439]

Macmillan pondered on how best to approach the young president,
with his ideas about the 'problems which face us in the world'.[440] His diary
entry of 1 January 1961 read, 'I worked about 7 or 8 hours yesterday on the
Memorandum, Problems of 1961. I feel it is going to be a dramatic year for
good or ill'.[441] Macmillan spent that year seeking to break the deadlock in
East-West relations, and sent a full survey of his thoughts in a seven-page
letter on 4 January. Encouraging Kennedy to aim high, he wrote, 'I believe we
should make a supreme effort in the field of disarmament and nuclear tests…
finding a way out of the maze… there are moments in history when it is better
to take a bolder choice and put a larger stake upon a more ambitious throw'.
Underlining the need to take action, he advised, 'It is easy to do nothing at
all or do nothing in particular, but on the whole it is not the things that one
does in life that one regrets but rather the opportunities missed. With warm
regards, yours very sincerely, Harold'.

Macmillan saw this moment as a maximum time of danger; the
destruction of mankind was at stake if they failed to act. When composing his
letter, writing draft after draft until he was satisfied, Macmillan had chosen
to read Churchill's *Marlborough*. He was now urging Kennedy to be a leader
like Churchill. Guided by his cousin David, the Prime Minister believed he
was doing no more than encouraging the President to become the man he

wanted to be. He was delighted with Jack's reply. 'A very good letter from Mr Kennedy', he recorded. 'He obviously liked my letter and deals at some length with my ideas. He would like a meeting at the end of March'.[442]

To have reached this meeting of minds on Macmillan's bold and ambitious ideas was a credit to years of constant exchange between David and Jack.

When David had arrived for the UN General Assembly meeting in September 1960, Jack had invited him to spend a weekend at Hyannis Port. Renewing what Jack called their 'twenty-five-year conversation', David, now an expert on disarmament leading Britain's talks on nuclear weapons in Geneva, focused on restarting negotiations by using a more sophisticated and flexible approach with the Russians. David brought with him ideas developed with Eden and Macmillan and based on Churchill's views of Russia and the post-war world. Jack had as congressman displayed the standard anti-communist hard line; and not yet the flexibility and subtlety that might be needed. With his knack for asking questions, Jack quizzed David as Jackie took notes. David saw the big appeal that ideals exerted on Jack. The understanding they had found in their student days made David certain that he knew the kind of man Jack wanted to be. Confident in each other, they talked about the great things that he as President might now accomplish.

That December, Jack asked David to meet him for lunch at Washington's Carlyle Hotel. Macmillan and his Foreign Secretary were keen to get a view of Kennedy's ideas on a range of issues, and tasked David with a long agenda,[443] but gave him the freedom 'to proceed as he thought best'. David now started to walk that delicate line between close personal friend and representative of a foreign government.

David's report, resting in Foreign Office files at the National Archives, is overwritten, 'He obviously got on very well with the new President',[444] by the Foreign Secretary. Any traces of awkwardness that had arisen from Jack's new monumental status had clearly vanished. They had bantered and joked as friends. With a shared frame of reference, they got through a lot of work in an hour and a half. David ended his report: 'In spite of his father, I believe Kennedy has a genuine affection and respect for the British. He is not enthusiastic about his other more powerful allies'.[445]

David was ready to play his part in directing the current and, 'move events in certain directions which I believed in'.[446] Nuclear weapons had been the focus of his political life, and years of experience in Soviet affairs were now at

Jack's disposal. The President-elect asked David to help American disarmament negotiators formulate fresh proposals.

David's subtle influence was described by Arthur Schlesinger (Press Counsel), 'David had not only great personal charm but exceptional intelligence and integrity. Indeed only two men of notable character could have so delicately mingled personal and official relations for each remained at all times the firm and candid advocate of the policies to his own nation'.[447] Robert Kennedy saw David as 'part of the family'.[448] Jackie said, 'David Gore was the brightest man he'd ever met – he used to say that he and Bundy were. But he'd say that David more so than Bundy because Bundy's intelligence is so highly tuned that he often couldn't see the larger things around him. I mean David was more rooted, more compassionate'.[449] And as she would later confirm on tape, "And of all Jack's friends now David Gore's the one, I'd say next to Bobby and me, he's the one. Perhaps that's not fair but he's the friend that I'll always see for the rest of my life."[450] In his *Classic Biography*, Jack's Special Adviser, Sorensen, confirmed, 'The President consulted with the British Ambassador as he would be a member of his own staff, saying, "I trust David as I would my own Cabinet".'[451]

The Prime Minister and ambitious peacemaker believed he still held powerful cards. Britain could play a vital role in confronting the threat of the Soviet Union through its relationship with America.[452] Macmillan's letter on approaching the Soviets had struck a chord with Jack, but the possibility of political damage still worried him. He could not allow Khrushchev to make a fool of him. Whilst the President was not willing to risk a summit with the Soviet leader, he told David he could agree to send a joint letter to Khrushchev on 7 February, asking the Soviets to join in a 'supreme effort' at the disarmament talks about to restart in Geneva.

David and Jack next met on 24 February. The two friends, sitting in comfortable White House chairs in the family room, now swapped ideas as once before, when they had been students in their rapid back and forth style. Should leaders follow opinion and wait for the public to catch up, like the easy-going Baldwin? Or take the lead in educating the electorate like a heroic Churchill, even if that meant risking popularity at the polls? Jack could see that if he were to become a statesman, this would be the measure by which he would be judged.

David reported on the difficulties that Jack as President faced but remained optimistic. 'There are many who confess themselves to have been

completely converted to our more flexible approach to East-West relations…
however there are also many old-style cold war warriors. But if the President
took it into his head to pursue a clear-cut policy on any of the important
questions that are likely to face us, his still immense prestige, coupled with the
formidable powers invested in his office, would ensure the vast Washington
machine answered to the helm'.[453]

But could Kennedy succeed in steering his vast ship of state? Jack wanted
his State Department officials to be more dynamic and to take a position 'one
way or the other'. He did not want them to become brainwashed by their
training 'not to give an answer – and simply be safe on both sides'.[454] He went
over and gave the State Department a talk, demanding that 'younger people
should get up quicker'.[455] He liked to put clever people with imagination in
charge to improvise solutions, preferring to trust a few first-rate generalists
to a number of second-rate specialists. He was inclined to place intelligence
above experience and established procedure. The White House became filled
with 'strikingly young and strong-willed individuals who pushed ideas and
policies, rather than being swept along by them'.[456] The mantra of Jack's
presidential campaign had been, 'Let's get this country moving again'. The
wife of diplomat Charles Bohlen saw the change: "All these young faces. The
atmosphere bubbles and sparkles like champagne."[457] The President had been
able to attract talented aides – 'Men with shining eyes and a great deal of
energy and ambition, marching forward in some very exciting and romantic
fashion. Jack enjoyed almost anyone from whom he could learn. Remarkable
people were coming to work together, and intersecting at a special time – a
perilous time, but one when nothing seemed beyond man's reach'. The White
House had become a deeply human place.[458]

Whilst brainpower was highly valued, so was a talent to amuse.[459] Jack
possessed a charming wit. But, 'some mistook humour, gaiety and gentle
urbanity as a lack of depth and mistook his cool calculation of the reasonable,
for a lack of commitment'[460] Sorensen would add, Jack's wit was something that
'flowed naturally, good-naturedly. One could see the eyes twinkling and the
smile breaking as he deliberated whether a particular barb should be cast'. Jack
respected and was stimulated by intellectuals and understood their limitations.
He had a profoundly realistic mind[461] and entertained no illusions about
himself or others. Long-time friend David Powers observed Jack, 'always got
what he wanted, persistently but diffidently, through a series of questions'.[462]
The President, whilst he gave 'a great impression of affection and congeniality,

he had immense reserve', said Arthur Schlesinger. This element of reserve and mystery remained a source of fascination and power for Jack. His restrained and detached reaction to enthusiastic crowds, only cranked emotions higher in the manner of royalty.

For Jack, each day presented a new adventure. One of his outstanding gifts was to bring idealism and excitement into public life. He wanted young people everywhere to develop their talents to the full. As with the ancient Greeks, Jack believed great achievements required society to give a high place to both physical vigour and individual hardiness. Jack's headmaster at Choate saw as early as February 1932, 'Jack, so pleasantly optimistic and cheerful, makes us all want to help him. He challenges the best that's in us – and we're giving it, with full confidence in the outcome'.

People responded to Jack in part because they saw a 'happy' president. Believing in Aristotle's idea that, 'Happiness is the full use of one's faculties along the lines of excellence',[463] his presidency offered everyone the opportunity to pursue excellence. His words were moving hearts and minds everywhere. Washington was no longer just the centre of power in the world. In the words of the Australian Ambassador Bruce, it was now a 'centre radiating civilizing impulses'.

Britain's prime minister and America's new president met for the first time in hurried fashion at Key West Naval Base, on 26 March 1961. The idea had been to meet in Washington on 5 April, but America's problem with Laos had suddenly become urgent. Six battalions of Soviet-supplied Pathet Lao forces were beginning to overrun a demoralised government army. The Pentagon was pressing for rapid military intervention, a worried Kennedy told David.[464]

When, at the end of March, the President heard Harold was 'nearby', he quickly sent him an emergency telegram. Macmillan recalls being woken in Trinidad. 'At 4am there arrived a telegram from Kennedy saying he was very anxious to see me without delay to talk about Laos, a crisis which was now causing the deepest anxiety. Could I come the next day – Sunday?'[465] It was a measure of Macmillan's character – 'cautious and careful with detail, yet deeply excited by the idea of rescheduling on a few hours' notice',[466] – that he readily agreed to fly 1,800 miles to luncheon in Florida. As Andrew Devonshire fondly recalled, "There was part of Uncle Harold that would have given almost anything to be the sort of man like Jack Kennedy, to whom the idea of going '1,800 miles for luncheon' seemed perfectly natural."

Harold, like Churchill, had the benefit of an American mother. But he was unsure how he would get on with America's new leader. At sixty-six he felt more of a contemporary of Jack's predecessor Eisenhower, but now there was a helpful family connection through marriage. Kick had been married to the eldest son of the eleventh Duke of Devonshire, and Harold had married the daughter of the tenth Duke. Debo, the Duchess of Devonshire, recorded that Jack 'was soon referring to the Prime Minister as Uncle Harold, like the rest of us,[467] over the phone when talking about family gossip or Anglo-American relations.'[468] The speed with which they 'clicked' and understood each other, would come as a surprise to both of them.

Macmillan described his first encounter. 'The next day, 26 March, was at the same time one of the strangest and one of the most interesting of my experiences. We touched down at Key West, the great naval station and airport at 11:30am. The President's plane came in just before us. The Guards of honour were lined up, a salute of 19 guns and a very large number of spectators. The President and I drove in an open car to the Naval Headquarters. Harold Caccia had come in the President's plane and I had time for a few words before the conference opened. The actual proceedings were limited to the detailed exposition by American generals and admirals and airmen, of whom there seemed to be a great number which included all their aides and attendants. There were excellent maps and a large blackboard... Kennedy only asked one or two questions and I continued silent. We then adjourned for luncheon. The President and I went into another room where we remained alone. Before our conversation had gone on for many minutes I felt a deep sense of relief. Although we have never met and belong to such different generations, he just 40 and I was nearly 70, we seemed really immediately to talk as old friends.'

'From all the accounts I heard, I was not surprised that I should take a vast liking to him. It was encouraging to find that he seemed to feel something of the same. We had hardly begun to eat the meat sandwiches provided when he turned to me and said, "What do you think of that?" I replied, "Not much, it is not on." I thought the very large-scale military plan was dangerous... During the conference I could get no indication of the President's reactions. He listened politely while bridges were flung across rivers, troops deployed on a grand scale and all the rest. But his silence was characteristic. Nevertheless it was evident that he was in control of the Pentagon not the other way round. He was clear and decisive.[469] The President was not at all anxious to undertake a military operation in Laos. If it had to be done, as a sort of political gesture...

First meeting between President and Prime Minister, at Key West Naval Base, 26 March 1961. 'Although we belong to such different generations, he just 40 and I was nearly 70, we seemed really immediately to talk as old friends'. (Courtesy Key West Museum, Florida Memory Archive)

he did not want to go it alone… I rather objected to anything on the scale of the present SEATO plans. They were to my mind unrealistic. The United Kingdom did not want to get involved in a big way. The President pressed me very hard on this… We then discussed alternative plans… 31,000 troops to be supplied by air… Although he did not say so, the President seemed to share my doubts'.

David had been instrumental in persuading Jack,[470] earlier in February for a change in US policy.[471] The final joint communiqué reflected this, and Moscow was asked to reply constructively to British proposals to end the fighting and pave a way for the creation of a neutral state. The ceasefire that followed allowed for meetings in Geneva, and the formation of a new government. At this time, Kennedy told Richard Nixon, "I just don't think we should get involved in Laos," and expressing his worry about, 'fighting millions of troops in the jungles', added, "Vietnam would be next. Then Thailand… etc."[472]

Before leaving Key West, Jack had talked about a successor to Ambassador Caccia, who had done a fine job restoring US/UK relationships badly shaken by Suez. The President 'was emphatic for David Gore',[473] recorded a delighted prime minister, eager to get David to Washington without delay.

Macmillan flew back to Trinidad having reassured Jack of his own instincts to oppose military action. Jack had discovered the same easy 'back and forth' style with Harold to run through his thinking, as he had with David. It was a good start, opening the chance for David 'to play a unique role of immense value to both countries, such as no Ambassador has had before'.[474]

Washington was in full blossom when Macmillan arrived for his second meeting with the President, in the first week of April. In the lead-up to the meeting, Jack had confided to David, that his new Laos policy 'might make him look like a weak President',[475] and had asked if Harold could write to Eisenhower, whom he had once belittled over national security and the missile gap, to urge him to avoid any talk of 'appeasement' over Laos. Whilst scolding Kennedy in private, Eisenhower gave a show of support in front of reporters.[476] The two topics closest to Macmillan's heart, Berlin and nuclear tests, could now be tackled freely amidst the White House trees in blossom.

Macmillan's diary records, 'At 2.45pm (6 April), I went to the White House, and had three quarters of an hour alone [underlined] – no one present at all – with the President… It was really most satisfactory [underlined], far better than I could have hoped… He seemed to understand and sympathise with most of the plans of what I call "The Great Design"… It was left that I should try and compile a secret Memorandum and send it to him, setting out my plan'.[477]

The Prime Minister noted Jack was 'courteous, quiet, quick, decisive – and tough. The President impressed us all, not only by his quiet confidence but his great courtesy. He listened well, did not talk too much and encouraged others on both sides to speak'.[478] Jackie would describe a lunch that day, 'just Sissy and David and Macmillan and Jack and I, which was so nice, and it was such a happy atmosphere and they would stay in and talk. That was a very rare and touching relationship'.[479] Henry V's 'band of brothers' principle –

loyal personal relationships and human warmth, rare at government level, had clearly taken hold.

The two leaders took their team of officials on a cruise on the Pontomac as far as Mount Vernon. Alec Douglas-Home, who recognised Jack as 'gifted with imagination', worked with his opposite number, Dean Rusk, a Rhodes scholar. Macmillan had great confidence in his noble Foreign Secretary. 'I was glad that Lord Home had been able to meet me in Washington for he contributed greatly to the success of this somewhat anxious meeting with the new Administration and spoke the next day with great force and charm'.

By the time they left Washington on 8 April, personal relations between the two leaders of the free world had risen to a new high. Jack presented Harold with a photograph showing him with raised hand, pointing forward over the White House gardens, and on which Jack had written, 'To Prime Minister Harold Macmillan who has "pointed the way" on this and many previous occasions. With high esteem and every good wish – John F Kennedy April 8, 1961'.[480] (Macmillan would use this on the cover of his *Memoirs*.)

Both leaders admired each other's intelligence, patrician bearing and political instincts. Despite the age difference, they shared a surprising sense of irreverence, often laughing between themselves. Jackie said, "Jack had this high sense of mischief and so did Macmillan, so I've never seen two people enjoy each other so. Obviously all the important things they were talking about alone; but when it ended up with Sissy and David and us and him… there was talk about a lot of family things… and always this wonderful humour underneath it all."[481]

David's destiny was to be the bridge between languid Uncle Harold and young, dynamic Jack. Bonding together as a 'band of brothers', this family came together at just the right time. At this dangerous moment for the free world, their lives were now intersecting and lining up as if guided by destiny.

Macmillan advised the Queen, 'The President, apart from his intelligence, has great charm. He is gay and has a light touch. Since so many Americans are so ponderous this is a welcome change'.[482]

Jack's light touch was about to be challenged in mid-April when he faced his first big crisis – a planned invasion of Cuba by 1,400 exiles devised by the CIA, before he came to office. Despite deep concerns about this CIA plan, the need for utmost military secrecy had held Jack back from sharing his thoughts with David and Harold, ten days earlier. New to his role and seemingly deferential to the CIA and military brass, he agreed their overconfident plans. The military establishment had pressed him hard, fearing that a young untested president might wish to appease America's foes, in the manner of his father. Jack had succumbed under intense pressure to respond militarily. Four days into the landings with over 1,000 Cuban exiles captured by Castro, Jack called off further US air support and the invasion as a whole, on 17 April. After this debacle, the President's anguish and dejection were evident to all. Charles Bowles saw him as 'quite shattered' at a Cabinet meeting, on 20 April. Jack felt responsible for the deaths of the valiant Cubans on the beaches. It was the biggest mistake of his presidency and he would describe the 'Bay of Pigs' as one of the worst experiences of his life.

From that moment, Jack was determined to broaden his sources of information and 'never to rely on experts'.[483] It was a lesson in not doing 'your intellectual homework', and in taking expert advice at face value.[484] Kennedy had assumed, as he told Schlesinger, "the military and intelligence people have some secret skill not available to ordinary mortals. How could I have been so far off base? All my life I've known better than to depend on the experts. How can I have been so stupid to let them go ahead?"[485]

Jack explained to David that he did not know yet who to trust, and told his counsel, Ted Sorensen, "I need someone who knows me and my thinking and can ask me tough questions."[486]

There had been other factors in play which had steered Kennedy's uncertain thinking on Cuba. Instinctively, he was always in favour of political rather than military solutions. His main goal as President, had been to try and shift the dynamics of East-West relations with a new approach, but his campaign pledges had painted him as tougher on communists than Eisenhower. He had already overruled military advice to pursue Eisenhower's tough policy on Laos, and now, faced being seen as 'soft' on communism. With this, on top of his father's legacy to contend with, being President, suddenly looked complicated.

Kennedy now started to subject his generals to tougher questions and regularly consulted Macmillan by telephone. The ceasefire in Laos had not been fully effective but, by May things had progressed enough to allow Jack to steer America away from any military intervention. After the failed invasion of Cuba, Jack saw a Gallup poll, which showed his popularity had increased to eighty-two per cent. He joked to Schlesinger, "The worse I do, the more popular I get."[487] But this failure was to bring deeper consequences.

Just before Jack celebrated his forty-fourth birthday with family, at Cape Cod, his friend David sent a long and positive letter of support urging him to regain focus on the big theme – to begin the lengthy process of defeating communism peacefully through contact, rather than combat. 'We need to rethink our strategies and tactics before we can hope to turn the tide of history in our favour. I am convinced... that Communism can be maneuvered into a fatal decline. I am fairly convinced that our best hope of beginning the process is during your Presidency'.[488]

On 25 May 1961, after the problematic start over Cuba, Jack 'reignited' his presidency. He gave a second State of the Union address[489] and instantly grabbed the nation's attention by announcing a $9 billion programme to put "a man on the moon by the end of the decade". As he famously explained, "We do these things not because they are easy, but because they are difficult." It seemed only fitting that this bold and daring endeavour – turning dreams and ideas into reality – would be declared by none other, than by Jack Kennedy.

The Soviets at this point were ahead in the Space Race. Jack presented the race as a battle between two systems, one of freedom, and one of tyranny. Sputnik 1, launched in 1957, was the first craft in space. On the campaign trail, Kennedy had bemoaned the fact that, "The first living creatures to orbit the earth in space, and return safely were dogs named Strelka and Belka, not Rover or Fido." The Soviets were first to send a manned spacecraft, piloted by Yuri Gagarin, into orbit. Three weeks after, Alan Shepard soared 115 miles into the upper atmosphere. Watched by a live TV audience, Shepard 'rode the hopes of the free world in a period of darkness', wrote *Time* magazine.[490] Jack had insisted on risking live television coverage, even when the scientists gave no better, than a seventy-five per cent chance of success. It paid off handsomely when the *Mercury* spacecraft landed safely 302 miles out into the Atlantic. Jack was hugely excited by such a daring and historic venture – as noble and stirring to man's soul as tales from King Arthur, and that ancient land of Camelot. It was to be man's most dramatic journey since he walked out of Africa 100,000 years earlier. (Shepard would later walk on the moon, courtesy of *Apollo 14*.)

"Man can be as big as he wants. No problem of human destiny is beyond human beings," Jack told students at the American University, in Washington. People seemed to sense the inner quality of this youthful president. Young but experienced, educated and vigorous, cultured and optimistic. He personified a new grace and optimism – a new sense of freedom. When the President spoke, his words were listened to. They meant something. The space programme was 'a measure of our excellence'. His confidence inspired confidence. He was authentic. The once impossible, now seemed possible. Fully at ease with himself, he was ready to transform our world.

At the end of May, Jack took off with Jackie for their first overseas visit, to Paris, Vienna and London. In that heady and optimistic summer of 1961, the couple would be met by huge cheering crowds, all yearning to catch a glimpse of America's new president and his glamorous wife.

18

"GET ME THE BRITISH AMBASSADOR"

Big crowds greet Jackie in Paris, Khrushchev bullies Jack in Vienna, Macmillan fortifies Jack with whisky soda, Queen's palace dinner, David's family arrive in Washington.

General de Gaulle stood tall and erect on the red airport carpet to welcome the President and First Lady. Surrounded by a fifty-strong motorcycle escort, they headed for Paris in an open-top limousine, with Jack standing up now and then to wave to the crowds who lined the road. The General had proclaimed a national holiday for the visit and crowds of around half a million had gathered along the route to cheer wildly, with shouts of "Zhaq-ee! Zhaq-ee!" and "Kenne-dee!" Their popularity in Paris was a sensation.

The thirty-one-year-old First Lady had prepared well for this first state visit by brushing up on her French with a tutor. Appearing on television, she spoke in impeccable French about her Gallic background and love of French culture. This did her own appeal no harm. Jack would often start his public appearances, "I am the man who accompanied Jacqueline Kennedy to Paris!" Boosting their informal and youthful image, they could often be seen breaking away from their police escort to plunge into crowds of well-wishers.

Jackie had spent time as a student in Paris and on her second night asked a Secret Service agent to drive her around at dusk, to see the Paris she had known as a college girl.[491] De Gaulle entertained them lavishly. Watching the Paris Opera ballet, Jackie exclaimed, "I thought I was in heaven. I have never seen anything like it."[492] On their final evening in Paris, she acted periodically as interpreter between de Gaulle and Jack in the candle-lit Hall of Mirrors in Versailles, where 150 guests joined them for a six-course dinner, served on Napoleon's gold-rimmed china.

The French leader pushed for American assistance on what *Time* magazine termed, 'do it yourself nuclear arms development', and was rebuffed.[493] General de Gaulle had hoped to place France, as equal partner to the United States and Britain to oversee the defence of Europe. Macmillan had forewarned Jack that 'conversations with de Gaulle are quite difficult to conduct', and had suggested he deal sympathetically with de Gaulle's ambitions, including giving some assistance to France's ambitions to develop a nuclear deterrent.[494] Jack rejected this, explaining that France's ambitions would require the approval of Congress for transferring technical know-how. "How then could this be refused to other Allies, and might not Germany after Adenauer ask for the same privilege?"[495]

Macmillan well understood de Gaulle's pride and 'his inherited hatred of England and intense vanity for France'. In one revealing instance, when Jack suggested Churchill and Macmillan must have inherited some qualities from their mothers, de Gaulle added grandly, "Pure English blood does not seem capable of producing a really strong man," citing Disraeli and Lloyd George. The Prime Minister had earlier encouraged the General to 'talk very frankly and fully' to Kennedy![496] Macmillan was able to record afterwards, 'Even though Jack carried out most loyally our arrangement and really did do everything I had asked him to do, de Gaulle was very avuncular... very oracular and very unyielding'. (Macmillan's observations were to be borne out later when de Gaulle blocked Britain's desire to enter Europe on reasonable terms.)

Now Khrushchev awaited Kennedy in Vienna. The nuclear question lay at the heart of East-West relations. The Soviets had tested their first atomic bomb in 1949, and the threat took on additional menace when they launched 'Sputnik' in 1957. It suddenly demonstrated how the Soviets could deliver nuclear weapons across the oceans in half an hour. Jack had fanned fears of a 'missile gap' in his election campaign. The two superpowers together with Britain, were now in a race to amass nuclear weapons. Talks in Geneva designed to control this nuclear race had been suspended when Russia shot down America's U2 spy plane twelve months earlier.

Jack's big aim in Vienna was to persuade Khrushchev to resume serious arms control negotiations. David pushed hard on this, believing that getting a test-ban treaty would be the first practical step towards nuclear disarmament. The day before he left for Europe, the President had sent word that he would appreciate it if David could be present in London, when he got back from Vienna.[497]

It was raining, but huge crowds turned out to greet the young couple in Vienna. 'It was incredible in that it was miles from the airport and back, and it was a dark grey day… and just to see those crowds going on for twenty-five miles mostly weeping and waving handkerchiefs. That was one of the most impressive crowds I've seen', Jackie recorded.[498] After attending Mass at St Stephens' Cathedral on Sunday morning, Jack and Dean Rusk headed to the Soviet Embassy for their first meeting.

The Soviet leader was dressed in a grey bulky suit with star-shaped medals above his left pocket. The heavily built and bald-headed Khrushchev seemed to have already formed his opinion of the new president, after the Bay of Pigs withdrawal and debacle as "a soft and not very decisive young man", in the words of the Polish Ambassador. Kennedy's light touch approach and charm would now merely serve to affirm the 'soft young man' image. And Jack's self-deprecating jokes about one's mistakes were seen as evidence of further weakness.

It became horribly clear to Jack, that Khrushchev had no intention of discussing a test ban. The Soviet leader only wanted the talks to ensure the signing of a peace treaty with East Germany, to guard against a united Germany. "If the United States refuses to sign a peace treaty, the Soviet Union will do so and nothing will stop it," Khrushchev declared. Kennedy stood his ground, indicating the United States would not be bullied into a peace treaty. In biographer Dallek's account, the Soviet leader was unrelenting. During a stroll in the embassy garden after lunch, the short and bull-necked Khrushchev was 'circling around Kennedy and snapping at him like a terrier shaking his finger'. According to an aide who witnessed this and later spoke to the President relaxing and recovering in a hot tub, Jack asked, "What did you expect? Take off one of my shoes and hit him over the head with it?"

The Soviet leader seemed blithely willing to accept that his demands for the end of Western occupation of Berlin and the recognition of two separate German states, could well lead to nuclear war. He threatened and taunted the President. "Force will be met by force… if the United States wanted war, that's its problem."

At this point, Jack responded, "Then there will be war, Mr. Chairman. It will be a cold winter."[499]

Later, at a banquet in the splendid rooms of Schönbrunn Palace built for Queen Maria Theresa, Jackie tried her best to jest with the bald Soviet leader.

"Oh, Mr. Chairman, don't bore me with statistics." This made Khrushchev relax and launch into his own favourite jokes. Before the relatively relaxed evening was over, Jack took the chance to thank his hosts, reminding them of his pre-war visit to Austria in 1938, and 'my ten-day enjoyable holiday, over twenty years ago in Carinthia on the Wörthersee'.

When talks resumed next day, in a quiet and understated fashion, Jack gamely pressed on with his critical issue – the possibility of war by miscalculation. But to no avail. Khrushchev exploded as Kennedy referred repeatedly, to the dangers of miscalculation. "Miscalculation! Miscalculation! You ought to take that word and bury it in cold storage and never use it again! I'm sick of it!"[500] Khrushchev believed he had smelled Kennedy's desperation, and in the words of diplomat Shevchenko, he believed America's young leader 'would accept almost anything to avoid nuclear war'. The Soviet leader with his bullying tactics and combination of external jocosity and internal rage had unnerved Jack.[501] He feared his meeting with the Soviet leader could turn into his own 'Munich' nightmare.

Flying out from Vienna on 5 June, Jack was relieved to land in London and be met by Macmillan. They were driven in an open-top car through the city. 'The young President with his lovely wife and the whole glamour which surrounded them both creating something of a sensation', noted the Prime Minister. 'The Kennedys were news on every level, political and personal'. They represented a change in the old order from behemoth wartime leaders, Eisenhower and General de Gaulle. (It would take another seven years and the student protests of 1968 in Paris, to hasten a change in French leadership.)

Jack was determined not to pretend Vienna had been a success. He remembered how Chamberlain had made that fatal political error in public, ignoring advice from his Private Secretary Alec Douglas-Home.[502] The image of Chamberlain declaring, "Peace in our time," haunted the President. He told Macmillan that Vienna had been 'the worst thing', and that he had been 'savaged' by the Soviet leader, who had 'beat hell' out of him. He divulged that the last few days had made him realise the problems of the world were far more difficult than he had imagined before it fell to him as President, to cope with them. Macmillan saw that Jack had been overwhelmed.

Recalling this moment, Macmillan wrote, 'A formal meeting had been arranged with the usual advisers… but it was very clear as soon as the President arrived that he wanted nothing of this kind. He wanted a private talk'. The

Prime Minister promptly took Kennedy upstairs in the Old Admiralty Buildings to his office. Fortified by sandwiches and whisky, and away from their advisers, the two leaders remained private and closeted from 10.30 to 1pm.[503]

In the words of the Prime Minister, the President 'seemed rather stunned – baffled, would perhaps be fairer. This was the real reason for his wish for a private talk. He was much concerned and even surprised by the almost brutal frankness and confidence of the Soviet leader… rather like somebody meeting Napoleon [at the height of his power] for the first time. In effect no progress was made on any issue'. Macmillan saw that 'Khrushchev had decided to take this offensive and even brutal line partly from a tactical point of view… to test the character of this new figure in the political world… Could he be intimidated or would he stand up boldly?'[504]

Going to see the Prime Minister was like being "in the bosom of the family", Jack told his friend, Henry Brandon. Macmillan's intelligence and dry quick wit, impressed and delighted Jack. The urbane prime minister had been able to cope with – even to the point of enjoyment – the Soviet leader's theatrics. Harold told Jack he thought Khrushchev's aim, had been to unnerve and test the character of the young president and suggested that when the time came, Khrushchev would in fact do nothing to block Western access to Berlin. But Macmillan also cautioned that threats made in Vienna, could be real. Jack and Harold agreed together that if Berlin became 'their Danzig', they would be left with little choice but to go to war. These leaders alone were left with the knowledge that they might soon be called upon to launch a nuclear attack.

It must have been a great comfort to the young president to be able to talk frankly to a fellow leader who shared his burden – someone who understood the magnitude of what Kennedy called his loneliness as President. He had enough detachment about himself and the magnitude of the problems that he confronted, not to allow negative perceptions or criticism, to control his public actions. It was that reflective temperament that set him apart from his father, and most American military. However, his performance in Vienna troubled him, and his anger and frustration were with himself as much as with Khrushchev. For the second time in three months, Jack believed he had acted unwisely. First, in approving the Bay of Pigs attack, and now in thinking he could reduce differences with Khrushchev by rational explanation. His behaviour had strengthened the Soviet leader's conviction, that he was an inexperienced and irresolute president who could be bullied into concessions over Germany. Worst of all, he feared his performance had increased, rather than diminished, the chance of an East-West war.[505]

After his private talk over whisky soda and sandwiches, Jack came downstairs with Harold to join his 'family circle' for lunch. Seated at one table were Andrew and Debo, Andrew's mother, Mary (known as Moucher), and David and Sissie Ormsby-Gore. At the other circular table sat Prince and Princess Radziwill (sister of Jackie), Sir Alec Douglas-Home and his wife, Elizabeth, Harold Caccia and Mr and Mrs Bruce (US Ambassador). Jack relaxed; he always did in the company of that warm aristocratic cousinhood which he and Kick had befriended in those pre-war days. There was no sign of that drained and devastated man from earlier that morning. He joked freely, referring to a news story about Jackie drinking, and asked Uncle Mac, "How would you react if somebody should say, 'Lady Dorothy is drunk'?"

Macmillan shot back, "I would reply, 'You should have seen her mother!'"

David Gore saw that luncheon day as marking the real beginning of an even deeper understanding between the two leaders.[506] Macmillan later told Jackie, "I shall never forget our talk alone in London when he was back from the first and bad visit to meet Khrushchev. He seemed to trust me and – as you know – for those of us who had to play the so-called game of politics – this is something very rare, but precious." Kennedy told his friend Brandon, "I feel at home with Macmillan because I can share my loneliness with him. The others are all foreigners to me."[507]

Jack was awed that Macmillan had worked with Churchill, during the war as a member of his Cabinet. The Prime Minister, in turn had been impressed with Kennedy's campaign speeches, containing Churchill's ideas and attitude that Jack had adopted.[508] Both leaders now facing the Soviets shared similar terms of reference, forged by British mistakes in the Rhineland and Munich. Both agreed with Churchill's conviction, 'A show of force and small action then might have persuaded the Germans that the British would fight and might have conceivably prevented the war'.

The London visit for Jack and Jacqueline finished with 'a small dinner' given in their honour by the Queen at the Palace. Jack who had previously met, and 'made time with the Princess' when she was thirteen, now shared presidential thoughts with 'Her Majesty'. David Ormsby-Gore and Lord Home, the man who had been at 'Munich', helped the President's staff prepare a draft of what he was going to say to the American public and world about

'Vienna'. During a break in the evening inside the Palace, Jack and David took a moment to huddle in a corner and refine the text of what he was about to say the next evening, on television from the Oval office.

This first visit to the UK, short as it was, had been a tonic for Jack. Macmillan recorded, 'The President's visit was a success from the point of view of our personal relations. We had a very gay luncheon at 1.30pm at Admiralty House – two round tables (ten each) – and lots of nice men and pretty women. Both families were in strength – Kennedys and their allies, Macmillan and their allies. He was kind, intelligent and very friendly… I find my friendship beginning to grow into something like that which I got with Eisenhower… This was now the third time that I had met Kennedy. Our friendship seemed confirmed and strengthened'.[509]

On the plane back home to America, Evelyn Wood, his secretary, clearing the President's desk of papers, found a note written in Jack's hand. 'I know that there is a God and I see a storm coming. If he has a place for me I am ready'.[510] This was the same reassurance Abraham Lincoln gave himself on the eve of the American Civil War.

When Jack went on television on the evening of June 6, he explained his obligation, 'to report candidly and publicly'. Calling the Vienna meeting a 'very sober two days', he stressed that no spectacular progress had been 'either achieved or pretended'. He ended his address by announcing an immediate enlargement of the military budget. Jackie watched him from the window of her dressing room. She looked, 'down onto the Rose garden – and his office and all the television cables… giving one of the grimmest speeches I've ever seen him make… and you just couldn't believe that you were sitting there thinking that, well, you really might have to go to war. I always thought with Jack that anything, he could make happen – once he was in control anything, all the best things would happen. In this childish way I thought, "I won't have to be afraid when I go to sleep at night or wake up." So I thought. I remember a couple of times just a little shooting pain of fright going through me thinking – "Cannot even Jack make this turn out for the best?"'[511]

Kennedy had failed to ease tensions in Vienna – his actions in the Cold War had gradually made the situation worse. Macmillan wrote 'The last half of 1961 brought a marked deterioration in East-West relations… in his new tactics, Khrushchev, so long accustomed to push, had forgotten how to parry. His methods were still crude'.[512]

Six days after Vienna, Khrushchev publicly released the demand he had presented privately to Kennedy. He insisted, on a peace treaty with Germany by December, that would alter Western rights of access to Berlin. Two days later, the Soviet delegation in Geneva dropped all pretence of serious interest in concluding a weapons agreement. Public opinion in the United States was moving not towards negotiation, but towards intransigence. 'Anyone who talks sense is called a coward or traitor', remarked Macmillan in his diary, adding ominously, 'We may drift to disaster over Berlin –(either) a terrible diplomatic defeat or (out of sheer incompetence) a nuclear war'.[513]

At a public rally at Bowood on 1 July, Macmillan issued a warning about Berlin. "In Europe the situation is threatening and sombre... our right to be in Berlin cannot be in question. I hope Mr Khrushchev will reconsider this matter. We have not forgotten the lessons learned so painfully if we are prepared to accept acts of force...This is an issue on which the peoples of the Western World are resolute."[514]

The President asked Dean Acheson, his Foreign Secretary, to examine and recommend how to respond to the Soviet demands. The American mood at that moment, as *Time* magazine reported, was that they would prefer to risk war over Berlin, rather than appear to give in to Khrushchev. This was at odds with Britain's preferred double-barrelled approach; combining a show of strength with negotiations at the same time.

On 8 July, the Soviets announced a halt to earlier planned reductions of their forces of more than a million men. Instead, they ordered a one-third increase in military expenditure.[515] President Kennedy, who had already ordered big increases in the defence budget, expanded the number of Polaris submarines from six to twenty-nine, and nuclear-tipped missiles aimed at Soviet targets, from ninety-six to over four hundred. He finally ordered a fifty per cent increase in B-52 strategic bombers flying on fifteen-minute ground alert missions.[516] Khrushchev's bluster in Vienna had left Kennedy no chance to stand down from the alarming arms race.

Ever since those threats in Vienna, Jack's back problem had become steadily worse. In late June, he had a fever that reached 101 – a symptom of his Addison's disease, brought on by stress. He had to use crutches, which he hated, for a few days. He left for Hyannis Port on 4 July to recover, taking with him, Dean Acheson's report on Berlin in his battered black alligator briefcase. On the face of it, Jack should have been enjoying a perfect Cape Cod weekend, replete with lobsters and fish chowder, sailboats and sun, and seeing the bare

feet of children running through the hedges. But now he had to absorb his
Foreign Secretary's report. It recommended America take extreme military
measures, to show American firmness. Acheson freely admitted this policy
might provoke a nuclear exchange. It was everything that Jack on coming to
office, had hoped to avoid.

Returning from a meeting with Jack in Washington, Lord Home told
Macmillan he was alarmed that the President might prove too weak to
withstand Acheson's report, which suggested negotiations be put off until a
possible catastrophic test of wills had been played out.[517] Macmillan himself
was worried at this point, and rather out of character wrote in his diary on
25 June, 'I feel in my bones that President K is going to fail to produce any
real leadership'. Jack's delay and failure to produce a timely response to Soviet
demands was beginning to raise serious doubts about his leadership. The New
York columnist Walter Lipman, who had given him high marks for his debates
with Nixon, now wrote, 'The President seemed unsure of himself'.[518]

Jack struggled with this huge decision. After the fiasco of Cuba, he was not
willing to be rushed. More than a month had passed since Khrushchev had
presented his demands on Berlin. On 12 July, Acheson called to say there would
be a revolt in Congress, if the President failed to provide strong leadership.
He repeated his views the next day to Kennedy, at a meeting of the National
Security Council. But the meeting ended without a clear word from the
President, one way or another. After Cuba, the suspension of test ban talks, and
shock at Vienna, people wondered if the President would recover his balance
and sense of where he wanted to take the country. Acheson was irritated; but
it was one thing to advise the President to prepare to launch a nuclear war, and
quite another to be the one who must carry out such a plan with the vast loss of
life it entailed. The President deliberated for another six days.

Jack went on television on 25 July to give his decision. He now gave a
masterly presentation,[519] finely balanced between competing options of a
readiness to fight, and a readiness to negotiate. He told his audience, "Our
response to the Berlin crisis will not be merely military or negative. It will be
more than standing firm. We will not permit the communists to drive us out
of Berlin, either gradually or by force... The steps I have indicated tonight
are aimed at avoiding war. To sum it all up, we seek peace – but we shall not
surrender. That is the central meaning of this crises, and the meaning of your
government's policy."[520]

Jack had clearly decided to seek not a military but a diplomatic solution. Coolness and reason were again guiding the President's decisions – he felt much happier this way. He refused to declare a national emergency and made very clear to Acheson he did not want matters to become 'so dominated by the military aspects that fruitful negotiations might become impossible'. In declining Acheson's hard-line suggestions, Jack had chosen not to be driven by any narrow effects on his own domestic fortunes. As he told his staff, "Domestic policy can only defeat us. Foreign policy can kill us." Jack's statesmanlike instincts, were now guiding him forward.

Khrushchev appeared furious about Kennedy's intention to rearm conventional forces and he exploded when he heard the speech. He told a visiting American delegate that the speech had been an 'ultimatum tantamount to war'. Khrushchev promised that the next war would be 'decided not by infantry but by rockets and nuclear bombs'. He boasted to the delegates that he had enough bombs already and predicted that whilst the United States and the USSR might survive, all of Europe would undoubtedly be destroyed. He conceded Kennedy seemed 'a reasonable young man full of energy', but then grimly prophesied that in the event of war, he would be, 'the last President'. British Ambassador, Sir Frank Roberts in Moscow suggested to his colleague the American Ambassador, that Khrushchev's fit of temper had been merely an act. The leader's apparent rage at Kennedy's speech had not been officially reflected – neither in the formal comments of Foreign Secretary Gromyko or by any Soviet officials whom the British Ambassador had met.

On 1 August, the President signed an order authorising a call-up of 250,000 reservists for active duty. A record number of refugees – over 2,000 a day – were now fleeing from the East to West Berlin. Early on Sunday morning 13 August, whilst Jack was at home in Hyannis Port, East German security forces put up barriers to block access between East and West Berlin. The Soviets had decided to erect a concrete wall.

Jack's response as he saw a thirteen-foot-high wall going up, was restrained. He viewed it as something of a godsend. "Why should Khrushchev put up a wall if he really intended to seize West Berlin? This is his way out of a predicament." Jack saw it as effectively neutralising the crisis that had begun in Vienna. "It's not a very nice solution, but a wall is a hell of a lot better than a war," he told his aide O'Donnell.[521]

In his diary, Macmillan records, 'A lot of telephoning, morning and evening to Alec Home about the Berlin crisis… all movement from East to West Berlin has been shut down… the flood of refugees has reached crises proportions… the situation is tense and may become dangerous', adding, 'The Foreign Secretary has behaved with remarkable sang-froid, and continues to urge the importance of taking at least the preliminary steps to a negotiation'.

Willy Brandt, Mayor of Berlin, appealed to Kennedy to demonstrate his commitment to Berlin and reinforce the US garrison. The President phoned Macmillan suggesting they both send more troops to Berlin. They agreed to send in 'a few armoured cars, etc., as a gesture', despite observing militarily that this was nonsense.

Vice-President Johnson arrived in Berlin to tell 300,000 cheering Germans to "maintain faith in yourselves and your Allies". With General Clay standing at his side, they watched 1,600 fresh US troops arrive. Kennedy stayed in Washington that weekend to monitor progress. He wanted to direct any response, as American soldiers moved down 110 miles of *Autobahn* from West Germany, to any confrontation with Soviet troops at their checkpoints. When cheering Berliners greeted the arrival of the unhindered convoy with shouts, tears and flowers, the President was much relieved.[522]

The Russians, then turning their attention from Berlin, announced they would resume hydrogen bomb tests. Macmillan and Lord Home raced back down to London from Gleneagles, where they had been playing golf, to speak with the President on the telephone. That same day, on 30 August, David Ormsby-Gore flew to Geneva to try one last time for a test-ban treaty. The next day, Kennedy and Macmillan issued a joint US-UK response to the Soviet leader that called for all three powers to cease atmospheric tests. In defiance of world opinion, the Russians' only reply was to explode another bomb. 'Naturally, this caused the Americans to get very excited and much pressure to be exerted from the Pentagon and from the Hill on the White House. The President gave in and has announced his decision to resume underground tests, but not atmospheric tests',[523] recorded Macmillan. 'Khrushchev is trying to frighten us and to divide us. Unfortunately, the Americans get mad at these tactics… Even President Kennedy, with all his political experience, behaves like a bull being teased by the darts of the picadors'.[524] The Berlin crisis that summer was evolving into the most dangerous moment for nuclear conflict since the onset of the Cold War.

On 14 September, Jack rang Macmillan to say testing underground of the hydrogen bomb would start the following day. It was a day the Prime Minister would not easily forget. 'Forty-five years ago, today, I was taking part in the 15th September attack by the Brigade of Guards in the Battle of the Somme. This was the first time that tanks were used. I was severely wounded – for the third time – and spent most of the last two years of the war in hospital'.[525] The Battle of the Somme, when troops advanced into the jaws of the German guns, had marked the greatest loss of life in a single day in British military history. Raymond Asquith was killed in the action that day with the Brigade of Guards. His inscription at Guillemont reads, 'Small time, but in that small most greatly lived, this star of England'. Kennedy's hero was thirty-seven – a symbol of a lost generation.

British and American tanks now stood in battle order facing each other in Berlin. With tanks lined up against each other at the border, the chance of starting an accidental war came ever closer. Kennedy phoned Macmillan and then sent a back-door message via Bolshakov asking Khrushchev to pull back his tanks, and promised he would do the same.[526] The Soviet leader had given a private indication that he was maybe not prepared to risk nuclear war, when he told Ambassador Frank Roberts, "Why should two hundred million people die for two million Berliners?"[527] Three days later, Russian tanks suddenly withdrew. The immediate military confrontation was over.

In London, the Ministry of Defence had made plans public, about the risks of nuclear fallout. Advice was given on providing dried milk for infants and iodine to all, if contamination from fallout should happen. Public tension reached a peak on the nights of 17 and 18 September, with massive 'Ban the Bomb' demonstrations at Trafalgar Square. Thirteen hundred sincere but 'misguided enthusiasts lying across the roads', as Macmillan put it, were arrested by the police.

On 22 September, the President was delighted to sign off a $40 million budget to set up, his very own idea for a 'peace corps'.

Three days later, after the peak of this East-West crisis passed, Jack appeared before the opening session of the UN General Assembly in New York. He told his global audience, "Mankind must put an end to war or war will put an end to mankind."

The newly knighted Sir David Ormsby-Gore with Sissy and three of their children aboard the *Queen Mary* sailed into New York Harbor at six in the morning on 24 October. Up well before sunrise, they all saw the Statue of

Liberty at the harbour entrance. When they got to Washington, David's family had hardly got through the front door of their new embassy home with its vast rooms and glittering chandeliers, when the President, 'very kindly rang me up… to ask how we were getting on'.

Jack was delighted that David was now close at hand. "He has been on the telephone at odd hours of the day and night frequently since," reported the Ambassador, back to London.[528] Following the Berlin crisis, the Soviets had exploded yet another thirty-megaton bomb. The 'lessons of Munich', which Jack and the cousinhood had debated two decades earlier, were once again very much in the air. The *New York Times* now ran a headline, 'Berlin in the light of Munich'. But at least it helpfully argued, there was perhaps sufficient leeway now in Khrushchev's position to make possible a negotiated settlement, without any Munich connotations.[529]

The new ambassador handed his note of formal introduction to Jack at a White House ceremony. The note focused on "another critical time of great challenge to the great principles we hold in common to our way of life". Delighted with the chance to renew 'his twenty-five year' conversation, Jack's formal reply stated, "I find it particularly pleasant that the Queen has seen fit to appoint you an old friend, as her representative… permit me again to extend a warm personal as well as official welcome to you and your stay which I hope will be an extended one in this country."[530]

In his first report to London, David highlighted the President's positive energy and stance. 'I found him extremely vigorous and he talked the whole time at a great rate and moved about without any apparent discomfort. In discussing recent events the President made no attempt to conceal his impatience with both the French and the Germans… he told me several times the immense satisfaction he got from working with you and how fortunate it was even without consultation, he and you seemed to come to very much the same conclusions'.[531] The new administration were keen to support the 'special relationship', which David was about to boost to extraordinary new heights. Feeling readily at home, he told Sir Alec, "We are all settling in well with the benefit of the most glorious autumn weather."[532]

David's family was at the heart of Britain's establishment. His father, the 4th Baron Harlech, had led Britain's delegation at the League of Nations in 1933. David gave the appearance of being laid-back and unemotional in a stereotypical English manner. David was an exemplar of what Schlesinger described as, 'English political society with its casual combination of wit, knowledge and unconcern'. David knew these features applied to Jack. "I think Jack had deep emotions but he very much disliked the display of them."[533]

David and Sissy, who had been especially close to Kick, now shared family weekends together with Jack and the First Lady and children at Hyannis Port. Jackie recalled, "We'd see them a lot – we'd always see them and we would have seen them every week if they hadn't been Ambassador."[534] Sissie had a statuesque beauty with porcelain skin and black hair. She was Catholic and as graceful on horseback as Jackie. With their husbands, they made an attractive and easy foursome.

David's unique relationship allowed him to emerge as a de facto member of JFK's cabinet. In the words of Dean Rusk, he was, the eleventh member! As one of the President's most intimate advisers, David was an exception – Jack usually kept 'friends' and 'advisers' keenly apart in separate circles. But as Robert Kennedy confirmed, David was 'part of the family'.

In a rare recorded interview in March 1964, Jacqueline talked about David. "Jack would talk more intimately with David, than with anybody in his Cabinet apart from Bobby. If I could think of anyone now who could save the Western world, it would be David Gore. But – well, they started as friends obviously in London, and Kathleen, who was Jack's favorite sister, was Sissy's best friend. And, I guess, David was the closest of all those friends then. Whenever David was here, we'd see him, and Jack used to say that David Gore was the brightest man he'd ever met. Well, we'd see them a lot. We'd always see them. They would stay with us usually on vacations, or they'd come for a weekend to Camp David, or the country or the Cape. Or they'd come for dinner maybe once a month or so. We used to do it rather spontaneously. And they'd always be talking on the phone. So many times, 'Get me the British Ambassador.'."[535]

That November, there was a lull in tensions over Berlin. After Adenauer was re-elected German Chancellor, Jack phoned Harold on 9 November, to agree on what line to take with Adenauer – and what they should attempt to persuade him to do.[536] A new secure telephone link had been set up between Downing Street and the White House. Macmillan found its use awkward. "You had to push a button after you had said anything to hear the reply. This made conversation somewhat jerky," complained Macmillan. But he continued to press Kennedy on the old problem that remained: how best to present a position of united strength yet still be flexible as regards possible solutions.[537] He felt it important that the Americans continued to put pressure on the Germans even though Kennedy was 'fed up' with both Adenauer and de Gaulle.[538]

The Indian leader, Nehru, had met Khrushchev earlier in September. He now told Macmillan that the basic factor exercising Khrushchev was the growing power of West Germany and "the fear of it gradually developing along the lines of Hitler's Germany. He could not tolerate this menace."[539] On this basis, Nehru was optimistic there was room for successful negotiations. Sir Alec agreed. On 13 November, the Soviets indicated their willingness to resume negotiations, sending a note that crossed with an almost identical British-American offer sent that same day.

It was at such pressured times that Macmillan took satisfaction that, 'at least my personal relations with Kennedy seemed to become daily closer and more intimate.[540] It was the gay things that linked us together and made it possible for us to talk about the terrible things'.[541] For his part, Jack felt, 'I am lucky I have a man to deal with, with whom I have such a close understanding'.[542]

Anglo-US relations and the 'special relationship' flourished at a level as never before and were closer at a personal level than those between Roosevelt and Churchill. When they had met for the first time "I fell for him," Macmillan told Jackie, "but much more inexplicably, he seemed to warm to me… We seemed to be able when alone to talk freely and frankly to each other as if we had been lifelong friends and to laugh (a vital thing) at our advisors and ourselves."[543]

Macmillan looked like the archetypal Edwardian gentleman with his trim moustache, silver hair and bespoke suits. He had a sophisticated and worldly outlook, built on a great sense of history. Macmillan had got on with Eisenhower, whom he saw, 'was an American soldier, trained as a soldier and talking that language. He did not find it easy to "discuss" a problem, although his instincts about how to handle it were generally right'. Macmillan had adjusted to the new president with a different mental background, 'who was quick, well-informed and subtle, and proceeded by asking questions rather than answering them'.[544] Debo, the Duchess of Devonshire, saw they were 'astonished by each other', adding that 'they were certainly dependent on each other'.[545]

David took close note of Jack's 'subtle' technique, at a White House dinner party on 8 November. A hectic and noisy debate ensued for an hour on

Vietnam, with each guest giving his own emphatic view on what to do about the deteriorating situation. As usual, Jack behaved inscrutably and David observed, 'Although the President constantly intervened on the debate with many pointed questions, he never gave anything like a complete summary of his views on any points, and no matter how hard he was pressed the final decision he was to take remained wrapped in mystery'.[546] It was in private that Jack would express his views candidly and forthrightly, as he did with David. Jack had a way of building bridges whilst never committing himself to any one point of view, before he had garnered all the facts. Jack told David Gore about Lord Melbourne, who said he would have liked 'to be sure of everything as his critics appeared to be'! He reminded David there were always two sides to every serious problem – a fundamental point always missed by zealots of left and right who demanded simple solutions.

That December, the Duke and Duchess of Devonshire visited Washington. Staying with David and Sissie at the Embassy, they were invited to a dinner at Joe Alsop's house, when the President dropped in. The National Gallery were to borrow a collection of Master drawings from Chatsworth, and Jack suggested, "Let's go visit," to the Director of the Gallery near midnight. "Our arrival caused great excitement," said Debo. "I don't think the President went to exhibitions as a rule the way Jackie did." As Jack got out in the rain and shook hands with a welcoming party, Debo recalls how "Lady Tweedsmuir, one of Britain's delegates at the UN, could not resist the unexpected opportunity to buttonhole the President on some pressing matter. 'Not now,' Jack replied. 'It's your turn tomorrow.' He had got rid of her, but in such a good-natured way that she could not take offence," recorded Debo. The President did not clock back into the White House until 1.16am.

Invited by Jack, Debo accompanied David and Sissie to the Army-Navy game in Philadelphia. Jack flipped a coin to start the game in plunging temperatures with around 100,000 spectators cheering on their smiling president. Jack looked even happier when the Navy won 13-7. After this victory, the President's party boarded a thirteen-long coach train back to Washington where Jack and David then peeled off from the group and headed for a long talk, much as they had done before and over many years.

Before his next meeting with the Prime Minister, Jack enjoyed reading his own ambassador's imaginative portrayal of Macmillan, sent from London on

2 December. 'Heavily lidded eyelids… shot through with Victorian languor. It would be a mistake to infer from this that he is lacking in force or decisiveness… or to deduce from what is called his "Balliol shuffle" that he is not capable of swift action. He represents Edwardian and eighteenth-century England in the grand tradition of the Establishment. He has charm, politeness, dry humour, self-assurance, a vivid sense of history, dignity and character'.[547]

When *Air Force One* touched down at Bermuda Airport, Harold the Edwardian gentleman stood erect in the tropical sunshine, retaining the ramrod posture of the Grenadier Guard he had once been. He shook Jack's hand and straightaway asked about his father. Days earlier, Joe had suffered a stroke which had left him speechless and paralysed down one side. Although Jack had moved long ago to be his own man, this was a big blow and Macmillan understood this new absence in Jack's life; the fatherly reassurance that a son enjoyed.

The two leaders drove past waving palm trees to a vast colonial residence set up on a ridge overlooking the capital. This building would not ordinarily have been used for such a conference, but Macmillan had chosen it to provide English country house conditions; somewhere the leaders could talk and take meals together. The Prime Minister commandeered an intimate drawing room where conversation could best flow freely, much as it would have done at Cliveden and other great houses that Jack had stayed at before the war.[548] And Harold presented Jack a gift of silver buttons from Chatsworth, which Debo had dropped off at Admiralty House. These buttons from 1766, had been worn by the footmen dressed in the buff and blue livery uniform of Chatsworth in homage to the uniforms worn by George Washington's soldiers. The Duchess Georgiana had openly supported the Revolution and its American rebels.[549]

Macmillan came to Bermuda with great purpose. It was the Prime Minister's fervent hope to secure a first-ever East-West agreement. He wanted Jack to share his belief that it was a leader's duty to risk everything for such a big cause. He had begun to worry about Kennedy's potential weakness as a statesman, after David had warned him of the President's concerns about being out of harmony with the views of his citizens. With Jack growing steadily more pessimistic about securing a test ban treaty, Macmillan came to Bermuda to persuade him that he must try once more.[550]

For all the Prime Minister's grand plans, the President had come with his own agenda. He proceeded to set the tone at Bermuda and pressed Macmillan for permission to use Britain's Christmas Island for atmospheric nuclear testing. (Jack did not want to have mushroom clouds seen over home ground in Nevada.) Macmillan stayed notably silent during the talk's early stages, with the President keen to focus on small practical details. When he spoke, Macmillan tried to draw the President on to wider issues. But Jack seemed keen to avoid debating the big picture with Macmillan in front of his team. This led Macmillan to note privately that 'he seemed rather lost' on the wider issues. But Kennedy had in fact been deeply impressed by Macmillan's passion for disarmament.

Whilst Senate scepticism for a test ban agreement dominated publicly, Kennedy was willing to accept risks and make compromises – more than he felt able to show. On the second day, Jack began talking about the bigger picture with Macmillan, who insisted they could not 'sit in an ordinary little room three days before Christmas, and talk about these terrible things without doing anything'. The Prime Minister told Jack the dangers were now so great that they trumped any consideration of any political self-interest. Using the Churchillian assumption that a first agreement would lead to others, he now pressed hard for a test ban treaty to reduce the terrifying prospects of an indefinite, and enormously costly arms race.

Jack had long been fascinated by moments in history when individuals had to take difficult decisions. Now, that part of Jack drawn towards duty as embodied in his hero, Lieutenant Asquith, took firm hold again. The final Bermuda communiqué read: 'The President and the Prime Minister continue to believe that no task is more urgent than the search towards effective disarmament… and to break out of the dangerous contest so sharply renewed by the Soviet Union'.[551]

Anglo-American meetings always had a spice of fun. In Bermuda, Lord Home had seen Jack's huge Stars and Stripes fluttering boldly on top of Government House, making Britain's flag alongside 'look like a postage stamp', and spoke to the Governor. Agreeing this would not do, they rapidly sent people into town to buy up as many Union Jacks as could be found to sew together, so that, "By next morning our flag was as impressive as theirs… honour was saved… and Kennedy was highly amused."[552]

The Prime Minister noted also the President's back had been hurting during their latest conference. 'He could not sit long without pain and could not bend down to pick up a book or a paper off the floor'.[553] The sixty-six-year-old prime minister commented he also had his own problems, and found that journeys tired him out 'more each time'.[554] Safely back in London in time for Christmas Eve, Harold sent Jack a warmly worded telegram. 'Greatly enjoyed talking with you… their value lies not so much in reaching precise agreements, as in the sense of understanding each other and discussing in an absolutely frank and open way the problems with which we are faced. Perhaps Bermuda, with its long British tradition and its American Naval base, is a good symbol of our partnership. The first half of 1962 cannot fail to be important, perhaps decisive. Let us hope that what we have planned, may have some success'.[555]

Jack's first year in office in 1961 had not been easy. David's official 'Annual Review' recorded, 'The new Administration were confident that a combination of brains, careful planning, good will, youthful vigour and hard work could get the country moving again after the stagnation of the Eisenhower years. After the brilliant inauguration speech, public expectation was high… The Cuban debacle shocked, puzzled and angered the Administration and the American public. It exacerbated a mood of nationwide frustration and bewilderment at the seemingly endless series of communist successes. Cuba became a symbol of Communist penetration… Subsequent Russian successes in space and the further Communist encroachments in Laos and Vietnam all gave Americans the galling sense of playing second fiddle'.

The Ambassador described the President's dilemma, 'The President's problem has been to impress Mr Khrushchev with the West's determination to fight if its rights are interfered with, while at the same time keeping right-wing opinion at home in check and preparing the American public for negotiations whose outcome may well be denounced in many quarters as appeasement. This latter remains his biggest immediate problem'.[556]

Macmillan was despondent. 'My great plan seemed to have failed; at least little progress with the French and none with the Russians'.[557] East-West relations for the first half of the year had been one 'of wild oscillation… high hopes before the Paris summit meeting; the despair that followed it; the dangerous crisis in Berlin; and a growing sense of Soviet pride and intransigence facing a Western structure. But at least it could not be held against the British Government that they had not done their best'.

The First Lady, Jacqueline recalled the constant worry. "I mean, that was a terrible time for him. There was nothing more that worried him through 1961/62 than all this testing. But it started so long ago. I can remember when David Gore came to Hyannis in the fall we were married – would be October or November 1953 – he was doing something at the UN on disarmament and he and Jack were talking then. Jack used to say in his speeches that it was a disgrace that there were less than a hundred people working on disarmament in Washington."[558]

The threat posed by the arms race and nuclear war, was a constant and daily concern for many people during the Cold War. For Jack and Harold, such worries were to reach a fearful zenith in 1962.

19

THE PRESIDENT'S DAY

*Orange juice, two soft boiled eggs and toast, walk to office with
Caroline, Swim/gym exercise, lunch and forty-minute nap,
bedtime prayer, Hyannis Port sailing and children's golf cart rides,
Champagne start to 1962, Soviet missile plans.*

How did Jack look after his health and manage his everyday life when facing the challenges of being President? In a taped interview with Arthur Schlesinger in January 1964, Jackie gave us a view of his normal routine.

"The day would start when Jack's long-time valet, George, brought in a tray of orange juice, two soft boiled eggs, toast with marmalade and coffee with milk and sugar, at around 7.30am. Then the children would rush to turn on the television set and you'd hear this roar full blast, of cartoons or that exercise man… and Jack would be sitting there reading those fifty morning papers and sheaves of briefing papers, and this racket around. Then he'd take a bath. And then he'd always come in before he went over to the office – I mean I'd only be half asleep or else I'd be having breakfast – and see me. And he used to take Caroline over to the office with him every day – and later on it used to be John's treat to walk to the office with him to the Oval Office".[559] The children sometimes returned to the office at night with their unflappable English nanny, Maud, for a pre-bedtime romp, when John would crawl through the 'secret door' under his father's desk!

Close friend William Manchester said the President was usually on his way to the office by 9am, "with Caroline tagging along, when he would meet with appointments and study documents until 1.00 or 1.15. Usually a business lunch would follow. During the middle of the day he would swim in the pool – its walls painted with a harbor scene and moon and stars above – and then enter the gym in the adjoining room for his fifteen minutes of exercise, usually with his old naval friends. After the swim and exercises and lunch, he napped for forty-five minutes or an hour. After his return to the office, he would work until 8pm or even later".[560]

Jackie was always surprised at how Jack was able to sleep like clockwork taking his regular forty-five-minute naps. "He'd always said that Winston Churchill used to do it, and he'd often say how much more staying power, you know, it gave him." Ted Sorensen noted he was always, 'able to relax as intensively as he worked, to catch up on his sleep or his sun or his golf, and to laugh at the children and the world and himself. He rarely had a cold and never a headache'.[561] He did not smoke, except to enjoy an expensive cigar after a meal, and enjoyed a daiquiri, a scotch and water, or a vodka and tomato juice before dinner, perhaps with a brandy, later.

The Oval Office was decorated now for a Navy man with framed pictures of tall ships and naval battles and a model of the USS *Constitution* over the fireplace. Jack's desk was made from nineteenth-century timbers from Britain's last wooden frigate HMS *Resolute*, a gift from Queen Victoria. Jack put his famous Pacific coconut shell with carved message on his often disordered desk. He had a table behind, covered with newspapers and magazines including *The Times, New Statesman, Spectator, Economist* and *Manchester Guardian Weekly*, treating them as though they were his household papers.[562] Tall French windows, almost twelve feet high, looked out onto a flower garden. Even on gloomy days, the Oval Office had light pouring through those big windows, which lit up cream-coloured walls. Jack's rocking chair stood between two sofas decorated in warm beige that helped create a quiet glow. There was a fireplace which Jack tried to light – but only once – after he filled the entire West Wing with smoke.[563] In winter when the trees were bare, he could see out to the Lincoln Memorial and the 555 foot tall Washington Monument, with its flashing red light.

The whole White House crackled with excitement under its young leader. Jack's advisers had to be 'quick, tough, laconic people'. He disapproved of anyone dull, ideological, earnest or emotional. On any given day, the President would be managing what adviser Clark Clifford called, 'the cockiest crowd I'd ever seen in the White House'. As Oxford don Isaiah Berlin said, "Kennedy's men had a great deal of energy and ambition, marching forward in some very exciting and romantic fashion," which, David Ormsby-Gore thought could be likened to that of a 'Tudor Court'.[564] Jack's preferred timeframe for meetings was fifteen minutes, and few lasted more than an hour.[565] Ted Sorensen found that around 7.30pm was the best time for dropping in on him, 'when he was usually then in shirtsleeves sometimes watching the news on TV or signing mail. He would sometimes stride out to Mrs Lincoln's office to read whatever was on top of her desk. He was at his reflective best in those hours, relating some crisis or anecdote of the day and asking me to look into some new problem or raising a question on which he sought my opinion'.[566]

Jack, who liked books on British history and romantic heroes of the battlefield, also enjoyed light reading; *From Russia, with Love* by Ian Fleming fascinated him.[567] When the CIA told him they were experimenting with some 'Bond gadgetry', he was captivated, especially with the tiny radio bleeper that could be attached to the underside of a car. Music was important for Jack, from those dance bands in London to those American crooners he listened to on his record player in the Pacific islands. His favourite music was from the show *My Fair Lady*, until *Camelot* came along and opened in Broadway just before he became President.

At weekends in Hyannis Port, Caroline and John always raced over to the President's helicopter to be picked up by him after he landed on the front house lawn. He would often drive his white and gold golf cart with up to eighteen or twenty children hanging on, and sometimes toppling off, to the local candy store.[568] There would be competitive tennis matches, swimming in the pool, turns in the Finnish sauna and then dinner with guests followed by a film in the Ambassador's basement theatre.

A sensitive stomach meant Jack usually ate carefully and often. He had great quantities of milk, creamed soups or chowder, sirloin steak, baked potatoes, ice cream and hot chocolate made with milk.[569] At the end of each day at home, Jackie recalled her husband used to say prayers. "But he'd do it so quickly, it was really a ritualistic thing. He'd come in and kneel on the edge of the bed – kneel on top of the bed and say them, you know. Take about three seconds – cross himself. But I thought that was so sweet."[570] Jack rarely fell asleep before midnight, and more often than not would reach for the phone to call his father or Bobby.

Events in the first half of 1962, saw no progress in East-West relations and remained steady without undue drama. Guests in the White House welcomed in the New Year, with Krug 1929 champagne and danced to *The Twist*.[571] *Time* magazine voted Jack as its 'Man of the Year'.[572] The Prime Minister, who had a cold over Christmas, spent the New Year staying at home and 'pondering and brooding in bed over a new plan to get general détente between the West and Communism'.[573]

In February, after John Glenn circled the earth three times, a delighted President went to congratulate him at Cape Canaveral. On Valentine's Day, the First Lady thrilled an audience of 46 million on CBS and NBC television, when she took them for a personal tour of the White House, and then took off on her own tour, to Italy, India and Pakistan. Arriving in Delhi on 12 March for what she called the 'most magic two weeks of my life', she viewed the Taj Mahal by moonlight and rode a camel in the Khyber Pass. Jackie got on well with Nehru, and also Ayub Khan, the military leader, 'magnificent in his uniform and easy to talk to, being educated in England like Nehru'.[574] On her way back, stopping to visit her sister Lee Radizwill, they all went to a small dinner party at Buckingham Palace.

Jackie did not generally involve herself in politics, but according to Kenneth Galbraith, helped Jack by distinguishing sharply between those who were serving him and those who were serving themselves.[575]

The President and First Lady both loved elegance and glamour. When visiting Buckingham Palace the previous summer, Jack had turned to his Chief of Protocol, Angie Duke, as they stepped out of their limousine and said, "Let's study, how they do it!" Within weeks, a fanfare of trumpets, would be heard as a marine band played *Hail to the Chief* whenever Jack and the First Lady led guests downstairs to the state dining room. It was monarchical and formal and America loved it.

That spring, the young couple gave a glittering state dinner for the Shah of Iran and his young wife, Empress Farah, who had come 'bedecked in jewels'. A few weeks later, forty-nine Nobel Prize winners came together for 'one of the most stimulating parties ever', reported the *Washington Post*. Jack, seated next to Ernest Hemingway's widow, got up and quipped, "This is the most extraordinary assembly of human talent and of human knowledge that has ever gathered together at the White House, with the possible exception of when Thomas Jefferson dined alone."[576] The evening ended, as a guest remembered, "with the Yellow Oval Room

JFK's birthday aboard the Sequoia *yacht with British actor friend David Niven (left) who personified dapper charm. Seated to the side of Bobby Kennedy is Fifi Fell (next to the President) and Enud Sztanko. (Courtesy JFK Library)*

filled with cigar smokers and their lady companions and the President, sitting back with a Havana, in his rocker chair, wreathed in smoke looking relaxed and contented". Jack was at home in the company of stars and celebrities. For his birthday in May 1963, he invited British actor David Niven, together with his Norwegian wife, Hjordis, aboard the yacht *Sequoia*. Dressed in yachting clothes, Jack tucked into roast fillet of beef with a 1955 Dom Pérignon champagne. First thing next morning, on Memorial Day, he was at Arlington placing a wreath at the tomb of the 'unknown' soldier. Together with Niven, who had served in a British commando unit during the war, Jack and his party then flew by helicopter to Camp David where, amid much laughter and comedy, the President piled into his birthday gifts, 'with the speed and attention of a four-year-old child'![577]

Jack, who always enjoyed 'the moment', told Jackie his best quality was curiosity. Irritability his worst. Jackie believed her husband would define himself as, 'an idealist without illusions'.[578] Arthur Schlesinger agreed. 'The President gave youth and intellect a world voice, with his extraordinary combination of idealism and reality'. Jack could reel off long Shakespearean passages taken from Richard II, or Henry IV, or King John which he would insert into his speeches. Given his clear fondness for *Camelot*, the First Lady said, "My husband was a romantic, although he did not like people to know that."

Jack had developed a good relationship with the media from the start despite Joe's warning – "Remember the press are not your friends." He began the first ever regular televised press conferences. The third one was watched in 21.5 million homes.[579] Jack's style, substance and savvy came together in a manner at these conferences, which set standards rarely equalled since. Harold Macmillan was annoyed by his own press coverage. 'The London press continues critical of the Govt. *The Times* is particularly smug and irritating. Happily, I think the press, with its gossip and sneering and pomposity and pettiness – as well as its downright lies – is losing influence every day'. Jack told him he was using television, to appeal to people over the heads of a broadly hostile press. Harold now wondered, 'whether a monthly press conference on American lines would be a good thing for me to try!'[580]

The Prime Minister came to Washington for his fifth meeting with Jack in the spring of 1962. Harold had been buoyed earlier by the First Lady calling on him on her way back from India. 'Very agreeable and flattering and assured me of the President's devotion to me.'[581] On arrival, Jack took Macmillan to the Sheraton Hotel, where an enormous gathering of a thousand people[582] were being entertained over dinner by British actor Peter Sellers. The comedy actor did a 'take-off' of the Prime Minister and the President. Jack then responded with a 'take-off' of himself. 'It was a very American scene – with all the American humour and good nature and a sort of hilarious schoolboy crudity which was engaging', noted Macmillan.[583]

After this light-hearted entertaining start, Jack valued the chance to talk freely the next day and give vent to his concerns about the recently stalled Geneva talks. The Prime Minister was surprised by the bitterness of Jack's feelings 'against the French and in particular de Gaulle's rudeness to Rusk'. The President asked, what can you do with a man like that?' Jack's positive mood soon returned when David, Sissy and Jackie joined them, with Jackie remarking she had never seen her husband so relaxed as in the 'complete family atmosphere' of lunch that day.[584] In this setting, Macmillan felt able to resume his gentle pushing of the President to take political risks. He was emerging as a mentor – even a father substitute – to the younger man.

In 'Uncle Harold', Jack had found someone he could instinctively trust. Someone to share his lonely burden of leading the free world. 'The President likes these private and confidential talks. He seems to want advice – or at least comfort',[585] recorded Macmillan in that last week of April. He accepted a book from Jack on blunders that led to WWI, called *The Guns of August*, which the President had told his top advisers and military to read. It emphasised what Jack firmly believed – that war is usually the result of misunderstanding and miscalculation.[586]

On leaving Washington, the Prime Minister reflected on his feelings about his special relationship. "The most striking thing seems to be a greater friendliness to the UK than I remember before.[587] The President went out of his way to do me honour. He met me at the airport; he put in a very impressive guard of honour; he took me to the White House in his helicopter; he came to dinner at the British Embassy on Saturday night – all these are really a breach of protocol for anyone not a head of state."

Macmillan appreciated David's special role. "The position of our Ambassador is unique. He is very close to the President and yet gets on well with the State Dept."[588] The Prime Minister noted Jack was "very secretive and suspicious of leaks, from the State Department or Pentagon intended to frustrate his policy. He is all the time conscious of this, as well of the difficulties with Congress. He looks to us for help – and this means not going too far ahead of him".[589]

These were indeed threatening times. The arms race, which Jack had hoped to avert, now resumed in earnest. Just after Easter, the United States conducted its first above-ground nuclear test, near Christmas Island. There had been none since 1958; now, there would be a total of thirty-six explosions.[590]

Such tense times often called for a light touch and cool sense of perspective. Lord Home once took along Sir William Penny, a scientific advisor on weapons, to meet the President, in New York. When Jack turned to Sir William and asked how many atomic bombs it would take to destroy the City of New York, Sir William in his broad Australian accent replied, "Ow, Mr President, give me two or three and throw in another for luck and I'd make a good job of it – m'y I have another gin and tonic please?"[591] The President's rocking chair apparently rocked well into the night, as the flavour of that moment kept coming back to him.

There was scant progress in Geneva. However, after these meetings with the urbane Lord Home, his counterpart Gromyko would say, "Despite no sudden breakthrough, each meeting left a civilised impression, that made the next one easier."[592]

That summer, Jack installed a secret tape recording system in his Oval Office where a flick of a switch under his desk, would allow him to record conversations. The first recording, on Monday 30 July, showed his advisers joking comfortably and happily expressing firm opinions. Jack complained about diplomats who, 'don't seem to have *cojones*', with Dean Rusk diplomatically replying, "Their appearance is somewhat deceptive." Jack then talked about a member of his father's staff in London. "Counsellor Johnson, an old lady if you ever saw one… He used to call my father Jeeves which drove my father mad."[593]

On 19 May 1962, for his forty-fifth birthday, Jack was at a Democratic fundraising rally, and in front of an audience of millions on television, he received an unexpected birthday greeting. As *Time* magazine reported, 'For one breathless moment the 15,000 people in Madison Square saw sashay onto the stage and attired in a great bundle of white mink Marilyn Monroe. She turned and swept the furs from her shoulders. There was a slight gasp from the audience as Monroe started to sing in a breathy and seductive voice, 'Happy Birthday Mr. President'. Grinning broadly, Jack went to the microphone, "I can now retire from politics, after having Happy Birthday sung to me, in such a sweet and wholesome way." Maria Callas, Harry Belafonte and Ella Fitzgerald all performed for the President that night.

While Jack was being entertained in Madison Square Garden by Marilyn and Maria Callas, Chairman Khrushchev was firming up plans with Gromyko in Moscow to install missiles on Cuba.[594]

20

CUBAN MISSILE CRISIS – JACK TALKS TO DAVID (1962)

Can't do that to me, David's pivotal suggestion, Jack keeps engagements with 'the cousinhood', Kick's vital force, daily transatlantic calls, Khrushchev backs down, joint family Christmas.

It was not until August 1962 that the White House began to get worrying reports of Russian military and equipment landing in Cuba. Ships had been seen unloading in the dead of night.

On 23 August, Jack called an urgent meeting, telling his Foreign and Defence Secretaries, Rusk and McNamara, to prepare a statement to serve as a warning to the Soviets. No sooner had this been done than American senators were starting to call for an immediate invasion of Cuba. As Jack prepared to leave for Newport for the weekend, he received more bad news: CIA photographs now revealed the construction of at least eight surface-to-air missile sites that looked like 'offensive' missiles. In order to give him time to reflect, Jack quickly instructed the CIA to put this information 'back in the box and nail it tight',[595] before he set off home taking a 'negotiating position' report he had requested from his advisers.

David and Sissie joined the President at Newport. 'We were the only guests except for Peter Thorneycroft who came to stay for Saturday night', reported David to the Foreign Office on 19 September.[596] Jack seems to have avoided talking about the latest CIA information. But he emphasised several times, 'how dangerous he considered Khrushchev's complacent attitude to be with regard to the West's likely response to Soviet pressure on Berlin', and pointedly asked for 'any suggestions we might have for trying to bring home to Khrushchev the tremendous risks he would be running'.[597]

The President and his house party went to see the start of the America's Cup yacht race. They saw big cheerful crowds all in fine summer holiday mood at Newport, before going on that Friday night to dinner hosted by the Australian Ambassador, Sir Howard Beale, with 300 guests in a vast marble and gilt dining room of their mansion. On Saturday morning, the *Honey Fitz* collected and took Jack's party from the dock of Hammersmith Farm to a waiting destroyer, named in honour of Jack's brother, USS *Joseph P. Kennedy*. With military planes flying overhead, the destroyer took them out fourteen miles to watch the race in progress. Returning aboard *Honey Fitz*, relaxed and laughing with their families, and seeing the President, dressed in blue yachting blazer with buttons gleaming in the sun, no one would have imagined here was Jack, contemplating the possibility of a world war.[598]

Jack had done what he could at this point. He had warned Khrushchev that he would take strong action if Cuba were to become an offensive military base. He knew and feared a crisis over Berlin was imminent. He showed David a report of Khrushchev telling several Western visitors that he could do whatever he liked in Berlin without fear of a fight. Khrushchev had even told the departing German Ambassador in Moscow that the Western Alliance would never go to war over Berlin! Jack knew he had to find a way of impressing upon Khrushchev that if provoked, the United States would fight.[599]

Not long after David got back to the Embassy from Newport, he hosted a lavish champagne party. The residence terrace was covered by a huge silk tent decorated with gold braid and ropes of hemlock and pine entwined with tiny white lights. The President and First Lady, and 600 guests, remained at the party until 2.30am.[600] The *Washington Post*, covering the glamorous event, told its readers, 'that the magnetism of the Kennedys has become the hub of the social universe'. But beyond the silk tents and gold braid of the British residence, over forty Cuban missiles were about to be pointed at America.

For thirteen days in October 1962, the world teetered on the brink. It faced the real possibility of a nuclear war. American spy planes had now pictured forty-two missiles in Cuba aimed at America. The scary sharp point of the Cold War had suddenly appeared.

On Tuesday morning, 16 October, Jack was in his dressing gown and pyjamas propped up against some pillows on his bed, when George Bundy arrived. He handed over the first hard photographic evidence showing 'offensive missiles' in Cuba. As the young leader of the free world stared at pictures of these missiles aimed at his country, Kennedy exclaimed, "He can't do that to me!"

The President was furious that Khrushchev had lied again. The Soviets had been advising that all weapons in Cuba were there merely for defence purposes. With mid-term elections due, Jack had been wary of sending U2 spy planes out at this time. After more CIA prodding, Kennedy agreed to further reconnaissance flights. Whilst he had anticipated a crisis, he had expected it to be after the elections and in Berlin! Kennedy now needed time to decide his next move without public pressure or panic. He would have to draw on all his experience, going back to London days on the eve of war, to avoid another war now.

Over the next six days, he held intense meetings in great secrecy. The National Security Council (NSC), which he had set up after the failed Cuban invasion, met for the first time on 16 October under its new chairman, Maxwell Taylor. He was a former military chief of staff whom Jack had specially called back to active duty. With the NSC reporting directly to the Defence Secretary, Jack was now able to keep the Joint Chiefs of Staff – whom he viewed as responsible for the Bay of Pigs disaster – at arm's length. When he finally met the Joint Chiefs of Staff, face to face on Friday, 19 October, they found that they were there, not to offer him advice; they were there so he could tell them what he intended to do – which was to institute a blockade. They tried to talk him into invading Cuba and assured him that the Soviets would not seize Berlin in retaliation. Kennedy told them they were wrong. He then headed for Chicago to carry on with his mid-term campaign schedule, sticking to much of his travel and speaking schedule.

On Saturday 20 October, the President was in Chicago when Bobby Kennedy told him the NSC were ready to present their positions; either to launch an air strike to take out the missiles or to settle for the milder remedy of a blockade. Cutting short his trip on pretext he had developed a cold, he called Jackie at Glen Ora, telling her to bring the children to the White House immediately, saying they were close to war. He wanted them to be nearby when he made the terrible choices that faced him.[601]

The idea of an immediate blockade, had been pushed by Defence Secretary Robert McNamara to show American resolve, whilst buying time and preventing additional weapons from reaching Cuba. McNamara had been specially chosen by Kennedy, despite his lack of experience from the Ford

Motor Company. (When McNamara said he did not have enough experience for the job, Jack famously replied, "Neither do I as President.")

The assembled generals and Air Chief Marshall, Curtis LeMay, now meeting Kennedy, wanted more direct action. The Air Chief unhelpfully compared a blockade, to appeasement at Munich. "You are in a pretty bad fix," LeMay said to Kennedy across the table at one point. The President asked him to repeat what he had just said. And then, solid as steel, Jack responded. "You're in there with me. Personally!"

On Sunday, 21 October, Jack asked David to arrive unseen at the White House around lunchtime. He then told him about the missiles in Cuba. He wanted to talk through the options open to him. As they had frequently done in the past, they went through Jack's reasoning. It was without question the most difficult moment of his life. One wrong move and Jack could set off a nuclear exchange that might end in annihilation for everyone. David, the first person to be consulted outside the US Government, saw serious drawbacks to an airstrike and confirmed that he too favoured a blockade – even though it might spur the Russians to act on Berlin. David told Jack, "Very few people outside the United States would consider the provocation serious enough to merit an American attack. Besides, action like that might provide a smoke screen behind which the Russians might move against Berlin. Some form of blockade is probably the right answer."

The Duke and Duchess of Devonshire were in town and staying with David to open an exhibition at the National Gallery, of old master drawings from Chatsworth. Coinciding with the missile crisis and by a curious move of fate, Jack had scheduled a family dinner for them that Sunday. It was the night before the President was to address the American people, but Jack as ever, was glad to run through his reasoning again with David that night, surrounded by old family friends.[602]

Leaving the Oval Office, Jack headed to the family quarters around 7.30pm. There he found Jackie chatting happily with Andrew and Debo, David and Sissie and Jakie Astor and his wife – his close circle from Kick's aristocratic cousinhood. Jack immediately relaxed in the company of his 'family', this cousinhood, whom he had known since youth, when they knew a dictator's bombs and bullets might snatch their lives away. As the evening progressed, Jack and David went upstairs to talk privately. Astor reflected back to those London days when a light-hearted Jack and David – the 'second sons'

– had seemed the least serious members of the group. Now those two fellows were going off together to confer about the imminent confrontation![603] Jackie went upstairs to see what had become of the two men. She found them both, 'squatting on the floor, looking at the missile pictures…', and found herself now rushing 'backwards and forwards to keep the party going',[604] as she put it.

Jack and David pored over dozens of aerial photos showing all the medium-range ballistic missiles pointed at them. They hurriedly selected a batch of pictures for immediate release to the world media. Top secret telegram 2622 records the moment. 'I had another long conversation with the President after a private dinner at the White House last night. I said that it was most important that the Americans provide really convincing evidence to the general public… he quite understood and after he had sent for a batch of photographs which should be published, I emphasised the need for clear explanatory notes to be attached. I had pointed out without such notes the uninitiated would have no means of telling whether the missiles depicted were six feet long and therefore defensive or sixty feet long and therefore offensive.[605]

'Halfway through our talk Bobby Kennedy joined us. He had just come from a secret meeting with the Russian Ambassador Dobrynin… The President and his brother asked me how I thought the whole affair would end. I said it seemed to me that there could only be two endings. Either action or counteraction, that would lead to war, or there would have to be some negotiated settlement. I imagined that everyone in their right mind would prefer the second alternative. But it was of the greatest importance to the West, that Khrushchev should be left in no doubt as to America's resolution. They both agreed with this summing-up'.[606]

As young men, Jack and David had felt the consequences in London of what had happened when no one seemed prepared to take early action to stop Hitler. That night, there had been no breakthrough with Dobrynin. The Russian Ambassador had looked ashen and in a state of confusion. He persisted in claiming there were no long-range missiles in Cuba. He denied knowing what orders Soviet ships had been given. He said he did know that a month ago the ships' captains had been told to ignore any possible blockade and to sail through to Cuba. At the end of his tether, Bobby had told the Ambassador to get on the telephone to Moscow and learn the truth!

That night, Jack confessed to David he did not know whether his choice of a blockade was the right one. There was no telling how the Soviet leader would react. Perhaps he should have approved an airstrike; perhaps he should have done nothing at all. For now, all they could do was live with excruciating uncertainty. And in such a condition the President maintained his 'unfailing good humour which kept everybody else calm and in a good-natured mood', wrote David.

Before the busy night was over, Jack managed to send his first message to Macmillan about the dangers they faced. 'I am sending you this most private message to give you advance notice of a most serious situation and my plan to meet it… I want you to have this message tonight so that you may have as much time as possible to consider the dangers we now face together.[607] I have found it absolutely essential, in the interest of security and speed, to make my first decision on my own responsibility, but from now on I expect that we can and should be in closest touch'.

After six days of secret deliberation, on Monday, 22 October the President finally went on television to address his citizens. Speaking for seventeen minutes, looking drawn but determined, Jack described the situation facing America. He demanded the Russians remove the missiles. He said there would be a blockade put around Cuba to stop any ships bringing more missiles. The largest audience ever for a president's address, tuned in that night. With grave words and matching demeanour, Jack referred to Britain's mistakes with Hitler in the 1930s, to explain his actions. "The 1930s taught us a clear lesson. Aggressive conduct, if allowed to go unchecked and unchallenged, ultimately leads to war. The United States could not tolerate this threat to its security and would henceforth quarantine Cuba to block off all offensive weapons from reaching the island."

Macmillan's diary entry for 22 October: 'The first day of the World crisis? He [Ambassador Bruce] brought a long letter from the President, as well as a great dossier to prove contrary to specific assurances given by the Russian Government and Gromyko in particular there had now been secretly deployed in Cuba a formidable armoury… a pistol aimed at America… that would not be tolerated. Ambassador Bruce, in his detached and quiet manner, did not attempt to conceal the excited almost chaotic atmosphere in Washington'.[608] Macmillan asked Sir Alec to come over to help work on a reply, supporting the President, 'in his determination to prevent the Russians getting away with this new act of aggression'.

The Prime Minister had agonised over what to advise. 'In my first draft, I had thought of advising him to seize Cuba and have done with it… but I felt this would be wrong. It seemed a risk that should not be taken. All the same, the Suez analogy is on my mind. If [Kennedy] "misses the bus" – he may never get rid of Cuban rockets except by trading them for Turkish, Italian or other bases. Thus Khrushchev will have won his point. He may even be able to force the frightened Americans to trade Berlin for Cuba'.[609]

The President stayed in close touch with regular night-time telephone calls. On Tuesday, 23 October, Macmillan scribbled down questions to ask Jack. 'How are you going to end this blockade; a, by occupying Cuba, or b, by conference?'[610] The telephone transcripts for that first call, see the Prime Minister supporting limited action, followed by negotiation. However, on this call and subsequent ones, Macmillan generally talked little. He remained mostly in listening mode, providing occasional encouragement and reassurance. Kennedy seemed to use these late-night (for Harold!) conversations, as a way of clarifying his own thinking.

Adlai Stevenson went to the United Nations on Tuesday 23 October, to show the world the CIA photographs. The President opened a secret direct channel of communication to Khrushchev by telegram and letter, shortly before the quarantine was to be put into effect.

Jack asked David to come to see him that Tuesday. McNamara had decided the quarantine line be placed 800 miles from Havana, out of range of Cuban weapons. Jack asked about this and David quickly suggested reducing the line to just 500 miles out. It was risky, David conceded, but it would give Khrushchev a few more valuable and perhaps crucial hours to back down. Jack immediately phoned Defence Secretary McNamara with new instructions for a 500-mile perimeter! With little more than twelve hours left, he then signed off the order for a 500-mile quarantine to go into effect at 9am Eastern time, Wednesday, 24 October.

Embassy telegram 2664 reported the Ambassador's thinking. 'I suggested that there were some disadvantages in the Americans going out of their way to make an early interception of a Russian ship sailing to Cuba... even a few hours might enable them to take decisions which would avoid a serious clash'.[611]

The President informed the Soviet leader in advance of his intentions. 'I hope you will issue immediately the necessary instructions to your ships to observe the terms of the quarantine... which will go into effect at 14.00 hours Greenwich Mean Time, Wednesday, 24 October'. Khrushchev gave a quick and vague reply. Jack responded immediately. 'I have received your letter of 24th, and I regret very much that you still do not appear to understand what it is, that has moved us in this matter… I ask you Mr. Chairman to recognise it is not I who issued the first challenge in this case…'[612]

As the blockade went into effect that Wednesday morning, Macmillan sent the President a short telegram as the perilous moment was arriving. 'The trial of wills is now approaching a climax… I shall expect to hear from you how things are developing. I agree that any initiative by me is all a matter of timing'.

Macmillan's diary: 'Woke early – 6.30am and "did the box", which I had left unfinished last night. A very confusing morning, with Lord Home, Harold Caccia and much sending and receiving of telegrams. An anxious day, too. For the first clash will soon begin, if the Russian ships sail on. Not much from Russia yet, except words'.[613] The German Chancellor, Konrad Adenauer, sent the President a message that Wednesday, promising, '*Dass wir in dieser gefarhlichen Zeit eng zussamenrucken*'. (*sic* We will at this dangerous time stick closely together.)

Bobby Kennedy spoke to Ambassador Dobrinyn again that morning, and he still continued to deny the presence of missiles. The Soviet ships were about to enter the quarantine zone. The leading Soviet ships – a convoy of fourteen observed carrying military cargoes – had not altered course. A Soviet submarine had taken up a position close to two of the Soviet freighters. The aircraft carrier USS *Essex* now headed towards the submarine. That morning, Britain's Minister of Defence and his Chief of Defence called for a meeting with the Prime Minister at 3.30pm.

The Soviet leader had been convinced after their meeting in Vienna, that the young American president would accept almost anything, if it meant avoiding nuclear war. He believed Kennedy did not have the stomach for a fight. Khrushchev staked his prestige on getting a settlement on Germany quickly. He was now apparently prepared to threaten and force this crisis on Kennedy, to get him to abandon any idea of German reunification and to withdraw Western troops from Berlin.

The President watched the USS *Essex* loaded with helicopters and depth charges that Wednesday morning move slowly across a large screen that was tracking each ship in the 'situation room' of the White House.[614]

The Navy were ready to intercept and engage. "I think these few minutes were the time of gravest concern for the President… Was the world on the brink of a holocaust? Was it our error? A mistake? His hand went up to his face and covered his mouth. He opened and clenched his fist. His face seemed drawn, his eyes pained, almost grey. We stared at each other across the table," Bobby Kennedy recalled. "For a few fleeting seconds it was almost as though no one else was in the room and he was no longer President. Inexplicably I thought of when he was ill and had almost died; when he lost his child; when he learned that our oldest brother had been killed; of personal times of strain and hurt… I didn't seem to hear anything until the President asked McNamara, 'Isn't there some way we can avoid having our first exchange with a Russian submarine? We had come to the time of final decision'."

At 10.25am, a messenger entered the situation room and handed a note to McCone, Head of CIA. He read it aloud. 'Some Soviet ships have stopped, dead in the water!' Dean Rusk with a sudden smile turned to Bundy. "We're eyeball to eyeball… and I think the other fellow just blinked."

McNamara then immediately left the situation room and headed for the Navy's control centre in the Pentagon. There, he asked Admiral Anderson, in charge of blockade logistics, if every US ship had someone on board who spoke Russian. The Admiral said he did not know. McNamara asked him what they would do if a Soviet captain refused a boarding party. A flustered Admiral waved a copy of the *US Manual of Naval Regulations* saying, "It's all in there."

The Defence Secretary exploded. "I don't give a damn what John Paul Jones would have done. I want to know what you are going to do. Now!"

Anderson countered, "Now, Mr Secretary, if you and your deputy will go back to your offices, the Navy will run the blockade." An unconvinced McNamara, still concerned about the ships and submarines, turned on his heel and left.

Jack phoned Harold at eleven that night. "Some of the ships we are interested in have turned round – but others are still coming on. We shall know in the next twelve hours."

Macmillan probed further. "How are you going to get the rockets out of Cuba – the ones that are there now?"

The President replied, "The judgement we have to make is whether we're going to invade Cuba and take our chances or hold off and use Cuba as a hostage in the matter of Berlin. Then, any time he takes action on Berlin we can take action on Cuba. That's really the choice we have now. What's your judgement?"

Harold hesitated and said, "I would like to think about this and send an answer." The unruffled prime minister, maintaining his wry humour after being asked about 'taking out Cuba', noted in his diary, 'It's just like *Beyond the Fringe* [television comedy] which takes off all politicians!'[615] On 25 October, Macmillan sent his answer. 'Events have gone too far now and… while such action [i.e., invading Cuba] may be right and necessary, I think we are all in a phase now where you must try to meet your objectives by other means'.

In London a nervous Soviet *chargé d'affaires*, Loginov, on 25 October, asked for an urgent call on Sir Alec at the Foreign Office. He implored the British Government 'to do all it could do in their power to avert developments on Cuba which could push the world to the brink of a military catastrophe'. Sir Alec asked Loginov, why the Russians had put missiles into Cuba. He replied he did not know what missiles were there, adding, "In any case, the American Government have put missiles in Turkey which were directed at my country." Sir Alec told the nervous diplomat, "What Russia has done was an act of power which has gone wrong and done them great damage. We are thinking hard about what to do to help in this dangerous situation, but Russia must first remove the weapons from Cuba before anything can be done."[616] Sir Alec declined to act instantly as a mediator, as the Russians had hoped.

The Soviet tanker *Bucharest* did not 'stop dead in the water' and crossed the quarantine line on Thursday, 25 October. The aircraft carrier *USS Essex* and a Navy destroyer went to intercept, but the *Bucharest* failed to cooperate. Deeming it unlikely that the ship was carrying offensive weapons, the Navy restrained itself from forcibly seizing the ship.

Then came the announcement the world was waiting for: 'At 08.00 hours this morning a Soviet vessel that was intercepted by the U.S. Navy was a tanker and it was allowed to proceed under the terms of the U.S. Quarantine. It now appears that a dozen Soviet vessels have turned back'. That announcement, from America's Defense Department was instantly relayed and repeated around the world, and created a tidal wave of smiles. At that moment, everyone felt able to breathe again.

The American Ambassador in Moscow received an emotional text from the Soviet leader, for the President. 'If you have not lost your self-control and sensibly conceive what this might lead to, then, Mr President, we and you ought to know, not now to pull on the ends of the rope in which you have tied

Arriving by helicopter at the White House just before the Cuba crisis in September 1962.
The President with Naval Aide Captain Shephard and Secret Service agent Bob Lilley. The
devoted private secretary to the President, Evelyn Lincoln, can be seen in the background.
(Courtesy JFK Library)

the knot of war… Consequently, if there is no intention to tighten the knot and thereby doom the world to the catastrophe of thermonuclear war, then let us not only relax the forces pulling on the ends of the rope, let us take measures to untie that knot. We are ready for this'.[617]

Khrushchev and his officials had in fact met earlier on Wednesday, and decided to remove the missiles if President Kennedy undertook not to invade the island. An exhausted Soviet leader cabled his rambling message along these lines to Kennedy on 26 October, followed by another on 27th adding a further condition – the removal of US missiles in Turkey. Kennedy ignored for the moment the second message and decided to focus on accepting the first offer. Bobby, who had already indicated that missiles in Turkey could be removed, repeated this, to the Soviet Ambassador. (The missiles were considered largely obsolete, but this part of the deal remained secret until recently.) The Soviet leader finally accepted all of Kennedy's demands on Sunday, 28 October.

A British diplomat living in Moscow, Christopher Mallaby, recalled the moment the ships turned back and saw it as the turning point in the Cold War. "The success in facing down Khrushchev in an extremely dangerous crisis restored initiative in the Cold War to the West."[618]

The diplomat's wife described the tension and her feelings then. "We saw risk of nuclear war, but we did not believe there would be a nuclear war. We were riveted, but not afraid."

The Cuba crisis had been a close-run thing. According to Bobby, the President himself believed, "There was a one in three chance of nuclear war happening then."[619]

The Duchess of Devonshire remembered Jack showing remarkable 'cool' throughout. Looking back to a White House dinner on Sunday, 21 October, she wrote, 'Jack was his usual self, showing no outward signs of the strain he must have felt! In the room where we met for drinks before dinner, photographs of the missiles were lying on the table and were being picked up and put down by dinner guests as if they were holiday snaps. I suppose some of us did not realise how near to world disaster we were. The atmosphere in the White House was unchanged from the previous year – a tribute to steady nerves. At one point, Jack suggested. "Why don't you call your sister in California and asked his switchboard to put me through to Decca in Los Angeles?" Over dinner, Jack and I talked about his family's years in London before the war and about old friends. I talked about Vice-President Johnson, trying to upstage Princess Margaret at the Jamaican Independence celebrations with the UK delegation, headed by Hugh Fraser. "Not our Hugh Fraser?" asked Jack, and then laughed at this promotion, much as Hugh might have laughed at Jack's new status. The next night, Jack went to address the nation on television about the situation in Cuba and called on Russia to remove the missiles or face retaliation'.

Keeping to nearly all of his social engagements, Jack would meet the Duke and Duchess a number of times that week, enjoying the chance to talk about his sister Kick, and student days in London. Debo writes, 'Jack and I were sitting talking and laughing about the old days, about his two sisters Kick and Eunice, and the girls he met twenty-four years before. He asked about the home life of various politicians. We moved on to war heroes – he wanted to know about Paddy Leigh Fermour and his capture of a German general in Crete in 1944. Suddenly he said, "Tell me about Percival." I said I did not know anything about him except that he had been the only British Prime Minister to be assassinated.

Jack stayed quiet for a while and then we went back to chit-chat. And of course Jack had stuck to all his social arrangements during the crises and we even called on him for half an hour during one of the Cuba meetings in the Oval Office. Harold Macmillan and the President were in constant touch by telephone the whole time. It was evident that Jack was seeking advice from the old boy, and the fact they were by now such friends, made a difference'.[620]

When the Duchess finally left, she recorded swimming with Jack, talking about Kick, and the relief felt by all. 'On Monday morning the President asked me to go for a last swim at the White House pool, where he swam every day to help his back. Again, we talked about the old times and especially of Kick. Afterwards I lunched with Eunice, Jean and Ethel, before leaving for New York where everyone was breathing a sigh of relief and there was a festive atmosphere'.[621] At this time, 'Jack's White House was so enjoyable and surprising!'.[622] The curious circumstance of fate having his London friends around him to enjoy and relax with when facing his biggest challenge as leader had been a stroke of fortune.

Jack's fondness to talk about 'the old times and especially of Kick', revealed the little-known but ever present role that Kick played in his life. Jack often drew strength when thinking about his 'kindred spirit'. His beloved sister had given Jack the vital force to drive him forward, more than anyone and even he consciously realised?

It was clear Krushchev had been surprised by Kennedy's unanticipated firmness and then feared an American invasion of Cuba. When Kennedy responded with a more modest quarantine, a relieved Khrushchev rejected a proposal by Dobrynin (only revealed in the 1990s), that they retaliate by blockading Berlin. "It would just add 'fuel to the conflict'," said the Soviet Premier.[623]

Macmillan wrote to congratulate Jack, "It was indeed a trial of wills and yours prevailed. Whatever difficulties and dangers we may have to face in the future I am proud to feel that I have so resourceful and so firm a comrade."[624]

Jack replied, "Your heartening support publicly expressed these past days and our daily conversations have been of inestimable value. Many thanks."[625]

The Queen was moved to write to Macmillan, 'In the end I suppose Mr Khrushchev's sudden announcement took the whole world by surprise'.[626]

This dangerous moment in the Cold War had tested Jack at his best. This was the critical moment for which he had been trained and armed in youth, by sharp experience. After this, the Russians abandoned their high-risk policy of brinkmanship. Khrushchev had misjudged Kennedy and there were no further ultimatums about West Berlin.

The lessons Jack and his friends learnt from London and Munich in 1938 and 1939 had rescued the world from another war. Harold Macmillan told the House of Commons that the Cuban Missile Crisis, 'represented one of the great turning points of history'.

Jack had triumphed to be the man that his sister Kick believed he could be. David sent his congratulations in a letter dated 30 October, that Jack would keep in his *Resolute* desk drawer in the Oval Office. David had expressed his deep admiration for 'the superb manner he had conducted himself in the tremendous days he had just lived through… receiving a mass of conflicting advice and acting at all times with perfect judgement'.[627]

The President took David with him on *Air Force One,* for the next meeting with the Prime Minister in the Bahamas on 19 December. They met to discuss the tricky problem of Britain's nuclear deterrent, which was giving Harold new worries. For this meeting, Harold suggested it should repeat the Bermuda model, with a sort of house party rather than a formal meeting.[628] The UK had anticipated getting the Skybolt missile – a system capable of being launched from under the wings of a plane. In November, the Americans had said they were abandoning Skybolt because development costs (to which the UK had been contributing) were running too high. Kennedy suggested putting Polaris missiles on British submarines as the alternative. This was acceptable, even though it would take years to build the submarines (which came into service in 1969). Kennedy stipulated they should be used as part of a NATO force, but Macmillan pressed to retain independence of action to maintain the appearance of Britain having its own independent deterrent. After two days, they agreed, 'a satisfactory compromise no other ally of the US could have achieved', recorded David. The tight bonds of their special relationship had come to the rescue, once again.[629]

During the talks, a surprise message arrived from Khrushchev. It indicated he was ready to make progress on a test ban treaty. As this could prove to be a historic milestone on the road to peace, the Nassau talks ended in a joyous mood of celebration. David and his family went back with Jack to Palm Beach to share a joint family Christmas, buoyed by Khrushchev's positive message of 19 December.

Jack's friends were all marked by a fierce loyalty to him. Shortly after becoming President, Jack said, "The Presidency is not a very good place to make new friends. So I'm going to keep my old friends."[630] Jack divided his friends by separate roles. Few, if any, with the notable exception of David Ormsby-Gore, ever crossed roles – especially that between 'family' and 'official'. Press counsellor Arthur Schlesinger said, "The President found the [British] Ambassador a companion for every mood, whether he wanted to sail in Nantucket Sound or brood over the prospect of nuclear annihilation. Their long relaxed confidential talks together at Hyannis Port or Palm Beach or on quiet evenings in the White House gave Kennedy probably his best opportunity to clarify his own purposes in world affairs."[631]

Jack and David grew to recognise the extent of their political and intellectual compatibility. David an expert in the intricate field of arms control had been advising Jack even before he sent his memo on nuclear arms negotiations for his presidential campaign. "Jack took a very keen interest. I know it did have some effect on his subsequent opinions," recalled Britain's Ambassador.[632] Bobby Kennedy went so far as to say he believed his brother would, "rather have his [David's] judgement than almost anybody else's". David attended some of Jack's campaign events, wearing a PT 109 tie clip.

As President, Jack stayed in regular touch with members of his British circle from student days; he kept alive his family link with the Devonshires throughout 1962, with numerous telephone calls to Chatsworth House. The Duchess remembers: "Jack sometimes telephoned with a question about Uncle Harold or another member of the government, or just for a chat. It was a convenient time for him but I was dead asleep when the telephone rang at 3am. 'Do you know it is the 4th of July?' he began one of these calls.

"'Is it?' I said, barely conscious.

"'Have you got all your loved ones with you?' he asked.

"'No,' I said. 'Why?' and so on…

"On another occasion he sounded exasperated. 'I got put through to a pub called the Devonshire Arms. It was closed.'"[633]

Jack entertained Hugh Fraser, now a minister in government, together with his wife Antonia, at the White House. The Fraser's would later accommodate daughter Caroline when she studied in London.[634] William Douglas-Home, another from the student circle who used to play with Jack at the Royal Wimbledon Golf Club, would join Jack and his wife on holiday in Cannes.

It was now William's brother Alec, who was playing a vital role in the 'special relationship.' His patrician style was appreciated and respected by Kennedy. Educated at Oxford, like David he had just scraped through university with a third-class honours, and working as a young Private Secretary accompanied Chamberlain to Munich to meet Hitler. When war broke out Alec had been struck down with polio of the spine and in 1940 had to undergo a back operation, which kept him in bed for almost two years. Replicating Jack's response to adversity in early life, when confined to bed, he surrounded himself with books. "Three different kind of books going at once – a history, a biography and a novel or detective story".

In a further dubious stroke of fate, whilst recovering at his father's estate at the Hirsel, Alec read 'all the books I could find on Communism'. Interest had been prompted by a Polish count, Starzenski of the Polish Armoured Division quartered on the Hirsel estate who had shown great bravery and adventure in escaping the German and Russian invasions – 'the tyrannies of the left and right', as he called it. Alec was soon convinced that the 'purpose of Soviet leaders was expansion through any chink of weakness that the West might reveal'.[635] However, unfazed by Khrushchev's mixed-up personality he even began to like him for his 'humanity which had come late to him in life, but it was there'.[636] His close understanding of communism would prove invaluable to Macmillan and Kennedy. He was also considered to be a calming influence on the Prime Minister and was often in the room for Macmillan's calls with the President. Jack in a memorable comment described him as 'polished wood covering steel'. Good fortune conspired to bring Sir Alec, with his talents into the 'special relationship' at this time.[637]

The Douglas-Homes came from a noble line whose ancestors included Lord Durham, who was Ambassador in Moscow and later Governor-General of Canada in 1838. Alec had three brothers who all went to war. William, brother George, who disappeared on a training flight in Canada, and Edward, taken prisoner by the Japanese. (After working on the notorious Burma Railway, Edward, despite being the 'most even tempered and charitable of persons', never felt able later to say a good word for his captors.)[638]

Alec had been an unusually gifted all-rounder, effortlessly popular at school, played cricket for Eton and married Elizabeth, the headmaster's daughter. In another eighteenth-century and Whig age, he would have probably become prime minister before he was thirty.[639] He was not personally ambitious and Deborah Devonshire would describe him as 'most unpolitical, with an almost saintly streak'.[640] Macmillan would tell the Queen, "Lord Home is clearly a man who represents the old governing class at its best… he is not ambitious in the sense of wanting to scheme for power, although not foolish enough to resist honour when it comes to him. He gives that impression, by a curious mixture of great courtesy and even if yielding to pressure, has underlying rigidity on matters of principle. It is interesting that he has proved himself so much liked by men like President Kennedy, and Mr Rusk and Mr Gromyko. This is exactly the quality that the class to which he belongs have at their best because they think about the question under discussion and not about themselves."

Together with the popular Dean Rusk an Oxford Rhodes scholar, the leading players in the special relationship worked seamlessly together. The 'special relationship' thrived on family bonds of shared experience and talent. This excellence was turning back the tide of communist ambition. "The tremendous advantage of a large family," Ted Kennedy remarked, "was that we were always reinforcing each other."[641] The Anglo-American family team aimed now, to break the deadlock in East-West relations with a treaty on nuclear weapons.

In his 'Annual Review of 1962', David warned that Kennedy's victory and his tough stand on Cuba could pose problems for future arms negotiations. 'It might simply reinforce the average man's view that toughness, rather than talk, is the proper way to do business with the Russians'.

For most Americans in 1962, the Cold War was still seen in greatly oversimplified terms. As David commented 'It is a matter of regret... the organs of public opinion in the United States with few exceptions continue to prove unequal to their responsibility of providing an intelligent analysis of world problems. Their jingoistic tone coupled with their bad guy/good guy interpretation of the East-West struggle makes it hard for the Administration to retain the flexibility needed to pursue a sophisticated policy calculated to advance the interests of the West'.[642]

David ended his 1962 report: 'There can be no question that we really now enjoy with the Americans an ease of access and intimacy of consultation which is unequalled. We have been the most influential and the most relied upon of America's Allies. In this sense a special relationship exists and must continue in one form or another'.[643]

Two days after the Cuban Missile Crisis was over, the President, looking to the future, told a meeting of congressional leaders, "There is no more threat from Russia – the threat in the years ahead will be China."

21

VISIT TO BERLIN AND BRITAIN, TEST-BAN TREATY SIGNED (1963)

Jack honours Churchill, the Peace Speech, 'Ich bin ein Berliner',
Pope blesses Jack, Irish ancestral visit, band of brothers meeting
with Macmillan, Test Ban Treaty signed.

For the first time in two years, Jack felt optimistic about prospects for peace. Whilst ordering a small increase in the Army, from 14 to 16 divisions, the President declared in his State of the Union Address that, "The tide of human freedom is in our favour… we have every reason to believe that our tide is running strong."

Seeing that the wave of Soviet expansion had been turned, Jack's ambition now moved to honour his great mentor Winston Churchill. He felt the nation's and his own intellectual debt to Britain's wartime leader ought to be repaid. The way Churchill had led the world, with a broad vision steeped in history, had made a deep mark on Jack. He understood how words and vision could be every bit as effective as arms, in winning wars.

On 9 April, Congress passed a Special Bill giving Winston Churchill honorary citizenship. Randolph, his son, accepted the award in the garden of the Oval Office, seen by a worldwide television audience. Speaking against the pink and white background of cherry blossom, Jack told his audience, "In the dark days when Britain stood alone and most men, save Englishmen, despaired of England's life, he mobilised the English language and sent it into Battle. The incandescent quality of his words illuminated the courage of his countrymen."

In reply, Randolph spoke about his father's theme of the English-speaking peoples and a democratic heritage, kept alive in a 'special relationship'.

"Our past is the key to our future. Let no man underrate our energies, our potentialities, and our abiding power for good."[644]

Watching from a second-floor window of the White House sat Joe, with five-year-old granddaughter Caroline, peering down on the 200 people assembled below. He must have reflected proudly on the success he had achieved as a father. Winston watched on television from the front room of his townhouse in London with his wife, Clementine, courtesy of the new era of live satellite television. Winston was 'a child of both worlds', as his wife would say, of England and America, and never more so than on this day. His son Randolph, who then struck up a fresh new chord of friendship with Bobby and his family, spent the weekend at the Kennedy compound in Hyannis Port.

Throughout the first six months of 1963, Kennedy and Macmillan exchanged ideas about nuclear weapons. On 16 March, Macmillan sent a thirteen-page letter marked both 'Top Secret' and 'Personal'. 'Dear friend… After much thought, I am impelled to write to you to give you my ideas about the question of nuclear tests and the possibility of an agreement to ban them'.[645] He urged 'his friend' to move boldly forward, stating that a test ban would be, 'the most important step you can take towards unravelling this frightful tangle of fear in East-West relations'.[646]

Achieving a treaty would mark the first expression of trust between the superpowers since the war. As a first step, it could lead to further agreements and herald the end of a closed Soviet society, which Churchill always believed, was the way to defeat communism. Harold Macmillan decided to stiffen Jack's resolve, 'before it is too late'. With exquisite tact, rather than tell Jack what he ought to do, Macmillan indicated his duty as world leader: 'A duty to try and change the course of history and guide it in a direction… which would be of benefit to the people'.

After Cuba, and as David predicted, the American public were not in a 'negotiating mood'. Kennedy and his State Department officials were reluctant to be bold – they worried about political pitfalls for Jack's re-election. Would Jack be able to live up to the high purpose called for in his inaugural speech – 'A new beginning in East-West relations'? Would he take that step, to be the statesman he longed to be – the type of hero he admired and who set principle above self-interest?[647]

As so often in Jack's life, events seemed to line themselves up like the stars in heaven, to motivate and guide him. On 9 April, David chose the day when

Looking into John Glenn's Mercury spacecraft 'Friendship7' at Cape Canaveral, 23 February 1962. Six days earlier Glenn had become the first American to orbit the earth. (Courtesy JFK Library)

Prime Minister and President looking over the White House lawn. Macmillan came to discuss "those moments in history when one must put everything at risk in order to change the course of events" on 29 April 1962. (Courtesy JFK Library)

David Ormsby-Gore presenting credentials as Britain's Ambassador on 26 October 1961. "He would rather have his judgement than that of almost anybody else. He was part of the family" recalled Bobby Kennedy. (Courtesy JFK Library)

'Family' gathering before taking lunch in the White House. The President with Harold and David together with Jackie and David's wife, Sissie, comfortable in each other's company, 29 April 1962. (Courtesy JFK Library)

Jack raising a point with David on the south lawn of the White House. 'David fitted exactly between Uncle Harold and Jack Kennedy. They were all completely out of the same hat.' (Alamy)

22 October 1962 – President Kennedy announcing a Naval blockade of Cuba to the world on evening television. "Our goal is not the victory of might, but the vindication of right, not peace at the expense of freedom, but peace and freedom. God willing that goal will be achieved." (Courtesy JFK Library)

President Kennedy rides with Mayor Willy Brandt into Berlin, to be greeted by cheering and expectant crowds wherever he went. (Alamy)

The President addresses the massive crowd at Rudolf Wilhelm Platz on 26 June 1963. "All free men, wherever they may live are citizens of Berlin and therefore, as a free man I take pride in the words, 'Ich bin ein Berliner'." (Alamy)

Commander in Chief during his visit to Germany greets his troops in the Mess at Fliegerhorst Kaserne, Hanau Air Base on 25 June 1963. (Alamy)

RAF Guard of Honour at Gatwick Airport as Jack is escorted by the Prime Minister on 29 June on his last visit to the United Kingdom. Macmillan would tell the President, "We have been in part equal to the Churchill-Roosevelt relationship at the most critical moment of history." (Alamy)

Jack celebrating with Caroline to his side and Ambassador David Ormsby-Gore to the right on 'Honey Fitz' off Hyannis Port, after the nuclear test ban treaty had been signed in Moscow. 28 July 1963. (Courtesy JFK Library)

Jack giving the Kennedy children and friends their regular treat on his golf cart at the family compound, Cape Cod, 3 September 1962. 'This was a man who all his life was at home with women and kids and human situations.' (Courtesy JFK Library)

Family Portrait at Hyannis Port taken by White House Press photographer Cecil Stoughton, a favourite of Jacqueline Kennedy, 4 August 1962. (Alamy)

The President plays in the Oval Office with Caroline and John, July 1963. (Courtesy JFK Library)

the President was bestowing honorary citizenship on Winston Churchill, to remind him about Macmillan's letter. Jack, who had been galvanised by the Rose Garden ceremony, realised in that moment that if he was to take up Churchill's mantle, he was going to have to act regardless of political cost to himself. Two days later, he called London and agreed to send a joint letter to the Soviets urging progress. He made just one caveat. He did not wish to risk the possibility of a summit meeting. Instead, two emissaries were to be sent to Moscow – Harriman and Lord Hailsham. Both men had suitable experience. One had been Roosevelt's personal emissary in London; the other had participated in the 'King and Country' wartime debates at the Oxford Union.

Khrushchev responded unhelpfully to the joint Anglo-American proposals. The Soviets wanted just three inspections a year and did not agree to UK/US demands for 'no fewer than eight or ten'. Having been lied to by the Soviets before, the President was not inclined to take chances. Worrying that Kennedy would give a hasty response, Macmillan called David back to London after the President agreed to delay action.

In London, David met Violet Bonham Carter, the sister of the late Raymond Asquith, and suggested she call on Jack, during her forthcoming visit to America. Sitting on a sofa a few days later and opposite him in the Oval Office in his rocking chair, Violet was delighted to hear Jack recite Churchill's lines about her brother – "The War which found the measure of so many, never got to the bottom of him." Jack asked if Churchill had made any impression on trying to educate the public with his warnings in the 1930s. "None," said Violet. "The country wanted poppy and mandragora. The governments gave in. Awakening came with the fulfilment of the doom he prophesied."[648]

As he had promised, Jack made no reply to Khrushchev whilst David was away. The President had been reminded by Violet, of the sort of man he wanted to be. He discarded a State Department draft letter likely to doom the talks' initiative. On David's return, Jack instructed his State Department to work from Macmillan's original draft to Khrushchev, making 'as few changes as possible'.[649] A delighted Prime Minister wrote to his ambassador. "I hardly know how to thank you sufficiently for all your help over the test ban proposals. It is remarkable that we have reached such a complete agreement on the text of the message. This is very largely due to both your wise advice to me and the skill with which you have handled all the personalities in Washington. I am deeply indebted to you".[650] The President finally gave his press conference on 22 May, and against the initial advice of his officials announced that he intended 'to push very hard for a test ban'.[651]

In late spring, domestic events now shared centre stage in public for both leaders. A campaign of civil disobedience led by Martin Luther King in Alabama was making the headlines, while in London the Press were highlighting a 'call girl' scandal involving the Defence Secretary Mr Profumo and a Russian Naval attaché. Despite such pressure, both leaders pressed on with negotiations.

Jack was horribly aware of the need to make urgent progress. Visiting a military command bunker, he told graduates of the US Air Force Academy, "We have already a total destructive capacity sufficient to annihilate the enemy twenty-five times and he has the power to destroy us ten times. Between us we are in a position to exterminate all human life seven times over. The nuclear load in only one of our B-52s now in the air – at this minute somewhere above us or over the Arctic – is probably greater in terms of destructive power than all of the explosives used in all of the previous wars in human history."[652] A fanfare of publicity then followed Jack's appearance on the aircraft carrier *Kittyhawk*. As reported by the *New York Times*, 'this once junior naval lieutenant now sat in the Admiral's cushioned chair on the flight deck, having a cigar and drinking coffee as jets roared overhead, and missiles seared the sky'.

On 10 June 1963, in front of students at the American University, just a mile from the White House, Jack, made what became known as his groundbreaking 'Peace Speech'. Calling for an end to the Cold War, he announced a fresh way of thinking with a new approach to the Russians. He asked American and Soviet people to examine their common hopes. "In the final analysis, our most basic common link is that we all inhabit this small planet. We all breathe the same air. We all cherish our children. And we are all mortal." The President said he was suspending the testing of nuclear weapons, and announced that Britain's Premier and the Soviet leader would hold discussions with him on a test ban treaty.

The June 'Peace Speech' surprised and seemed to convince the Soviets, that Kennedy was serious about wanting better relations. It was to be another major turning point. As Jack saw it, agreeing a treaty would be, 'a first step towards peace – a step towards reason – a step away from war'.

In late June, the President set off on his last visit to Europe. His aim to strengthen the Atlantic Alliance would take him to Germany, Italy and Ireland, finishing with a brief twenty-four-hour visit to Britain, to discuss the test-ban strategy. (Given the French President's, 'Non' to Macmillan in his bid to join the Common Market, he purposely omitted France.)

The President arrived in Berlin on 26 June 1963. More than one and a half million Germans, from a population of just over two million Berliners, lined the streets to see John Kennedy, standing and waving in his open-top car together with the city's Mayor Willy Brandt. When he reached the centre he climbed onto a podium close to 'the wall' in front of a huge gathering of Berliners, in front of his biggest crowd ever. After taking a long look at the twelve-foot-high barrier topped by barbed wire, Jack spoke into his microphone. "There are many people in the world who really don't understand or say they don't, what is the great issue between the Free World and the Communist World. Let them come to Berlin! Two thousand years ago the proudest boast was *civis Romanus sum.* Today, in the world of freedom, the proudest boast is, *Ich bin ein Berliner!* A million people roared their delight.

"Freedom has many difficulties and democracy is not perfect. But we have never had to put up a wall to keep our people in. To those who doubted the superiority of democracy over communism, I say, *Lass sie nach Berlin kommen!*" Jack's words flowed through the crowd and struck a chord of deep emotion.

"All free men, wherever they may live, are citizens of Berlin and therefore, as a free man, I take pride in the words, *Ich bin ein Berliner.*" Hearing this, the near million strong crowd went delirious. They cheered in a seemingly never-ending way. This call to the people standing in Berlin's Rudolph Wilde Platz, marked one of those moments in history. It became a defining moment in the Cold War. Dean Rusk said it was an unforgettable moment to those who were there. It would become unforgettable also, for the many millions listening to Kennedy on their radios and watching him on black and white television sets at home.[653]

The Berlin speech for a free and better future for Europe revealed Jack's heroic nature. He had talked with his speechwriter, Sorensen, on the plane to Berlin and asked for, 'a phrase to reflect my union with Berlin. What would be a good word for it? I really am a Berliner?'[654] The final choice of words demonstrated that, "Jack had an extraordinary knack for capturing people and changing them. It was his most inexplicable quality."[655]

After a stop, inspecting an American military base in Frankfurt and a visit to Bonn, the President took off for his ancestral home, Ireland, from where his

great-grandfather Patrick J Kennedy, had sailed out in 1848. Jack was greeted
wherever he went by enthusiastic and happy crowds, who nearly crushed him
once when climbing gleefully out of his car. When he escaped the melee,
running freely up the American Embassy steps, he looked back and, smiling,
yelled out, "They love me in Ireland!"

Speaking to the Irish Parliament, Jack quoted George Bernard Shaw's
approach to life: "Other people… see things and say, why? But I dream things
that never were – and I say, why not!" Jim Reed remembers Jack saying that
the visit to his ancestral home had been the happiest two days in his life. As
he took off from Shannon airport John F Kennedy was at the height of his
powers and happiness, and bound for England was now carrying some flowers
for Kick.

Instead of going directly to the Prime Minister's country home, Jack's military
helicopter headed to the green lawns of Chatsworth. At the last moment, he
had secretly decided to visit the grave of his beloved sister who had always
believed in him. In her own short life Kick had achieved much and was adored
by everyone who knew her. As a friend wrote, 'No American, man or woman
who has ever settled in England, was so much loved as she, and no American
ever loved England more'.[656]

Andrew and Debo Devonshire were there to greet Jack as he stepped out
of his helicopter to show him to the small nearby church at Edensor. He went
on alone over a wooden bridge and into the churchyard, holding those flowers
for Kick. One can only imagine the memories from childhood and youth that
flooded in at this private moment before he returned to Andrew and Debo and
stepped back into his presidential helicopter, which then rose high above the
tiny church and grounds of Chatsworth heading to the Prime Minister's home.

Harold knew that his country home at Birch Grove would give Jack the
family setting he always enjoyed. He was delighted to see Jack refreshed and,
'in the highest of spirits, with his humour puckish and mischievous'. The talks
that followed, proved a big success and were described in Foreign Office files
as if taking place between a band of brothers. A joyful Harold took the unusual
step as Prime Minister to add a personal memorandum to the official record:

The 24 hours during which the President spent at Birch Grove house was one
of tremendous activity… this was an international meeting of a quite unique
character because it could only have taken place between the British and American

Governments. It is inconceivable that a series of agreements could have been reached on such a wide number of difficult topics except by people who regarded themselves almost as partners and even brothers in a joint undertaking.[657]

The Prime Minister told the Queen that the meeting (to be his last with Jack) represented, "a remarkable tribute to the relations that exist between Britain and America... We understand each other; we do not seek to take points against each other; we do not try to deceive each other; and if we disagree we do so openly and honorably".

Referring to the test ban treaty, Macmillan recorded, 'The President and I were in complete agreement. He is as keen about a success as I',[658] adding that, 'President Kennedy showed a greater degree of authority now, and his staff had a lesser tendency to try and impose their views on him. The President's authority seemed stronger than ever'.[659]

The Prime Minister noted Jack had 'come down on our side and was clearly willing to risk a great deal to do what he thought was right'. He was enormously buoyed by this. 'Full steam with Moscow talks – Test Ban to be no.1 priority'.[660]

Jack had relished the family atmosphere and also the food at Birch Grove and told Dorothy Macmillan, "The food was of the sort that would make my wife ask if the cook would like to live in the United States!" Jackie had advised Dorothy ahead of the visit, to think of Jack "as someone David Gore is bringing down to lunch and do whatever you would do in your own house. His tastes are distressingly normal – plain food, children's food, good food – he likes anything".[661]

On Independence Day on 4 July 1963, Macmillan wrote to Jack about 'the great success at Birch Grove... a wonderful example of the way in which countries, and perhaps even more, individuals, who trust each other can work rapidly and effectively together'. The Prime Minister told Jack, 'It has been of great pride to me to feel that... we have been in part equal to the Churchill-Roosevelt relationship at the most critical moment of history'.[662,663]

The last person Jack was to call upon in England was Lady Nancy Astor. Now eighty-three, she had been responsible for first introducing Kick at Cliveden, to the 'aristocratic cousinhood'. Over tea, Jack and Nancy talked fondly about the cousinhood and the two joyful summers full of drama and excitement, back in 1938 and 1939.

It had been a remarkable time to which he owed much. From Palace to Parliament, from Chamberlain to Churchill, and journeys across Europe as borders were closing – all had made a deep impact on Jack. American-born Nancy and Kick had helped create those bonds of family and friendship amongst England's upper class, that had proved so valuable. Joe Alsop the veteran New York columnist and friend, was convinced that 'Jack always felt, that his time in England with Kick, to whom he was closer than any of the rest of the family, had more influence on him than most people thought'.[664] The American writer Gore Vidal would say of Jack, "I've always thought he was more of an English nobleman than he was an American."[665]

After Birch Grove, Jack flew to Rome with a one-night stopover in Villa Serbeloni, a retreat overlooking Lake Como amidst the hills. After arriving in Rome to meet the Italian President and to be blessed by Pope Paul VI, Jack bought himself a 500 BC figure of 'Heracles and the skin of a lion' for his Oval Office desk. For Jackie, he bought a Roman Imperial head of a young satyr. On this, the final leg of his European tour, he was cheered by massive Italian crowds. In Naples, 'women absolutely threw themselves at him – were projected over the crowd to try and get at the President', noted a journalist. On the plane back, a contented Jack, 'just kidded about it all and slept most of the way home'.[666]

This European tour had in many ways been the most powerfully charged journey of his life. And he was now returning home, having given Europe the greatest gifts in the world: hope and promise.[667]

Back in Hyannis Port, Jack resumed playing golf and was out on the course every weekend. He felt well. His visit to Europe had thrilled him, and he had his family and friends, view three newsreels of the trip. "He was watching the Berlin speech, and he started clapping," Jim Reed recalled. "He was not being egotistical. He was transported outside of himself to the movie image."[668]

On 2 July, at an appearance in East Berlin, the Soviet leader announced he would accept a limited nuclear test ban. On 15 July, Averell Harriman and Lord Hailsham started their negotiations in Moscow; and after accepting the reality of being unable to push for a full test ban treaty they made rapid progress. Jack and David finished a final game of golf that Sunday and returned to Washington next morning to monitor progress.[669]

Macmillan was overcome when on the morning of 25 July, with David at his side, Jack called him to say the treaty was being initialled at that moment in Moscow. He wept at the news.[670] It meant everything to the ambitious statesman. 'When the President gave me the news we had not yet got, I had to go out of the room. I went to tell D and burst into tears. I have prayed hard too for this, night after night. We have worked so hard and for so long for a test ban and it has (until a few weeks ago) seemed so hopeless that I can hardly yet realise what has happened'.[671]

Jack wrote to thank the Prime Minister: 'What no one can doubt is the importance in all of this of your own persistent pursuit of a solution. You have never given up for a minute, and more than once your initiative was what had got things started again. I want you to know that this indispensable contribution is well understood and highly valued'.[672] President Kennedy went on television on 26 July to announce the Treaty as a 'shaft of light that had cut into the darkness'.

Jack considered this treaty as the most important achievement of his presidency. Without David, it is arguable this historic milestone might not have been reached.

The President celebrated Jackie's thirty-fourth birthday on 28 July. Joining them in the sunshine and summer sea breeze off Cape Cod, were David and Sissie, Lem Billings, Chuck Spalding and the Radziwills. Jack could not have felt more carefree, and always at his happiest on water, he took everyone on a three-hour cruise on the *Honey Fitz*. A memorable photo taken aboard *Honey Fitz* captures his relaxed mood with daughter Caroline leaning back onto his shoulder, and David to one side wearing sunglasses and sipping a drink. That evening, they dined at the Brambletyde. There, Jackie looking radiant in the tranquility of her favourite home, loved to paint at her easel, looking out onto the setting sun. She read *Kim*, by Rudyard Kipling and *Civilizations of Rome*, by Grimal.[673]

Over the weekend, Jack, Bobby and David walked along the beach to chart their next move. As the trio stood together in the calm water, Bobby suggested that Jack's next step might be to go to the Soviet Union. David ventured that if the Russian people were able to see for themselves an American leader who 'lacked horns and a tail', East-West relations would be very different. In November and over a dinner at the White House, Jack surprised David[674] by saying he had finally made up his mind to go to Russia, adding it would have to wait until after the election in 1964.[675]

*Foreign Secretary Sir Alec Douglas-Home with Ambassador David Ormsby-Gore meet a
relaxed and cheerful President on 4 October 1963.
(Courtesy JFK Library)*

Dean Rusk, Sir Alec and Andrei Gromyko signed the Test Ban Treaty
in Moscow on 5 August[676] and the President signed the instruments of
ratification on 7 October. He told David Powers that this was the happiest day
of his life. On 26 October, Jack announced to Congress, "For the first time we
can limit the dangers of the age. We have a new beginning."

Equipped in youth to understand war, Jack had avoided war. He had reached
Churchill's goal – an agreement with the Russians.[677] Advisor Sorensen wrote,
'Nothing gave him greater satisfaction in the White House than signing the
Nuclear Test-Ban Treaty'. [678] Jack had become the statesman he aimed to be.
    Albert Schweitzer told Jackie that the reason he admired the President
was his bravery. "Because he had the courage to search for a solution to
the agonising problem of atomic weapons. On this issue, he put us on the
right path."[679] For his friend David, the achievement represented the most
'outstanding example of co-operation between Britain and America'.[680]

The President, idol of the young and idealistic, had seemed able to forge reality from impossible dreams. The Kennedy era was a time of daring optimism tempered with realism. Jack had moved hearts and minds to new levels of excellence. He made public service and politics exciting and noble. Whilst inspiring the best in us, he made being President look fun. The American White House became a civilising centre radiating grace and energy.

It was a time when curious destiny had chosen to align stars from an aristocratic cousinhood to those of a boy born in Boston in May 1917. It was a shining moment when the world was led by a free and extraordinary man. A brief moment that still shapes our world today.

22

FLOWERS FOR KICK

On Saturday 29 June, 1963, Andrew and Deborah Devonshire were there to greet him as the grey-and-white-topped military helicopter descended slowly onto their green lawn. Jack had finally come to see the grave of his beloved sister and kindred spirit – the girl who had fallen in love with England.

Looking trim and youthful in a dark blue suit, Jack stepped down from his helicopter and walked across the soft summer grass. After warmly greeting Andrew and Debo, he walked alone over the temporary footbridge leading to the small churchyard of Edensor. He carried a small bunch of flowers tied together in silver foil. He stopped and knelt, looking up and saw the words written on Kick's headstone: 'Joy she gave. Joy she has found'. He felt her eyes looking at him smiling at the man she knew he had become. He stood up, and with sparkling eyes, strode back to his friends from London days.

Five months after placing flowers on English soil, Jack Kennedy's thousand days as America's youngest president giving joy to the world, ended to become a shining legend.

Epilogue

LETTERS TO JACQUELINE KENNEDY IN NOV/DEC '63

After Jack's death – when the world seemed to stand still – a million letters and telegrams suddenly poured into the White House addressed to Jacqueline Kennedy, in November and December of 1963.

(22 November 1963)

Dear Mrs. Kennedy,

We've just heard that President Kennedy died a few minutes ago and we want to tell you how sad we are.

President Kennedy was a good president and a great man.

Our country will miss him very much.

Sincerely,

The third grade, Douglas School, Galesburg, Illinois

———————

(22 November 1963)

We are numbed by the shock of Jack's death. Nothing we can say can console you. All we can do is to send you our best love.

Harold and Dorothy Macmillan

———————

Overwhelmed by terrible news

Moucher Devonshire (mother-in-law to Kick)

Dear Mrs Kennedy,

Never have I been so filled with revulsion, anger and sorrow as when I heard of your husband's death.

On this great and good man were set the hopes of humanity… I would like you to know that throughout the world, and in England especially, all men who prize Freedom and hope for Peace share your loss.

Winston S Churchill

(8 December 1963)

———————

Madame,

I want to tell you what respect and friendship I felt for your husband, the President. He was a noble personage. He had the will to make the most of the duty which devolved on him from a high position he occupied.

He was a great and noble president. Thus, he will enter history.

I admire him particularly because he had the courage to search for a solution to the agonising problem of atomic weapons. On this issue he put us on the right path.

He was a blessing not only for his homeland but for the entire world.

Your devoted

Albert Schweitzer

Milton, Massachusetts

(December 31, 1963)

———————

Dear Mrs. Kennedy,

I wanted to write to you because I am a neighbour of yours at Hyannis Port. As a child I played with Jack and Joe there – 'battled' is perhaps a more accurate description of what we usually did. We also lived very close to their house in Brooklyn in the winters, too, the first dozen years of our lives. Almost the first people I can remember other than my immediate family were Joe and Jack. Life was never… dull around them.

I remember a black eye I got, circa eight, by being pulled out of a tree by Joe and Jack… and remember too being chased by the two boys down a snowy street, frightened but feeling in full flight that this time it was just – they were defending valiantly their nursemaid, who, I had just said rashly, had a nose like a turnip!

I remember the summer his family first came to Hyannis Port. I was walking up the pier, aged eight or so, rejoicing in the lovely vista and summer ahead – when there on the beach just at the head of the pier I spied two familiar boys. At home in Brookline, we would have sprung to arms instantly, but in a new setting and all of us at the moment lacking playmates, we greeted each other with at least muted enthusiasm. There followed probably the longest truce of our childhoods, which finally terminated in a great naval battle in rowboats…

I wish I knew now why there was so much conflict between us… it does not matter now except as a foil of what came afterwards.

When Jack ran for President, I remember all too clearly the aggressiveness and the will to dominate of the child. I questioned in my mind his ability to handle the overwhelming power of the office. Would he be tempted in a crisis to use that power to overwhelm opposition, in a destructive way…?

What I saw was the true wonder with the growth that had intervened. The small boy whose heart had been set on winning without much regard for his opponent's rights… had become the man who could use power wisely, magnanimously, for peace and justice for all mankind. The old strength of will there – but tempered with understanding and concern for others. This was in truth a glorious victory, a victory of mind and heart and character.

He was a good and great man, through inward growth and achievement as much as through outward power and position.

Perhaps when one's childhood foe can say this, in deep respect and living appreciation, it is about as complete an accolade as can be granted.

Sincerely

Esther Edwards

Address to the American Community (in Jordan)
(November 28, 1963)

My fellow Americans,

For all of us, the past few days have been almost indescribably sad.

We mourn the loss of an intensely human and attractive person – the first president born in this century – and an ornament to our time and era.

We cannot really believe that at the age of 46 this man is no more... and gone with him are so many other of his qualities we so admire.

His undeniable capacity for leadership,

his zest for his job,

his gallantry, charm, gaiety and humour,

his way with words,

his Lincolnesque self-confidence combined in that strange Lincolnesque manner with genuine and affable humility,

his ability to lift up our hearts,

and above all his reassuringly courageous conviction that through sacrifice, wisdom and steadfastness, an enduring and just world peace may yet be achieved.

Yet as I speak to you today, I am mindful of the further quality... A sense of perspective... most often expressed in a few casual Boston-accented words – and an accompanying grin.

And today I am sure he would want us to retain our own perspective too... to remember that, despite our grief, we still do have much to stop, and to consider and to be thankful for...

Ambassador William Macomber

(US Embassy, Amman)

Acknowledgements and Reflections

I would like to thank family, friends, and colleagues from HM Diplomatic Service, who with their ideas and encouragement, helped me complete my book.

I wish to thank staff at the National Archives at Kew, who provided access to Cabinet and Foreign Office papers, including transcripts of the MacMillan-Kennedy telephone conversations, and the staff at the Bodleian Library in Oxford. After visiting Boston, I wish to express my thanks for the guidance and help received from the John F. Kennedy Presidential Library finely located with its invigorating views across the Atlantic. A special mention must go to Maryrose Grossman, for her imaginative help, and to Jennifer Quan from the Kennedy Foundation, for permission to use photographs from the family collection and for her advice on using Jacqueline Kennedy's private letters.

I am grateful to Elizabeth Hayley Clark (Society of Authors) for her legal expertise, Jemima Hunt (Writers Association), Dynasty Press and Piers Russell – Cobb (Literary Agent). Mention must also be made of the late Michael Valentini who inspired me to edit his autobiography, "Fly Like an Eagle.'

I would like to thank my American friends, Donald and Stephanie Wagner, for their advice and support; Paula Hornbostel for her comments from New York; retired Diplomatic colleagues, Sir David Manning (ex-Washington), Michael Atkinson (ex-Bucharest), and the two colleagues whom my brother consulted, Sir Ivor Roberts (ex- Trinity College, Oxford), and Sir Jeremy Greenstock (ex- UN, New York, who came up with the book's title). I must thank Michael Hall, Lady Margaret Bullard and Alan Charlton, who shared their book publishing experiences with me, and those friends who gave their time to help with proofreading.

It was a great help to be encouraged by my brother Peter, (with his two daughters, Laura and Julia; their mother Kathy and grandson Lorenzo.) He kept pushing me, to 'get on with the book' and engaged enthusiastically with many acquaintances, including the late President, FW De Klerk. A few years earlier, my brother displayed admirable energy and passion, launching and creating an exhibition, 'Aquileia: The Great Lost City', which he held at the Royal Geographical Society in the heart of Kensington in 2015. I use this chance, to thank a number of friends who have influenced me over the years; Alfred and Gusti Eder, Ali Saleh, Carol Mosolygo, Donatella and Andrea Savonitto, Eric and Janet Mattey, Jane and Michael Philips and family, Michael Culme-Seymour, Othmar and Monika and Christian and Eva Gypser, Pamela Ansell, Pietro Esposito, Regina Herren, Samantha Becker-Crownover and family, and Simone Marshall.

Working in HM Diplomatic Service, I have been fortunate to have met remarkable people, many of whom had that rare quality -to inspire others. First and foremost, and with a direct connection to President Kennedy, was Sir Alec Douglas-Home. I met the Foreign Secretary, whom Kennedy described fondly as 'polished wood on steel' during his visit to Moscow in December 1973 when I was serving in the Embassy under our popular Ambassador, Sir John Killick who had worked in Washington during the Kennedy years. It was in Moscow where I met the outspoken Prince Philip. I will never forget introducing the duke at a reception to a Russian general wearing an impressive display of military medals. Prince Philip refused to shake hands, until he had walked a full circle around the bemused and well-rounded general, to tell him he was just checking to see if there were more medals on his back! Lady Mary Soames, Churchill's daughter who had remarkable blue eyes was very gracious when I accompanied her on a trip to Bumi Hills (where the elephants roamed freely across the airport runway) when I worked in Rhodesia, then temporarily governed by Lord Soames.

While we sometimes look outside and to others for inspiration, it is surprising how often it can be found within family. In light of this I would like to mention, my ever-cheerful grandfather, George William Marshall, who served in the First World War in Egypt, and on the beaches of Gallipoli (wounded at the Third battle for Krithia and shipped to Malta to recover) and on the Western Front. He served with 1/2 East Lancashire Field Ambulance, (Royal Army Medical Corps), and then joined the Royal Navy to experience the Baltic Campaign, aboard HMS Dauntless, in 1919. Following his example, my Mancunian father, known as Bill, joined the Lancashire Fusiliers in occupied Austria in 1946 where he met my mother and then served in the Royal Signals in Germany, and Cyprus during the EOKA crisis. Dad ended his career serving as a NATO civilian for twenty-five years at JHQ in Rheindahlen, Germany. My Austrian mother Elizabeth and known as Elsa, kept family comforts and created a cosy home in the many army bases we moved to. She had a remarkable sister, Annie. I mention her because she found and rescued her husband, Lieutenant Fritz Guadernack, with great courage and determination, from a Russian prisoner of war camp. He had served in Rommel's Afrika Corps, and after the war, needless to say, my Dad and Fritz got on very well. Another inspiring figure in my youth was John Lavender, my Royal Wanstead School headmaster, who as a Gurkha officer, represented the very model of an officer and gentleman.

President Kennedy was the only politician I can recall from schooldays, who immediately created any real interest and excitement. The smiling young president, often with his glamorous wife, simply looked and sounded quite different to other Leaders, whenever they appeared in newspapers or on black-and-white televisions, and 'Pathe' Newsreels. I can still picture their bright faces looking out from an open top car, surrounded by huge cheering crowds in Paris wherever they went. I remember too, racing to the school library, to see newspaper headlines counting down the days to a possible nuclear war on Cuba.

Naturally I recall the awful shock which hit us on a late November day, in 1963. I was in the middle of doing my evening homework when John Davis, a schoolmaster, suddenly appeared at the classroom door and shouted, "President Kennedy's been shot". Twenty-two boys sitting at their desks simply stared at one other. Even at that age of fifteen we felt the significance of the moment. The door was closed and the teacher was gone.

Five years later, I stayed up all night in at my parents' home at the army base in Germany, to watch the funeral service of Robert Kennedy. The hope of another era of youthful leadership had been taken away. It was a loss that was keenly felt by that idealistic and vigorous student class of 1968. That summer, on Monday 22 July, my brother and I joined the Foreign Office.

I was delighted to join the Diplomatic Service with its prestigious history, traditions and life that promised overseas adventure. We felt rather special and full of youthful idealism. With a sharpened sense of freedom common to many in those days, I remember vaguely thinking, how we might fit in, and use the chance to add fresh colour to established ways. The ways of government, proved to be more flexible and friendly than I had imagined. In my first week, Sir Paul Gore-Booth, the retiring head of the Diplomatic Service, came around to shake hands, with each and every one of us. I remember his broad and homely smile, traditional pin-striped waistcoat, and very bushy eyebrows! I recall being surprised when told that we did not usually address colleagues as 'Sir'. We were also encouraged to push open heavy oak office doors, without hesitating to knock first. And, we were expected to give our views and to speak freely if needed. Such small details make a big difference. Joining the Foreign Office, seemed like becoming a member of another family.

As good fortune dictated, I was sent in my first year to work in North American department, to be surrounded by the same desks and cabinets where urgent papers had been flying about five years earlier, preparing for President Kennedy's visit to Britain. In that delightful summer, I lived in a civil service hostel in South Kensington, at 71 Princes Gate. It was not many yards from where student diplomat Jack Kennedy had lived with his parents in the embassy residence, at 14 Princes Gate. In another moment of serendipity, I discovered that Jack and his sister Kick had spent ten days on holiday at lake Woerthersee, in Austria. My mother, I'm sure (!) was bound to have seen them, as it was only a mile or two from the British Military hospital where I was born ten years later.

This is not the right place to give details of career highlights with the Foreign Office, but those interested in seeing perhaps what helped shape my outlook (and approach to writing this book), may wish to look at the website I set up, to pursue my active interest in John Kennedy;– www.jfkinlondon.org. uk.

I retired from the Service after thirty-six years of having enjoyed an adventurous and privileged life. I remained in touch with the Foreign Office, interviewing candidates for their 'Stabilisation' programme. And, it was when I worked with the government's Chevening scholarship programme to select foreign students with leadership potential, that I began to think back to my schoolboy hero. The youthful president had brought idealism and excitement to public service that I had felt in my career. I wanted to find out what had helped shape John F Kennedy. Was his outstanding leadership quality, something he had simply been born with, or shaped by events and the choices he made in life? Could his early life and his example, inspire and serve young people today?

I have kept a daily diary, partly because of a fascination in how environment and early experience shape you. Very few biographies I had read, drew attention to John Kennedy's formative days in London, and the lifelong impact it had on him. After a career promoting and representing Britain, I felt of course I had to explore and write about this largely untold story, of how the UK helped shape JFK.

I visited the Presidential library to have access to private family letters, photos and diaries, and to stroll around Harvard and local streets to get a glimpse of life as seen through young Kennedy eyes, to understand the things that shaped his thinking. As I explored his early and then his formative years, it came as a fascinating surprise to see how Joe Kennedy's appointment as Ambassador in London, had completely changed the course of the Kennedy family.

It was the Ambassador's daughter Kick, who first, and before Jack, became a star. I dwell on her life in some details in the book because I felt she provided the secret motivation, and backdrop, that helped drive her brother forward. David Ormsby-Gore was part of the aristocratic cousinhood which Kick had joined, and was Jack's best friend from that student circle. He became the key individual and constant influence, outside of Jack's family. It is perhaps no exaggeration to say that without David and Harold Macmillan, there would have been no nuclear arms treaty. And without those London days of glamour and danger, to provide an education in formative youth, John Kennedy might not have become the statesman and peacemaker, who turned the tide in the Cold War.

New York columnist and friend, Joe Alsop, famously maintained that Kennedy was "intrinsically more English, than American. Harold Macmillan told the president on 4 July 1963, that their relations 'had been in part equal to that of Churchill - Roosevelt at a critical time in history'. The love and mutual admiration between Jack and Harold, was especially brought home to me, when I saw the original four-page letter Jacqueline Kennedy wrote to Harold Macmillan in January 1964. Composed in striking black ink, it conveyed the 'love' and respect that her husband felt for the Prime Minister, when they worked together for the 'best things' in a 'brief shining moment,' which she likened to 'Camelot'. Unfortunately, after the JFK Foundation consulted the First Lady's Will, I was not able to include her letter in my book.

I hope my book helps convey the magic of Kennedy's leadership, and how Britain had played its part in this. It was a time when we were aiming for the moon, when we were inspired by an extraordinary man who made us feel that nothing was beyond our reach.

It was no surprise that John Fitzgerald Kennedy seemed so utterly right as President. London had been at the core of his education as statesman. Friends and family had come together as if by curious destiny, at critical moments in his life. Personal family bonds had become the beating heart of a winning 'Special Relationship' at the height of the Cold War.

Although it has been nearly 60 years since those one thousand days of inspiring leadership ended, that brief moment of grace and optimism shines like a bright star in our uncertain times today.

Bernard A Marshall
19 August 2023
Southfields, London.
www.jfkinlondon.org.uk

Reference Sources

The National Archives, Kew (PRO)
The John F Kennedy Centre, Presidential Library and Archives, Boston (JFKL)
Museum of the Kennedys, Auguster Strasse 11, Berlin
Bodleian Library, Oxford

"The Kennedys Amidst the Gathering Storm 1938–40" Will Swift 2008
"Jack Kennedy – The Education of a Statesman" Barbara Leaming 2006
"Grace and Power" Sally Bedell Smith 2004
"Reckless Youth" Nigel Hamilton 1992
"The contents of Glyn Gywarch" Bonham Auctions Catalogue 2016
"The Life and Words of John F Kennedy" Country Beautiful Magazine 1964
"Kick" Paula Byrne 2016
"An Unfinished Life" Robert Dalleck 2003
"The Macmillan Diaries 1957–1966" Peter Catterall
"Harold Macmillan – Pointing the Way" 1959–61 Harold Macmillan
"The Letters of Joseph P Kennedy – Hostage to Fortune" Amanda Smith 2001
"When Lions Roar – the Churchills and the Kennedys" Thomas Maier 2014
"Rose Kennedy" Barbara Perry 2014
"The Kennedy Men" Laurence Leamer 2001
"The Kennedy Women" Laurence Leamer 1994
"One Brief Shining Moment" William Manchester 1983
"Kennedy the Classic Biography" Ted Sorensen 1965
"Jack, A Life Like No Other" Geoffrey Perry 2002
"Profiles in Courage" John F Kennedy 1955
"Prelude to Leadership: The Post-War Diary of John F. Kennedy" Hugh Sidey 1995
"Dear Mrs Kennedy" J Mulvaney and Paul de Angelis, 2013
"Living the Cold War" Christopher Mallaby 2017

"Munich" David Faber 2008

"Wait for Me" Deborah Devonshire 2010

"The Young Melbourne" David Cecil 1939

"A Thread in the Tapestry" Sarah Churchill 1967

"The Way the Wind Blows" Lord Home 1976

"Travellers in the Third Reich" Julia Boyd 2018

"JFK's Camelot" Daily Mirror 2013

"Jacqueline Kennedy – Historic Conversations" A Schlesinger 2011

Endnotes

1 W Swift p72
2 Barbara Perry, Rose Kennedy, p48
3 N Hamilton p42
4 N Hamilton p44
5 Reckless Youth, Hamilton p41
6 ibid p47
7 ibid p54
8 Hamilton p54
9 Hamilton p57
10 ibid p55
11 G Perret p20
12 Perret p24
13 L Leamer Kennedy Women p47
14 L Leamer Kennedy Men p14
15 B Perry, Rose, p82
16 N Hamilton, p46
17 N Hamilton p46
18 ibid p48
19 Hamilton, p49
20 ibid p49
21 L Leamer Kennedy Men p67
22 Dalleck p36
23 L Leamer p68
24 L Leamer p85
25 ibid p86
26 R Dallek p32
27 Hamilton p47
28 Byrne p33
29 L Leamer Kennedy Women p201
30 Byrne p37
31 Byrne p8
32 Perret p28
33 Hamilton p89
34 Hamilton p99
35 Perry p80
36 Hamilton p87
37 Hamilton p108
38 Hamilton p103
39 Hamilton p98
40 Hamilton p101
41 L Leamer Kennedy Men p43
42 Hamilton p93
43 Perret p41
44 Hamilton p110
45 Hamilton p104
46 Hamilton p102
47 B Perry, Rose, p86
48 Hamilton p135
49 Perrett p45
50 Dalleck p28
51 ibid p133
52 Hamilton p60
53 Byrne p31
54 Leamer p 81
55 N Hamilton p220
56 Bryne p55
57 Bryne p55
58 Bryne p57
59 Bryne p 58 Smith p182
60 L Leamer W p 216
61 Byrne p60
62 L Leamer, Kennedy Women p217
63 ibid p 225
64 ibid p 218
65 Hamilton p241
66 Hamilton p165
67 L Leamer, Kennedy Men p102
68 Hamilton p166

69 L Leamer KW p 219
70 N Hamilton p170
71 N Hamilton p222
72 N Hamilton p180
73 Hamilton p181
74 Hamilton p183
75 Hamilton Page 189
76 Hamilton p187
77 Hamilton p190
78 Hamilton p191
79 ibid p192
80 Hamilton p193
81 ibid p194
82 ibid p198
83 ibid p186
84 Hamilton p185
85 P Byrne p71
86 Hamilton p186
87 Hamilton p228
88 Dallek p54
89 W Swift p24
90 W Swift p26
91 ibid p28
92 ibid p28
93 Hamilton p226
94 David Faber, Munich p131
95 ibid p41
96 ibid p44
97 W Swift p44
98 David Faber Munich p45
99 David Faber p45
100 L Leamer M p119
101 L Leamer p249
102 Vincent Bzdeck, The Kennedy Legacy
    p16
103 W Swift p35
104 W Swift p35
105 Anne de Courcy, Debs at War p42
106 ibid p88
107 Anne de Courcy, Debs at War p28
108 Byrne p92
109 ibid p57
110 Byrne p88

111 P Byrne p65
112 Swift p60
113 Swift p61
114 Swift xxv
115 ibid xxvi
116 Swift p3
117 Hamilton p232
118 Hamilton p223
119 Bryne p96
120 Leaming p41
121 B Leaming p57
122 Swift p42
123 ibid p51
124 Swift p66
125 Byrne p107
126 Swift p78
127 Swift p78
128 Swift p77
129 Dallek p46
130 Byrne p106
131 Hamilton p236
132 ibid p237
133 ibid p237
134 Byrne p108
135 Hamiltoni p239
136 David Faber, Munich p 287
137 David Faber, Munich p289
138 David Faber, Munich p 288
139 Lord Home p69
140 W Shirer, Berlin Diary p115
141 W Shirer p115
142 Lord Home p65
143 David Faber, Munich p415
144 Lord Home p66
145 Lord Home, Way the Wind Blows p67
146 Lord Home p66
147 Faber, Munich p412
148 ibid p412
149 J Boyd p341
150 Faber, Munich p422
151 Swift p69
152 Swift p72
153 Swift p72

154 Swift p72
155 Byrne p101
156 Anne de Courcy, Debs at War p49
157 Ann De Courcy, Debs at War p48
158 Laura Thompson, "Take six Girls" p270
159 W Swift p97
160 W Swift Gathering Storm p97
161 ibid p43
162 ibid p43
163 Lord Home, Way the Wind Blows p68
164 W Swift, The Gathering Storm p99
165 Maier p382
166 David Faber, Munich p434
167 Byrne p117
168 B Leaming p46
169 Byrne p116
170 Byrne p116
171 Byrne p114
172 W Swift p124
173 W Swift p125
174 B Leaming p50
175 Hamilton p251
176 Hamilton p255
177 W Swift p129
178 W Swift p203
179 Perret p72
180 W Swift p138
181 Hamilton p257
182 W Swift p145
183 W Swift p145
184 Swift p147
185 ibid p147
186 Hamilton p257
187 Hamilton p257
188 W Swift p153
189 Hamilton p259
190 Hamilton p263
191 Hamilton p267
192 Perret p74
193 Hamilton p164
194 Rose Kennedy Diary 4 May (Perry p139)
195 Swift p 161
196 W Swift p168

197 Leamer, Kennedy Womern p278
198 W Swift p172
199 W Swift p172
200 W Swift p174
201 W Swift p174
202 Hamilton p268
203 Cecil p8
204 W Swift p176
205 W Swift p169
206 W Swift p169
207 Hamilton p278
208 W Swift p177
209 Perry p75
210 Byrne p132
211 Hamilton p270
212 Hamilton p 271
213 Hamilton p276
214 Joseph Kennedy diary 24 Aug 1939 (
    Bryne p183)
215 Hamilton p278
216 Hamilton p278
217 Hamilton p 277
218 Hamilton p279
219 Hamilton p279
220 JP Kennedy diary 3 Sep (Hamilton
    p249)
221 Leamer p140
222 Perret p76
223 Hamilton p282
224 Hamilton p 285
225 W Swift p194
226 JP Kennedy despatch of 11 Sept '39 to
    President. Smith p376 (Swift p194)
227 W Swift p194
228 Smith p376 Democrat chairman Jim
    Farley recollection (Hamilton p287)
229 Hamilton p288
230 Brendan Simms, Hitler p552
231 Smith p376 (Swift p194)
232 W Swift p198
233 Smith p371 (Swift p194)
234 Kick Kennedy to JP Kennedy 18 Sept
    1939, Smith p381 Bryne p142

235 Hamilton p297
236 Hamilton p286
237 Hamilton p287
238 ibid p286
239 Leaming p74
240 Leaming p74
241 Dallek p55
242 Hamilton p307
243 N Hamilton p320
244 Dallek p64
245 Hamilton p301
246 Hamilton p300
247 Maier p225
248 Hamilton p312
249 Leamer KM p141
250 Leamer KM p140
251 FDR to Roger Merriman 15 Feb 1939
    Library of Congress
252 Nancy The Story of Lady Astor, Adrian
    Fort 2012
253 Maier p229
254 L Leamer p143
255 Hamilton p309
256 Smith p392
257 L Leamer p142
258 W Swift, p219
259 Hamilton p311
260 ibid p312
261 Maier p231
262 ibid p258
263 Hamilton p324
264 W Swift p276
265 W Swift p278
266 W Swift p276
267 ibid p276
268 ibid p278
269 Anne de Courcey, Debs at War p107
270 L Leamer KW p338
271 Smith p466
272 W Swift p278
273 W Swift p287
274 Maier p271
275 ibid 271
276 W Swift p291
277 Smith p489
278 W Swift p292
279 PRO 371/24251
280 Maier p273
281 Hamilton p392
282 Smith p517
283 L Leamer KW P300
284 Hamilton p422
285 Hamilton p423
286 Hamilton p431
287 Hamilton p461
288 L Leamer KW p333
289 ibid p443
290 Hamilton p441
291 Hamilton p474
292 ibid (Diary Entry 27 February 1942)
293 Harold Nicholson Letters and Diaries
    1939–1945
294 Leaming KM p182
295 Hamilton p554
296 Hamilton p547
297 ibid p587
298 Hamilton p590
299 Thomas Maier, When Lions Roar p344
300 Hamilton p594
301 Leamer p186
302 Hamilton p543
303 Hamilton p544
304 Hamilton p613
305 Hamilton p550
306 Perret p119
307 Hamilton p549
308 Byrne p195
309 Hamilton p647
310 Perrett p121
311 L Leamer p342
312 Maier p332
313 Bryne p120
314 Maier p332
315 Bryne p188
316 Byrne p187
317 Bryne p208

318 Sarah Churchill p65
319 Sarah Churchill p66
320 Nancy, The story of Lady Astor, Adrian Fort p221
321 Byrne p192
322 L Leamer p264
323 Byrne p194
324 Byrne p193
325 Byrne p202
326 L Leamer KW p346
327 Maier p383
328 Maier p385
329 Hamilton p651
330 Hamilton p650
331 Byrne p232
332 Byrne p229
333 L Leamer p336
334 JFKL, Kick's and Billy's diaries
335 L Leamer p196
336 Maier p392
337 Maier p395 and B Leaming Kick p162
338 Leamer KW p377
339 Byrne p248 as per Capt Waterhouse letter to The Times
340 B Leaming, Kick p173 and Maier p396
341 Byrne p253
342 Bryne p255
343 Bryne p255
344 B Perry p182
345 B Leaming p170
346 Perrett p124
347 Perrett p124
348 Perrett p125
349 B Leaming p174
350 Perret p129
351 Sidey, Prelude to Leadership, page headed at front 'Dedication'
352 B Leaming p166
353 B Leaming p174
354 B Leaming p178
355 B Leaming, Education p177
356 B Leaming, Kick p202
357 Leamer KM p228
358 Leamer KM p228
359 B Leaming p181
360 Maier p391
361 Hamilton p780
362 Maier p421
363 Maier p427
364 Hamilton p776
365 Hamilton p781
366 Hamilton p765
367 ibid p757
368 Perret p137
369 ibid p729
370 ibid p778
371 Vincent Bizdek, The Kennedy Legacy'
372 Hamilton p730
373 Sorensen p23 and p27
374 Leamer KM p390
375 Sorensen p18
376 L Leamer KW p394
377 L Leamer KW p394
378 Thurston Clarke 'JFK's last hundred days'
379 Maier p427
380 Smith p630
381 B Leaming p189
382 B Leaming p190
383 Maier p450
384 Tim Bouverie, Appeasing Hitler, p68
385 Maier p453
386 ibid p451
387 Leamer KW p403 and Maier p454
388 Maier p455
389 Maier p459
390 B Leaming, E p194
391 Byrne p285
392 Sarah Bradford, America's Queen p129
393 Bryne p286
394 B Leaming p194
395 Hamilton p791
396 Hamilton p791
397 Sidey, Intro xx1x
398 L Leamer p424
399 Maier p481
400 Maier p481

401 Cecil p12
402 ibid p48
403 Cecil p267
404 ibid p 59–60
405 Sidey p xxii
406 ibid p xxii
407 Maier p 482
408 Leaming p215
409 Leaming p215
410 Maier p 486
411 Leamer Kennedy Women p429
412 Leaming E 218 and Sorensen p59 (on Seaway Bill)
413 Leamer Kennedy Men p350
414 Leamer Kennedy Men p354
415 Wood, The Life and Words of JFK p46
416 Sarah Bradford, America's Queen p163
417 Sarah Bradford, America's Queen p161
418 C Mallaby , Living the Cold War p43
419 Reg Gadney, Kennedy p130
420 Bedell Smith p78
421 Leaming p256
422 Leaming p452
423 Bedell Smith p78
424 Sarah Bradford, America's Queen p186
425 PRO Macmillan to Eisenhower 10 Nov 1960, PREM 11/3609
426 New York Herald Tribune 19.10.60, PRO PREM 11/3609
427 PRO JFK to PM Telephoned to Chequers PREM 11/3609
428 S Bedell Smith p65
429 ibid
430 Jacqueline p152
431 Jacqueline p155
432 Debo Devonshire ,"Wait for Me', Appendix p341
433 Debo Devonshire p342
434 Debo Devonshire p343
435 Sarah Bradford , America's Queen' p225
436 PRO Macmillan to JFK 25/1/61, PREM11/3609
437 PRO Caccia tel to FCO 21/1/60, PREM 11/3609
438 Leaming p260
439 Maier p577
440 Macmillan Diaries Vol 11, Nov 11 1960 p335
441 Macmillan Diaries Vol 11, I Jan 1961 p351
442 Macmillan Diaries p353
443 PRO, Gore to Sir Alec 5 Dec 1960 FO 371/152108
444 ibid Memo Sir Alec to PM 13 Dec
445 PRO, Gore to Sir Alec, 9/12/60 FO 371/152108
446 Leaming p264
447 Schlesinger "A Thousand days" p379
448 ibid p266
449 Jacqueline, Historic Conversations p254
450 Jacqueline p255
451 Sorensen p561
452 Macmillan, Diaries Vol 11, p351
453 PRO Gore to Sir Alec, 24/2/61 FO 371/14394
454 Jacqueline p316
455 ibid p316
456 Bedell Smith xxix
457 Bedell Smith p77
458 Bedell Smith xx
459 Bedell Smith xxiv
460 Ted Sorensen, p369
461 Bedell Smith p49
462 Bedell Smith p82
463 Ted Sorensen, Kennedy, p366
464 Bedell Smith p182
465 Macmillan, Pointing the Way, p329
466 Barbara Leaming p334
467 Debo Devonshire, Wait for Me, p225
468 Debo Devonshire ,Wait for Me, p221
469 Macmillan p336
470 PRO, FO 371/163115
471 B Leaming p268
472 Sally Bedell Smith p193
473 Macmillan ,Pointing the Way, p339

474 Macmillan , Pointing the Way, p339
475 Barbara Leaming p280
476 ibid p287
477 Macmillan Diaries Vol 11, p372
478 Barbara Leaming p276
479 Jacqueline p 213
480 Macmillan , Diaries Vol 11, p373
481 Jacqueline p 215
482 Macmillan ,Pointing the Way, p353
483 Robert Dallek p368
484 Bedell Smith p191
485 Robert Dallek p368
486 Bedell Smith p192
487 Bedell Smith p190
488 B Leaming p304
489 Bedell Smith p195
490 Bedell Smith p196
491 Bedell Smith p207
492 Bedell Smith p207
493 Bedell Smith p265
494 Macmillan, Pointing the Way p355
495 ibid p355
496 Bedell Smith p198
497 Barbara Leaming p304
498 Jacqueline p198
499 Barbara Leaming p 312, Dallek p406
500 ibid p308
501 Sally Bedell Smith, p208
502 B Leaming p313
503 Macmillan, Pointing the Way p356
504 Macmillan, Pointing the Way p357
505 Bedell Smith p211; Dallek p414
506 Leaming, E p314
507 Sally Bedell Smith p211
508 Leaming E p274
509 Macmillan p359
510 Robert Dallek, p 470
511 Jacqueline p 235
512 Macmillan p388
513 Macmillan Pointing the Way p389,
    Robert Dallek p418
514 Macmillan Pointing the Way p389
515 Dallek p 421

516 Dallek p342
517 B Leaming p 323
518 B Leaming p322
519 Dallek p423, Leamer KM p540
520 Dallek p424, Leaming E p326
521 R Dallek p428
522 R Dallek p428
523 Macmillan Pointing the Way p396
524 Macmillan p397
525 Macmillan p400
526 Barbara Leaming E p346
527 Dallek p421
528 PRO, Gore to Home, 4 Nov 1961
    PREM 11/ 4166
529 Leaming p 343
530 PRO FO 371/156510
531 PRO PREM 11/4166
532 PRO Gore to Sir Alec 4 Nov 61 PREM
    11/4166
533 Bedell Smith p181
534 Jacqueline p254
535 Jacqueline p255
536 Macmillan Pointing the Way p407
537 Macmillan p409
538 Macmillan p408
539 Macmillan p398
540 Macmillan p409
541 Dallek p415
542 Dallek p415
543 Bedell Smith p183
544 Macmillan p 359
545 Bedell Smith p183
546 PRO , PREM 11/4166
547 FRUS Foreign Relations of US
    1961–63,Vol X111
548 Barbara Leaming p360
549 Barbara Leaming p360
550 Barbara Leaning E p361
551 PRO, Meeting 20–23 Dec Bermuda,
    PREM 11/3782, and Leaming p364
552 Lord Home, Way the Wind Blows, p179
553 Macmillan, Diaries Vol 11, p437
554 ibid p437

555 ibid (FCO Tel no 9862 to Washington)
556 PRO, FO 371/162578
557 Macmillan, Pointing the Way p358
558 Jacqueline p246
559 Jacqueline p161
560 William Manchester p144
561 Sorensen p28, 42
562 Bedell Smith p119
563 Sorensen p376
564 Bedell Smith p xx
565 Bedell Smith p85
566 Sorensen p374
567 H Sidey p xxxv111
568 L Leamer p156
569 Sorensen p41
570 Jacqueline p102
571 Bedell Smith p250
572 Bedell Smith p251
573 Macmillan Diaries Vol 11 p438
574 Bedell Smith p261
575 Bedell Smith p 217
576 Bedell Smith p162
577 Bedell Smith p365
578 Jacqueline p28
579 Manchester p135
580 Macmillan, Diaries Vol 11 p437r
581 Macmillan, Diaries, Vol 11 p462
582 ibid p466
583 ibid p467
584 Leaming p382
585 Macmillan Diaries Vol 11 p467
586 Leaming p273
587 PRO, PREM 11/4052
588 Macmillan Diaries Vol 11 p468
589 Macmillan Diaries Vol 11 p468
590 Barbara Leaming p380
591 Lord Home, Way the Wind Blows, p179
592 Wikipedia on Lord Home
593 Smith Bedell p284
594 Leaming E p388
595 B Leaming p394
596 PRO, FO 371/166970
597 PRO, FO 371 /166970
598 B Leaming p397
599 B Leaming p398
600 Bedell Smith p 297
601 B Leaming p402
602 B Leaming p494
603 B Leaming p497
604 Bedell Smith p317
605 PRO, PREM 11/3689
606 PRO, PREM 11/3689
607 PRO, PREM 11/3806
608 Macmillan Diaries Vol 11 p508
609 Macmillan Diaries Vol 11 p509
610 PRO,PREM 11/3806
611 PRO FO 598
612 PRO, PREM 11/3690
613 Macmillan Diaries Vol 11 p511
614 PRO FO 598 and Sorensen Classic
    Biography p710 and Gadney p151
615 Macmillan Diaries Vol 11 p513
616 ibid Confidential tel Home copied to
    PM 26 October
617 Kennedy by Reg Gadney p153
618 Christopher Mallaby, Living the Cold
    War
619 Robert Kennedy, Thirteen days, p87,110
620 Bedell Smith p320
621 Debo Devonshire , Wait for me, p225
622 Debo Devonshire p223
623 Bedell Smith p322
624 PRO FO 598
625 PRO FO 598
626 PRO, FO 371/162590
627 JFK Library, JFK/POL/9/7/64
628 PRO, PREM 11/3691
629 Bedell Smith p334
630 Sorensen p36
631 Schlesinger "A thousand days" 1965
    p379
632 ibid p 82
633 Debo Devonshire p226
634 Lord Home, Way the Wind Blows, p87
635 Lord Home p89
636 Lord Home p157

637 Lord Home p179

638 Lord Home, p85

639 Cyril Connolly, "Enemies of Promise" 1938

640 Deborah Devonshire, Wait for Me p349

641 W Swift, p70

642 PRO Annual Review 1962, FO 371/168405

643 PRO Annual Review 1962

644 Sorensen p717 and Maier p580

645 PRO PREM 11/4593

646 PRO PREM 11/4593

647 Barbara Leaming p438

648 ibid p432

649 Barbara Leaming p432

650 PRO FO 371/171216

651 B Leaming p432

652 JFK Library, jfkpp-036-009 and Dallek p630 for Treaty 'milestone'

653 Bedell Smith p382 and Maier p587

654 L Leamer p680

655 S Bedell Smith p459 Epilogue

656 Sarah Bradford, America's Queen, p119

657 PRO, PREM 11/4586

658 ibid

659 PRO Macmillan memo 1 July '63

660 Macmillan Diaries Vol 11, p575

661 Bedell Smith p380

662 PRO, PREM 11/4586

663 PRO, PREM 11/4593

664 Maier p486

665 Sarah Bradford, America's Queen, p108

666 Bedell Smith p384

667 L Leamer Kennedy Men p680

668 Bedell Smith p388

669 Barbara Leaming p435

670 B Leaming p435

671 Macmillan Diaries Vol 11 p582

672 B Leaming p435

673 Bedell Smith p389

674 Barbara Leaming p436

675 Reg Gadney, Kennedy p128

676 Reg Gadney, Kennedy p155

677 Barbara Leaming p438

678 Sorensen, Kennedy, The Classic Biography p26

679 Mulvaney and Angelis, 'Dear Mrs Kennedy' p132

680 PRO Annual Review 1963 FO 371/174261